D1740369

Languages and Identities in a Transitional Japan

This book explores the transition from the era of internationalization into the era of globalization of Japan by focusing on language and identity as its central themes. By taking an interdisciplinary approach covering education, cultural studies, linguistics, and policy-making, the chapters in this book raise certain questions of what constitutes contemporary Japanese culture, Japanese identity and multilingualism, and what they mean to local people, including those who do not reside in Japan but are engaged with Japan in some way within the global community. Topics include the role of technology in the spread of Japanese language and culture, hybrid language use in an urban context, the Japanese language as a lingua franca in China, and the identity construction of heritage Japanese language speakers in Australia. The authors do not limit themselves to examining only the Japanese language or the Japanese national/cultural identity, but they also explore multilingual practices and multiple/fluid identities in "a transitional Japan." Overall, the book responds to the basic need for better accounts of language and identity of Japan, particularly in the context of increased migration and mobility.

Ikuko Nakane is a Senior Lecturer at the Asia Institute, the University of Melbourne.

Emi Otsuji is a Senior Lecturer at University of Technology, Sydney.

William S. Armour is an Honorary Senior Lecturer in the School of Humanities and Languages, UNSW Australia.

Routledge Research in Transnationalism

Languages and Identities in a Transitional Japan

From Internationalization
to Globalization

**Edited by Ikuko Nakane, Emi Otsuji,
and William S. Armour**

Routledge
Taylor & Francis Group

NEW YORK AND LONDON

First published 2015
by Routledge
711 Third Avenue, New York, NY 10017

and by Routledge
2 Park Square, Milton Park, Abingdon, Oxon OX14 4RN

Routledge is an imprint of the Taylor & Francis Group, an informa business

© 2015 Taylor & Francis

The right of the editors to be identified as the authors of the editorial
material, and of the authors for their individual chapters, has been
asserted in accordance with sections 77 and 78 of the Copyright,
Designs and Patents Act 1988.

All rights reserved. No part of this book may be reprinted or reproduced or
utilised in any form or by any electronic, mechanical, or other means, now
known or hereafter invented, including photocopying and recording, or in any
information storage or retrieval system, without permission in writing from
the publishers.

Trademark Notice: Product or corporate names may be trademarks or
registered trademarks, and are used only for identification and explanation
without intent to infringe.

Library of Congress Cataloging-in-Publication Data

Languages and identities in a transitional Japan : from internationalization
to globalization / edited by Ikuko Nakane, Emi Otsuji and William S. Armour.
pages cm. — (Routledge research in transnationalism ; 31)
Includes bibliographical references and index.
1. National characteristics, Japanese. 2. Language and languages—Study
and teaching—Japan. 3. Second language acquisition—Japan.
4. Globalization—Japan. I. Nakane, Ikuko, editor. II. Otsuji, Emi,
editor. III. Armour, William S., editor.
DS830.L36 2016
303.48'252—dc23
2015015019

ISBN: 978-0-415-72037-3 (hbk)
ISBN: 978-1-315-86683-3 (ebk)

Typeset in Sabon
by Apex CoVantage, LLC

Printed and bound in Great Britain by
TJ International Ltd, Padstow, Cornwall

Contents

Figures

Tables

Foreword

In Japan, the conceptual transition from internationalization to globalization, which has, to some extent, occurred over the last three or four decades, has not always proceeded smoothly. The move from the initial grappling with the meaning of internationalization in the 1980s to engaging with the present-day consequences of globalization has resulted in sometimes farsighted, sometimes confused thinking and policy outcomes. The precise meanings of the terms "internationalization" and "globalization" have been the subject of wide discussion, ranging from the internal/external internationalization discussions (understood, broadly speaking, as a "we-do" process, i.e., a process in which Japan is seen as the chief actor, controlling the progression of events) to a more finely nuanced understanding of the meaning of globalization (understood more as a "done-to-us" process, i.e., a whole-of-globe process over which Japan cannot hope to retain sole control).

One theme that has remained constant in the debate has been the importance of language and, more widely in recent scholarship, the shifting nature of the link between language and identity in national and international contexts that are evolving to conform to, or in some cases resist, the encroaching consequences of globalization. Global population flows both into and out of Japan have resulted in changed language environments requiring considerable thought and effort to manage. Within Japan, this has meant mostly a focus on the linguistic needs of migrants in terms of learning Japanese through both top-down and bottom-up processes; the potential contribution to be made by the first languages of those migrants to the Japanese linguistic landscape, however, has been somehow overlooked in the mix. Outside Japan, the influence of Japanese soft power resources on Japanese language pedagogy and the diverse needs of heritage learners in non-Japanese education systems have created their own instances of globalization and its (sometimes) discontents.

As this book shows us, globalization has brought about an incipient weakening of the premises underlying the long and staunchly held ideology of Japanese monoculturalism, monoethnicity, and monolingualism as borders have become increasingly porous and both community demographics and linguistic practices have resulted in more fluid concepts of Japanese identity both in and outside of Japan. We find here research that elucidates the weakening of the old fixed hierarchies of language and identity cherished in Japan's view of internationalization, which do not take account of the daily realities of globalization. Hybridity, transculturalism, and translingualism are now for many the largely unremarkable norm, as the once fixed ideological boundaries between Japan and the rest of the world lose ground under the border-transcending influence of information technology and transnational population flows.

What is the underlying link between Japanese courtrooms, Australian educational institutions, programs for language minority children in Japan, and the influence of Japanese mass culture products on Japanese language learning in Australia? How do the ideologies and practices at play in each of these contexts challenge and confound conventional beliefs about the nexus between language and identity? In the context of globalization and Japan, this book contends that nexus now needs to be understood as much more wide reaching and infinitely more complex than was the case when ideas of language and nation were more simplistically linked in the configurations typical first of modernity and then of Japan's view of internationalization.

The chapters here presented raise interesting questions about how different manifestations of language use link with and contribute to identity formation in a wider range of spaces, both in Japan and overseas, than was accepted in the context of internationalization. The use of multilingual resources in the everyday lives of urban dwellers, for example, produces a linguistic space which challenges the traditional idea of a society as a bounded space characterized by use of a particular language. Foreign defendants in Japanese courtrooms can no longer automatically be assumed to need interpreter services, as the connection between Japanese nationality and the ability to speak Japanese well becomes more fluid. The English language, Japan's most widely taught and highly esteemed foreign language, is found not to have much practical value as a lingua franca for the mostly non-English-speaking migrants in Japanese communities or for Japanese people working abroad in Asia; in other words, the English taught as a tool for internationalization is not, as thought, a sine qua non in today's globalized work and community settings, and the fixed belief that the Japanese and English languages can between them account for all Japan's linguistic needs is called into question by the elucidation of actual linguistic needs and practices.

Uncritically accepted orthodoxies are here challenged and sometimes found to be wanting. An often discussed aspect of globalization with regard to Japan, for example, is the international success of its popular culture, something both private and public sectors have been eager to capitalize on. The influence of manga, anime, and other manifestations of popular culture has spread into a wide range of fields: art, fashion, design, and hospitality, to name only a few. To a large extent, this has been a deliberate commodification of culture intended to reap both economic and political profit and prestige and has been hailed as a successful attempt by the Japanese government to control Japan's image abroad. The question this book raises, however, in a chapter critiquing such soft power, is whether any potential gains to be made for Japan through cultural diplomacy of this sort will be limited by a reluctance to embrace the full meaning of globalization and open up beyond the limitations of the homegrown concept of internationalization, which might be argued to place greater emphasis on protecting cultural barriers than on transcending them. And further, argues another chapter, the impact of soft power resources on teaching the Japanese language outside Japan, often uncritically celebrated as a means of attracting and inspiring students, must in fact be carefully monitored given that information technology can now almost replace the teacher as a central facilitator of student learning about Japan and its language.

Focusing on the often overlapping cultural, ideological, and pedagogical aspects of the language and identity dichotomy now in transition, the studies collected here investigate at both macro and micro levels arguments and practices that depart from and often outright reject the standardized beliefs that have hitherto held the spotlight. The chapters on language and Japanese living abroad engage with a central concern of the book, namely how people who do not live in Japan but are nevertheless engaged with Japan in some way make sense of the relationship between identity and multilingualism, confounding the orthodox Japan-versus-the-world dichotomy. And not only those outside Japan: the chapter on metrolingualism highlights the casual ludic role multilingual interpolations can play in the negotiation and formulation of a user's urban identity and the constituting of concepts of place and space.

The investigation of multiple and carefully observed issues offered here covers a wide canvas and presents us with a new way of thinking about globalization and its effect on the synthesis of language and identity in today's world. It will repay careful reading and reflection.

Nanette Gottlieb
University of Queensland

1 Languages and Identities in a Transitional Japan

Ikuko Nakane, Emi Otsuji,
and William S. Armour

TRANSITIONAL JAPAN

Globalization has brought various challenges as well as opportunities to Japan. The collapse of the 'bubble economy' in the early 1990s led to a long period of recession, and the nation has faced the competitive and harsh realities of a broader world market that is moving faster than ever before. More recently, the rise of China as the world's second largest economy has, in part, contributed to tensions concerning the region's stability. In addition to this, it is common knowledge that Japan's birth rate has been decreasing, which has resulted in a younger population to sustain a similar Japan to what is presently taken for granted. As the unemployment rate is high, this also projects a worrying future of a society not capable of sustaining the welfare of the aging population. To offset this particular issue, since 2008, Japan has invited nurses and caregivers from Indonesia, the Philippines, and Vietnam with sufficient Japanese language skills to work in Japanese hospitals. On the other hand, the number of Japanese language learners and institutions overseas has grown steadily (The Japan Foundation 2013), Japanese food has become part of the cosmopolitan lifestyle in many parts of the world (Bestor 2000; Hamada 2011), and Japanese popular culture resources such as anime, manga and fashion have been embraced by millions of consumers around the world. As Daliot-Bul (2009: 247) points out, Japan's image associated with *kigyōshakai* or enterprise society has "gradually been replaced with that of 'Cool Japan.'" Under the trend, Iwabuchi (2010: 89) argues these recent discourses of 'Cool Japan' helps to disengage us from the following more crucial questions about

> whether and how the consumption of Japanese media culture enhances a deeper understanding of the complexity of Japanese society and culture; whether and how it reproduces one-dimensional and stereotypical views of "Japan" as an organic national-cultural entity; and whether and how power relations operate to divide some groups and keep others intact.

For instance, Tokyo has been selected as the host city of the 2020 Olympic Games (see http://tokyo2020.jp/en/), which gives Japan, through its capital city Tokyo, an optimal opportunity to promote its positive image to the rest of the world through what Iwabuchi (2010: 90) calls "brand nationalism" or "uncritical, practical uses of media culture as resources for the enhancement of political and economic national interests."

As such, in the Contemporary Period of globalization,[1] Japan has gone through significant social changes, which include issues of language and identity. With increasing mobility of people and transcultural flows in the globalized world, the idea of Japan as a monolingual, monocultural, and monoethnic nation is becoming gradually demythologized (e.g., Gottlieb 2012a, b; Heinrich & Galan 2011; Maher & Yashiro 1995; Willis & Murphy-Shigematsu 2008). Along with the transnational and transcultural practices brought about by globalization (Blommaert 2010, 2013; Heller 2011; Pennycook 2010), Japan is facing new challenges not only within its geopolitical boundaries but also elsewhere beyond the borders. This is not to say that globalization is new to Japan, as it 'opened up to the world' more than once in its history (Befu 2000), nor is it a totally new phenomenon anywhere else. Akin to superdiversity (Vertovec 2006), which accounts for the increasing diversity in Europe, globalization brings about intense mobility and diversity to Japan, resulting in the refashioning of languages and identities. As Coupland (2010) suggests, trends in globalization such as the rapid spread of communication technologies and increasing mobility have implications for language and identity that warrant fresh scholarly inquiry.

Against the backdrop of these challenges and opportunities, what has globalization meant for languages, identities, and Japan-in-transition? While there is no agreement on what globalization *is* (cf. Bauman 1998; Bartelson 2000; Steger 2009), there are useful frameworks for understanding globalization in terms of what it *involves* or *does*. Steger defines globalization as a "set of social processes that appear to transform our present social condition of weakening nationality into one of globality" (2009: 10) and as "the expansion and intensification of social relations and consciousness across world-time and world-space" (ibid: 18). His understanding of globalization reflects the global economic, political, cultural, and environmental interconnections and flows (ibid: 9–10), but he also refers to the cultural dimension, in particular, globalization languages (ibid: 100–103). His work, therefore, elucidates important relations between language, identity, and globalization. Bartelson (2000) discusses three ways to conceptualize globalization: *transference, transformation, and transcendence*. Transference involves global flows in a sense of transfer from or exchange between distinct units or systems (such as nations), which is in line with the concept of internationalization (see the next section). On the other hand, transformation entails global flows disturbing the integrity and distinct identity of existing units or systems. Transcendence is one step further than this, where the disturbed boundaries are diffused and the world as one whole takes the form of "networks of flow" (Coupland 2010: 7). As Featherstone (1990: 2) pointed out, globalization entails "cultural integration and cultural disintegration processes which take place not only on an interstate level but processes which transcend the state-society unit and can therefore be held to occur on a trans-national or trans-societal level."

Change associated with globalization that has implications for language and identity include the rapid expansion of communication technology via the Internet, resulting in faster and easier access to information (Friedman 2007), proliferation of consumer culture and commodification (Coupland 2010: 3; Iwabuchi 2002), diffusion and hybridization of culture (Eades 2000), and increasing ethnic diversity and demographic mobility (Coupland 2010), to name a few. Speaking from the perspective of transformation and transcendence, some of the major consequences of the earlier mentioned global phenomena are 'hybridity' and 'multiplicity' (Coupland 2010), 'translanguaging' (García & Wei 2014), 'translingual,' and 'transcultural' phenomena (Canagarajah 2013; Pennycook 2007, 2010). Rather than taking hybridity of language and cultural practices as new and exceptions, these studies take them as the norm (Blackledge & Creese 2010; Blommaert 2013; García and Wei 2014; Otsuji & Pennycook 2014). There is a growing literature on Japan that shows this trend, (e.g., Willis & Murphy-Shigematsu 2008; Heinrich 2012a, 2012b). However, the focus of inquiry should also extend beyond the borders of Japan and examine 'Japan' in the global sphere, transcending the 'Japan-and-the-rest-of-the-world' ideology. This implies the importance of scrutinizing the relations between the local (Japan) and global practices. While 'global' has been the central theme in the discussion surrounding globalization, interfaces between the global and the local have also been explored (Hannerz 1990, 2001; Kraidy 2002; Robertson 1994). In the field of sociolinguistics, the study of these interfaces has brought to light a further understanding of how language and identity practices may have both local and global implications (Rubdy & Alsagoff 2014; Blommaert 2010, 2013; Pennycook 2010). As Pennycook (2010: 4) puts it, "the local is always defined in relation to something else regional, national, global, universal, modern, new, from elsewhere." His statement clearly points to the importance of looking at language and identity issues in a transitional Japan by linking both the local and global as well as the grassroots and policy level.

FROM INTERNATIONALIZATION TO GLOBALIZATION

The aim of this book, then, is to unpack what has been taking place in Japan in the process and as a consequence of internationalization or *kokusaika*, and to explore how the limits and opportunities engendered by *kokusaika* led to the current discourse and practice of globalization. The term *kokusaika* has been defined and interpreted in different ways. The two significant approaches to *kokusaika* relevant to our discussion are, on the one hand, about Japan's increased involvement in economic, cultural, and educational exchanges, etc., while on the other hand, it is about transcending cultural and national boundaries, with changes in the attitudes and mind-set of

Japanese people (Hook & Weiner 1992; Sugiyama 1992). Language has been a central issue in Japan's internationalization (Gottlieb 2000), and the major focus of this policy was on English language education (Gottlieb 2012b; Kubota & Mckay 2009) uncritically reinforcing the language ideology of the linguistic imperialism of English (Phillipson 1992). Given that the hegemony of English is so visible in the globalizing world, Japan cannot be the only nation whose language policy has been driven by a strong association between internationalization and English. The Japan Exchange and Teaching (JET) Program, a major government initiative that began in 1987 with the aim of enhancing English skills of Japanese students and of promoting international exchange is a clear example of the ideological underpinning of Anglocentric internationalization.

The ideology of English as the language of internationalization has also been critiqued as another instance of Westernization rather than internationalization in a sense of transcending cultural boundaries (Kubota & Mckay 2009). The problem with the exclusive focus on English is that, despite the sharp increase in their number since the 1970s, the language needs of migrants within Japan have not been addressed (Gottlieb 2012b). A need for 'internal internationalization' was strongly felt by communities that were receiving a large number of migrants; but often languages other than English, such as Filipino, Portuguese, and Chinese, were their first languages. Thus there is a disjuncture between the ideology of English as the language of internationalization and the foreign languages required for 'internal' internationalization of Japan.

Children of migrants require Japanese language skills for their education in the Japanese school system, which has meant that Japanese as a second language (JSL) support has to be provided. However, as Burgess (2012) points out, the language policy of Japanese as a second/foreign language (JS/FL) has until recently focused on the promotion of Japanese language education overseas but has neglected the language needs of migrants in Japan (see also Gottlieb 2012b). The reality of the rapid increase in the number of migrants since the 1980s and a lack of central government policy about this has left communities housing large migrant populations with their own '*tabunka kyōsei*' (multicultural coexistence: Ministry of Internal Affairs and Communication 2006) initiatives to address community-specific needs to provide language assistance (Shikama 2008). Therefore, an ideology of Japanese as a second/foreign language for 'foreigners overseas' appears to have prevailed, while it has taken a long time for JSL within Japan policy to take a shape. In fact, language issues faced by 'older' minority groups such as Chinese and *zainichi* Korean populations have not been recognized as much. Even after *tabunka kyōsei* superseded *kokusaika* as the main government policy since the 1990s, the *tabunka kyōsei* policy has also had its own ideological trap. Heinrich (2012a: 19) argues that "the idea of multicultural coexistence is found to perpetuate the assumption that Japan is linguistically and culturally homogeneous. In consequence, it reproduces the Japanese-verses-foreigner binary which is antithetical to the integration of immigrants." *Tabunka kyōsei* is then based on modernist assumptions about nation, language, and ethnicity.

The modernist approach is still ubiquitous when it comes to policy notwithstanding the fact that language and cultural practices are 'transcending borders' on the local level, as a result of the mobility of people/language/ artifacts as well as the advancement of technology. The roles that languages other than English and Japanese play within Japan and in encounters in the global sphere have not been legitimately acknowledged, despite an intensifying focus on English, as the government has been campaigning and securing Trans-Pacific Partnership agreements to revitalize its standing in the world economy. Under the *English Education Reform Plan Corresponding to Globalization* undertaken in Japan by the Ministry of Education, Culture, Sports, Science & Technology (MEXT), when English was introduced in primary schools for the first time since 2014 it was uncritically assumed to be the lingua franca of the world, thereby reinforcing a narrow, monolingual view of globalization (Kubota, 2014). The reform plan includes: "東京オリンピック・パラリンピックに向け、児童生徒の英語による日本文化の発信、国際交流・ボランティア活動等の取組を強化 (The building up of younger (lit. child/juvenile) students' *English* for transmitting Japanese culture, international exchange and volunteer activities, etc., for the Tokyo Olympics and Paralympics; underline added for emphasis)" and "日本人としてのアイデンティティに関する教育の充実 [伝統文化・歴史の重視等] (Enhancing education in relation to Japanese identities [emphasizing traditional culture, history, etc.])." This is another acute version of a monoglossic internationalization discourse, which seems to ignore the linguistic and cultural diversities within Japan. While some contemporary studies with a 'transcendence' approach to globalization are beginning to look at the complex phenomenon of border transgression by decoupling of language, ethnicity, culture, and nation-state, as well as by examining what it means to be 'Japanese' and speak 'Japanese' in current culturally and linguistically diverse Japan (Gottlieb 2012a; Willis & Murphy-Shigematsu 2008), Japan is still a milieu full of contradictions and dilemmas in the face of globalization.

Another important language-related contributing factor for the shift from internationalization to globalization is the teaching of Japanese as a Foreign Language overseas. The Japan Foundation, which was established in 1972 under the Foreign Ministry, was given the role of promoting Japanese culture, arts, language, and studies of Japan, as well as cultural and intellectual exchange. As Japan's international presence grew, the number of learners of Japanese overseas increased during the 1980s and 1990s and is still growing today according to a survey by the Japan Foundation (2013). In fact, Burgess (2012) suggests that JS/FL has contributed to the protection of an independent and unique Japanese identity, as its purpose was mainly to promote "the 'correct understanding' of Japan abroad" (p. 45). In relation to Japanese language education overseas, it is worth noting that the impact of the rapid spread of the Internet and online resources for learners, which is taken for granted today (2014), were yet to be experienced in the 1980s and early 1990s. This has meant that JS/FL overseas relied on teachers, textbooks, and the most basic of audiovisual materials, which allowed for a traditional transmission of 'Japanese language and culture' as a model, thereby maintaining the identity positioning of 'Japan' and 'the rest of the world.'

The Internet and the advancement of communication technology has enabled the expansion of Japanese soft power across the globe. Learners of Japanese are no longer passively instructed in the language; as they consume Japanese popular culture, the language becomes a tool for them to access these products. The model of JS/FL in which Japanese language education is for a "correct understanding of Japan" (Burgess 2012: 45) cannot be sustained in globalization and there has been a shift away from the conventional view based on 'linguistic nationalism' (Miller 1982; Gottlieb 2000, 2005) that Japanese is a uniquely difficult language to learn for foreigners. For many, it is Japanese popular culture (such as manga, anime, video games, television dramas, and music) that has provided *the* reason for learning Japanese (e.g., Northwood & Thomson 2012). This particular phenomenon, termed the Japanese popular culture effects argument by Armour and Iida (2014), seems to reflect a shift from the nationalistic discourse of *kokusaika* to more open attitudes toward the global spread of the Japanese. The popularity of Japanese pop culture, however, was again deployed pragmatically by the Japanese government to promote the country as 'Cool Japan' (e.g., Daliot-Bul 2009).

Learners are also changing. There are those who achieve a high level of proficiency in Japanese without going through formal language instruction. There is a growing number of so-called 'heritage' speakers of Japanese in the Japanese diaspora around the world (Kondo-Brown 2006; Oguro & Moloney 2012) and children moving between spaces, languages, and categories of language learning (Kawakami 2011). The ideology that foreigners do not speak Japanese well and Japanese nationals do is far from the reality in modern Japan and across the globe (cf. Burgess 2012). As García (2009: 8) argues, there is a need for pedagogical practices "firmly rooted in the multilingual and multimodal language and literacy practices of children in schools in the 21st century." For those learners, it is not so much about mastering a target language as about manipulating the various linguistic resources available to them. This approach resonates with 'symbolic competency' (Kramsch 2006, 2008), which is premised on the ecological approach to language teaching and claims that what is needed for these learners is "a particularly acute ability to play with various linguistic codes and with the various spatial and temporal resonances of these codes" (2008: 664). Yet despite the hybridity, multiplicity, and diversity at the policy and public awareness levels, ideologies about language and identity in the 'internationalization' framework, or globalization as *transference*, still seem to have a strong grip on Japan.

We have yet to see the development of the recent move toward a systematic approach to the need to support the education of non-Japanese-speaking-background children in Japan, among other language-related support initiatives. Japanese language is also becoming more 'international/global' (cf. Gottlieb 2000), and it has become far more than a language of international economic exchange: a tool to consume popular culture and to pursue personal interests in the global market of the 'Japan brand.' These trends emerging in globalization necessitate inquiry into languages, identities, and Japan-in-transition-in-transition. Coupland (2010) highlights the importance of social relations and identity for research into language and society in relation to globalization, because the relationship between language and identity has become more complex now than the traditional notion that language and identity are associated with distinct communities. Accordingly, for a comprehensive account of transitional Japan, it is important to scrutinize the interfaces between the local and the global levels as well as grassroots and policy levels of language and identity practices (Blommaert 2010; Pennycook 2010). The collection of chapters in this book in varied ways debunk the ideology of language and identity that Japan has retained beyond its era of internationalization; it may have no other choice but to relinquish such an ideology in the globalizing world. The book takes an interdisciplinary approach covering education, cultural studies, linguistics, and policy making and uses a combination of global and local perspectives. The central theme, languages and identities in a transitional Japan, is approached through critical discussions of global trends, policies, and public discourses, as well as through analysis of associated local practices. We ask what constitutes contemporary Japanese culture: how people, including those who do not reside in Japan but are engaged with Japan in some ways, and the global community make sense of identity and multilingualism.

A TRANSITIONAL JAPAN: DECENTERING PERSPECTIVES

In our exploration of languages, identities, and a transitional Japan, we identified three major areas of transition: *cultural, ideological,* and *pedagogical.* The first domain of transition is *cultural.* Rapid spread of the Internet and communication technology has accelerated access to Japanese popular culture products outside of Japan. In Chapter 2, Burgess gives a critical appraisal of the Japanese government's 'Cool Japan' diplomacy as its globalization strategy. While the government policy is aligned with the popularity of Japanese popular culture, Burgess warns against the ideologies underlying the Cool Japan diplomacy, critiquing the overreliance on the 'Japan brand' promotion despite a thin identity connection between the nation and the pop culture, and the policy makers' lack of global perspectives. Burgess' chapter also gives a context to the analysis of the impact of cultural and technological transition on Japanese as a second/foreign language outside of Japan, presented in some of the chapters in the collection. Armour, reviewing the development of Japanese language education in Australia, shows in Chapter 3 that with the powerful impact of Japanese popular culture and the spread of the Internet, Japanese language no longer exclusively 'belongs to' the geographical boundaries of Japan, but is used as a medium for consumer activities around the globe. Learners overseas are now able to use multiple resources available online, which they can access during class and outside of class hours. This has shifted the roles of teacher and student substantially, and Armour warns of the consequences of this transition in language programs and the future of JS/FL in its relationships with the popular culture products and available technology.

The second domain of transition is *ideological*. The chapters in this domain challenge the ideology of dichotomized categories of languages as distinct entities and their one-to-one identification with particular groups of users. In Chapter 4, Kubota critically discusses a powerful ideology that Japanese speakers are expected to use English as a means of international communication, drawing from examples of Chinese-Japanese business communication in China. She finds that actual communication practice does not entail the use of English as a lingua franca. Kubota also juxtaposes this finding with ideologies emerging from her ethnographic interviews with the Japanese residents in a Japanese town with a relatively high percentage of migrant population, demonstrating a disjuncture between the realities of 'borderless communication' in the globalizing world and the ideologies held by Japanese locals. This dichotomized view of Japanese versus non-Japanese speakers is also problematized in Nakane's chapter (Chapter 5). It shows that linguistic practices in Japanese criminal court proceedings take account of the fact that many defendants are able to use Japanese as a second language, though not to the extent of understanding highly technical legal genres. It is argued that the practice and discourses around language-related issues in a legal context ignore the problems faced by defendants and witnesses who speak Japanese as a first language. Otsuji, in Chapter 6, challenges the language ideology behind multilingualism, which is often premised on the conventional static correlations between nation, language, and ethnicity by applying a 'metrolingualism' framework (Otsuji & Pennycook 2014; Pennycook & Otsuji 2014). Otsuji argues that language ideology based on accountability does not allow for transcultural realities of language use in the globalizing world. Subsequently, in her analysis of everyday language use by Tokyo urbanites, she focuses on capturing the productive space provided by the contemporary city.

The third category of transition is *pedagogical*. Chapter 7 by Moloney and Oguro discuss an underresearched topic of heritage Japanese learners and their transcultural identities. They explore the trajectories of two second-generation Japanese Australians' identity negotiation in relation to their informal and formal language learning experiences. Although migrant children's language and identity developments are important to their transcultural lives as well as to their families, Moloney and Oguro point out that the educational system does not always support heritage learners' language and identity developments, as was the case with their interviewees who were not able to pursue formal Japanese language education beyond certain points due to their transcultural history.

In Chapter 8, Ōhashi and Ōhashi discuss two case studies of JFL in Australia, one at a university with a large proportion of international students and the other at a tertiary vocational education institution. Through the case studies, they consider a potential humanistic value of Japanese language education in a multicultural society such as Australia, sending a strong message that communicative competence in Japanese should not be the only objective of language education. While challenges do exist in their endeavor, the potential of language education to embrace diversity and empower learners debunks the idea of JS/FL as a means to enable transfer or exchange of information and instead casts it as a process of transformation and transcendence. In Chapter 9, Taniguchi and McMahill take a critical approach to policies of language and internationalization and beyond in Japan. In discussing problematic assimilation-oriented measures for migrant children's educational needs, their chapter gives an illuminating example of the struggles of an NPO in trying to support minority language maintenance of migrant children within the institutional framework of the Japanese education system. The NPO's approach to involve Japanese-speaking-background children to nurture their understanding of multiculturalism was not successful, an outcome that suggests lack of enthusiasm toward *transformation*.

While the book is organized into three parts according to the domains of transition outlined earlier, these three domains overlap and are interrelated. Cultural transition interacts with language pedagogy, while the ideological transition will result in pedagogical changes and vice versa. The discussion in each of the chapters of this book, in one way or another, also involves multiplicity and hybridity of languages and identities within and outside Japan and in transcultural and transnational spheres. With the global and multiple perspectives, one of the important aims of this book is to 'decenter' Japan through the discussion of languages and identities in relation to Japan-in-transition. We ask: What role does Japanese play outside Japan? What languages are used and in what way are they used in various transnational and transcultural contexts related to Japan in the globalizing world, and how are identities negotiated? In addressing these questions, therefore, this book attempts to challenge ideologies about languages and identities deeply rooted in a Japan-versus-the-outside-world dichotomy. The combination of macro and micro approaches is intended to highlight the gap emerging between ideologies about language and identity and their associated local practices in this crucial transitional period for Japan.

NOTE

1. Steger (2009) divides 'globalization' into five periods: Prehistoric (10,000BCE–3,500BCE), Premodern (3,500BCE–1500CE), Early Modern (1500–1750), Modern (1750–1970), and Contemporary (1970–present).

REFERENCES

Armour, W. S., & Iida, S. (2014). Are Australian fans of anime and manga motivated to learn Japanese language? *Asia Pacific Journal of Education*, 54–71. doi: 10.1080/02188791.2014.922459

Bauman, Z. (1998). *Globalization: The human consequences*. Cambridge: Polity Press.

Bartelson, J. (2000). Three concepts of globalization. *International Sociology, 15*(2), 180–196.

Befu, H. (2000). Globalization as human dispersal: From the perspective of Japan. In J. S. Eades, T. Gill, & H. Befu (Eds.), *Globalization and Social Change in Contemporary Japan* (pp. 17–40). Melbourne: Trans Pacific Press.

Bestor, T. C. (2000). How sushi went global. *Foreign Policy, 121*(Nov.–Dec.), 54–63.

Blackledge, A., & Creese, A. (2010). *Multilingualism: A critical perspective*. London: Continuum.

Blommaert, J. (2010). *The sociolinguistics of globalization*. Cambridge: Cambridge University Press.

Blommaert, J. (2013). *Ethnography, superdiversity and linguistic landscapes: Chronicles of complexity*. Bristol: Multilingual Matters.

Burgess, C. (2012). 'It's better if they speak broken Japanese': Language as a pathways or an obstacle to citizenship in Japan? In N. Gottlieb (Ed.), *Language and Citizenship in Japan* (pp. 37–57). New York: Routledge.

Canagarajah, S. (2013). *Translingual practice: Global Englishes and cosmopolitan relations*. New York: Routledge.

Coupland, N. (2010). Introduction: sociolinguistics in the Global Era. In N. Coupland (Ed.), *The Handbook of Language and Globalization* (pp. 1–27). Oxford: Blackwell.

Daliot-Bul, M. (2009). Japan brand strategy: The taming of 'cool Japan' and the challenges of cultural planning in a postmodern age. *Social Science Japan Journal 12*(2), 247–266.

Eades, J. (2000). Introduction: Globalization and social change in contemporary Japan. In J. S. Eades, T. Gill, & H. Befu (Eds.), *Globalization and Social Change in Contemporary Japan* (pp. 1–16). Melbourne: Trans Pacific Press.

Featherstone, M. (Ed.). (1990). *Global culture: Nationalism globalization and modernity*. London: Sage.

García, O. (2009). *Bilingual education in the 21st century: A global perspective*. Oxford: Wiley-Blackwell.

García, O., & Wei, L. (2014). *Translanguaging: Language, bilingualism and education*. London: Palgrave macmillan.

Gottlieb, N. (2000). *Word processing technology in Japan: Kanji and the keyboard*. Richmond: Curzon.

Gottlieb, N. (2012a). Language, citizenship, and identity in Japan. In N. Gottlieb (Ed.), *Language and Citizenship in Japan* (pp. 1–18). New York: Routledge.

Gottlieb, N. (2012b). *Language policy in Japan: The challenge of change*. Cambridge: Cambridge University Press.

Hamada, I. (2011). The Japanese restaurant as an exotic genre: A study of culinary providers' practices and dialogues in Melbourne. *New Voices, 5*, 84–102.

Heller, M. (2011). *Paths to post-nationalism: A critical ethnography of language and identity*. Oxford: Oxford Universtiy Press.

Hannerz, U. (1990). Cosmopolitans and locals in world culture. In M. Featherstone (Ed.), *Global culture: Nationalism, globalisation and modernity*. London: Sage.

Hannerz, U. (2001). Thinking about culture in a global ecumene. In J. Lulle (Ed.), *Culture in the communication age* (pp. 19–36). London: Routledge.

Heinrich, P. (2012a). After homogeneity: Maintaining unity in a linguistically diversifying Japan *Language and citizenship in Japan*. New York: Routledge.
Heinrich, P. (Ed.). (2012b). *Making of monolingual Japan: Language ideology and Japanese modernity*. Bristol: Multilingual Matters.
Heinrich, P., & Galan, C. (Eds.). (2011). *Language life in Japan: Transformations and prospects*. London: Routledge.
Hook, G. D., & Weiner, M. A. (Eds.). (1992). *The internationalization of Japan*. London: Routledge.
Iwabuchi, K. (2002). *Recentering globalization: Popular culture and Japanese transnationalism*. Durham: Duke University Press.
Iwabuchi, K. (2010). Undoing inter-national fandom in the age of brand nationalism. *Mecademia 5*, 87–96.
The Japan Foundation. (2013). *Survey Report on Japanese—Language Education Abroad 2012*. Retrieved on June 30, 2014, from http://www.jpf.go.jp/j/japanese/survey/result/dl/survey_2012/2012_s_excerpt_e.pdf
Kawakami, I. (2011). *"Idōsuru Kodomotachi" no Kyōikugaku* [*Research in Education of "Children on the Move"*]. Tokyo: Kurosio.
Kondo-Brown, K. (2006). Introduction. In K. Kondo-Brown (Ed.), *Heritage Language Development: Focus on East Asian Immigrants* (pp. 1–12). Amsterdam: John Benjamins.
Kraidy, M. M. (2002). Hybridity in cultural globalisation. *Communication theory, 12*(3), 316–339.
Kramsch, C. (2006). From communicative competence to symbolic competence. *The Modern Language Journal 90*, 249–252.
Kubota, R. (2014). Orimpikku to eigokyoiku: Hangurobaruteki kaikaku [The Olympics and English language teaching: An anti-global reform]. *Shukan Kinyobi, 975*.
Kubota, R., & McKay, S. (2009). Globalization and language learning in rural Japan: The role of English in the local linguistic ecology. *TESOL Quarterly, 43*(4), 593–619.
Maher, J. C., & Yashiro, K. (Eds.). (1995). *Multilingual Japan*. Clevedon, PA: Multilingual Matters.
Miller, R. A. (1982). *Japan's Modern Myth: The language and beyond*. New York: Weatherhill.
Ministry of International Affairs and Communication. (2006). Kokudo shisaku sōhatsu chōsa Kitakantōken no sangyō iji ni muketa kigyō jichitai renkei ni yoru tabunka kyōsei chiiki zukuri chōsa hōkokusho (Report on developing multicultural co-existence areas by cooperate and local government to sustain industries in North Kanto region). Retrieved on June 12, 2013, from http://www.mlit.go.jp/kokudokeikaku/souhatu/h18seika/04kitakantou/04kitakantou.html
Northwood, B., and Thomson, C. K. (2012). What keeps them going? Investigating ongoing learners of Japanese in Australian universities. *Japanese Studies, 32*(3), 335–355.
Oguro, S., and Moloney, R. (2012). Misplaced heritage language learners of Japanese in secondary schools. *Heritage Language Journal, 9*(2), 70–84.
Otsuji, E., & Pennycook, A. (2014). Unremarkable hybridities and metroingual practies. In R. Rubdy & L. Alsagoff (Eds.), *The global-local interface, language choice and hybridity: Exploring language and identity* (pp. 83–99). Bristol: Multilingual Matters.
Pennycook, A. (2007). *Global Englishes and transcultural flows*. London: Routledge.
Pennycook, A. (2010). *Language as a local practice*. New York: Routledge.
Pennycook, A., & Otsuji, E. (2014). Metrolingual multitasking and spatial repertoires: 'Pizza mo two minutes coming'. *Journal of Sociolinguistics, 18*(2), 161–184.
Phillipson, R. (1992). *Linguistic imperialism*. Oxford: Oxford University Press.

Robertson, R. (1994). Globalisation or glocalisation? *Journal of International Communication 1*(1), 33–52.

Rubdy, R., & Alsagoff, L. (Eds.). (2014). *The global-local interface and hybridity: Exploring language and identity*. Bristol: Multilingual Matters.

Shikama, A. (2008). Integration policy towards migrants in Japan with a focus on language. In P. Heinrich & Y. Sugita (Eds.), *Japanese as a Foreign Language in the Age of Globalization* (pp. 51–64). München: indicium Verlag.

Steger, M. B. (2009). *Globalization: A brief insight*. New York: Sterling.

Sugiyama, Y. (1992). Internal and external aspects of internationalization. In G. D. Hook & M. A. Weiner (Eds.), *The Internationalization of Japan* (pp. 72–103). London: Routledge.

Vertovec, S (2006) *The emergence of super-diversity in Britain*. Working Paper No 25, Centre of Policy, Migration and Society, University of Oxford.

Willis, D. B., & Murphy-Shigematsu, S. (Eds.). (2008). *Transcultural Japan: At the borderland of race, gender and identity*. London: Routledge.

Part I
Cultural Transition

2 National Identity and the Transition from Internationalization to Globalization

"Cool Japan" or "Closed Japan"?

Chris Burgess

> Whether it's that [we] do not like foreigners, or do not want foreign-
> ers, Japanese tend to be, shall I say, an extremely insular single ethnic
> group—it's because we don't have much [exchange] with the world.
> First, [to increase the number of tourists who visit Japan] we must
> open the country up, the Japanese must open their hearts . . .
>
> —Tourism Minister Nariaki Nakayama, September 2008
> ("Shinseiken" 2008, translation by the author)

INTRODUCTION

The disaster was "divine retribution" (*tenbatsu*) proclaimed Tokyo Governor
Shintaro Ishihara just days after the March 11, 2011 Tōhoku Earthquake
("Ishihara tochiji" 2011): "The Japanese people have become a selfish
(*gayoku*) people. We need to use the tsunami to wash away this egoism, to
wash away the grime accumulated over many years in the Japanese heart."
At first glance, Ishihara's words seem to have much in common with those
uttered by U.S. religious conservatives in the wake of natural disasters. For
example, in 2005, Pat Robertson and others portrayed Hurricane Katrina
as God's punishment for America's sins ("Religious conservatives" 2005).
In actual fact, Ishihara was not really talking about God at all; he was talking about Japanese national identity. His words can be seen as criticism of
what he perceives as a growing self-centeredness and materialism in Japanese
society, particularly among the younger generation. "American identity is
freedom," he explained in the same remarks, "French identity is freedom and
philanthropy. But Japan has nothing like that. Just selfishness, materialism,
and a desire for money" ("Ishihara tochiji" 2011, translation by the author).

Ishihara's negative characterization of the contemporary Japanese
national character does not seem to be shared by many outside Japan. In
September 2011, two of Japan's biggest popular culture exports performed
in China. SMAP (in Beijing) and AKB48 (in Shanghai) held concerts to

thank the Chinese people for their support following the March 2011 earth-quake and tsunami ("AKB48" 2011; "SMAP concert" 2011). The Beijing concert was significant because an earlier concert, originally planned for late 2010, had been canceled following the arrest of a Chinese fishing trawler captain in disputed waters near the Senkaku (Diaoyu) Islands in September of that year. The wave of anti-Japanese feeling that swept China then contrasted starkly with the excited fans and widespread public sympathy for Japan a year later. A Yomiuri ("Shinraikan" 2011) poll, for example, saw the number of Chinese respondents who thought Japan-China relations were "good" rise from 7% in 2010 to 48% in 2011, while those who thought Japan "could be trusted" grew to 55% from 15% a year earlier. In one online survey, conducted in late 2011 by Japanese advertising giant Dentsu, 65% of Chinese respondents said they had donated money or aid goods or offered encouragement via the Internet, while a majority viewed the Japanese as having positive characteristics, such as "orderly," "patient," "cool-headed," and "having solidarity" ("China's view" 2011). "The tone of the Chinese media coverage of Japan immediately after the disaster," noted the *Daily Yomiuri* ("China's view" 2011), "suggested opinions of this nation were being re-evaluated."

Praise of the Japanese after 3/11 was not confined to China. The international English language press also expressed admiration for the Japanese national character following the quake. One quality which was frequently highlighted was that of endurance and perseverance, often appearing in arti-cles in its original Japanese form, *gaman*. Elsewhere, I (2011: 31–39) analyze thirty articles containing the term *gaman* in major world publications in the six months following 3/11. The fact that a Japanese term (*gaman*) unfamiliar to most English speakers started to feature regularly in reportage of the quake demonstrates the importance the media attached to what was described as a "core value," a "distinctively Japanese mentality" ("Japanese character" 2011; "Why quakes" 2011). Like the Chinese survey noted earlier, many articles attributed the lack of "shouting, disorder, and looting" to the exis-tence of *gaman* ("Each time" 2011), contrasting Japanese orderliness with the chaos, looting, and violence seen in the aftermath of natural disasters in other countries (Choong, 2011; "Where are the Japanese looters?", 2011).

Of course, many of these stereotypes can be disputed, including the notion that there were no raised voices or crime (Burgess 2011: 39–40; see also "Crimes plunge" 2011). Elsewhere, I (2011: 40–45) have challenged the idea of *gaman* as a unique national identity trait in terms of (a) how Japanese actually see themselves, (b) the presence of similar traits in other countries, and (c) significant regional character differences. However, what is important here is not so much whether these discourses are "true" or "false," but what people believe and the discursive effects these beliefs have on their worldview (Burgess 2010). The social context determines how terms are interpreted and which interpretations become dominant, remind-ing us that choices and meanings of words are never ideologically neutral but always political. This is particularly well illustrated by national identity terms like *gaman*, which describe national "difference," terms which are evaluated negatively or positively depending on particular circumstances.

In a rapidly globalizing world, national images are extremely fluid and increasingly difficult to control. The positive images of Japan that arose spontaneously around the world post 3/11 might not last long; indeed, there are signs that much of the goodwill generated toward Japan post 3/11 may have already evaporated. China, for example, has complained that their support has not been properly appreciated ("Chūgoku shien" 2012). In particular, relations between Japan and China soured markedly after Japan's nationalization of three of the five Senkaku Islands in September 2012 ("Posturing" 2012). Anti-Japanese protests and boycotts of Japanese goods dominated the news in the ensuing months, and incursions by Chinese surveillance ships, planes, and even drones have become a common occurrence. China's muted reaction to Japan securing the right to host the 2020 Olympic Games—saying that success would depend on whether Japan recognizes past wartime aggression—was telling ("China" 2013). The current fluidity of the Japan-China relationship clearly shows how circumstances can quickly affect national images.

Japan-China problems aside, the positive media coverage of Japan in 2011 contrasts starkly with that of 1995, the year of the Great Hanshin Earthquake, but also fifty years since the end of the Pacific War. Despite five decades having passed since Second World War Allied propaganda portrayed the Japanese as a subhuman species (Dower 1986), Hammond (1997: xii) noted the apparent continuity in Western portrayals of the Japanese, describing the 1995 media coverage as "a media deluge of anti-Japanese chauvinism." Although the scale of the 1995 and 2011 disasters were not the same, this doesn't sufficiently explain the sea change in tone over the ensuing sixteen years. Specifically, how much has the emergence of Japan as a cultural superpower in the late 1990s influenced Japan's image abroad? Of particular interest here are recent government attempts to use popular culture as a soft power tool to exert and expand Japanese influence through a public diplomacy blitz known as Cool Japan. In the context of a shift from internationalization to globalization, this chapter asks how successful the attempt to capitalize on Japan's popularity and to ideologically control national images has actually been.

In attempting to answer these questions, the chapter proceeds as follows. The next section looks at the economic boom of the 1980s, "Japan-bashing," and the birth of *kokusaika*—Japanese-style internationalization. Following this, the chapter examines the post-bubble challenges of the 1990s and the switch from *kokusaika* to globalization. Then I trace the emergence of the Cool Japan movement, which, in its desire to control and manipulate national images, has echoes of earlier *kokusaika* ideology. The chapter then identifies some of the problems with the Cool Japan project. In the conclusion, I argue that Japan's reluctance to move beyond internationalization, embrace globalization, and truly open up severely limits any influence it hopes to obtain through its soft power diplomacy.

THE JAPANESE MODEL AND JAPAN-BASHING: THE BIRTH OF KOKUSAIKA IN THE 1980s

Japan's rapid economic growth from the 1960s to the 1980s—known as the Japanese economic miracle—saw the "Japanese model," particularly management practices, become the object of much admiration worldwide. For Vogel (1979), Japan offered the best example of a successful nation that America could learn from and mirror. In terms of Japan's relations with the world, the emphasis was firmly on "economic diplomacy" and globalization, when it was considered at all, was conceived "largely in the context of international competitiveness and the popular belief that the economy could be internationalized while maintaining Japan's unique cultural integrity" (Mouer 2004: 168, 180). In other words, Japan was both culturally confident and culturally closed, secure in its own insular identity. This changed over the course of the 1980s as Japan came to be viewed less as an ideal and more as a threat or problem: "Japan's supposed cultural uniqueness," writes Iwabuchi (2002b: 214), "had changed from an object of admiration to one of criticism." Morris (2011: 2, 3) notes that the term "Japan-bashing"—a label both describing and criticizing anti-Japanese rhetoric—was in widespread use in the U.S. by the late 1980s.

Faced with growing international criticism, Japan was forced to respond. In Japan, Morris (2011: 89, 137) argues that "Japan-bashing" was interpreted as "the product of widespread misunderstanding," a mutual perception or information gap rooted in ignorance and fear. The solution was to engage with the world to "actively promote 'correct' and positive images of Japan throughout the world" (Morris 2011: 90). Carried out under the umbrella term *kokusaika* (literally "internationalization"), these PR efforts were undertaken by a variety of actors, from the government to business leaders, from government-affiliated institutions (such as The Japan Foundation and Nichibunken[1]) to academics and the media (Morris 2011: 90). However, although the English term "internationalization" refers simply to contact and exchange with other countries and implies both a physical and psychological opening up, Japanese *kokusaika* is a far more complex term that highlights how language is a form of social practice. Goodman (2007: 71) refers to *kokusaika* as a "multivocal symbol" that means different things to different people, "the site of conflict as different interest groups compete to have their own interpretations accepted as the dominant one." Goodman (2007: 72) identifies two diametrically opposed meanings for the term *kokusaika*: a Japanese-only nationalism that reinforces a "closed" national identity and a more universalistic, global concept "transcending any idea of national identity." Elsewhere, I (2004) argue that the former "boundary-strengthening" interpretation rather than the latter "boundary-loosening" interpretation of *kokusaika* has been the dominant one.

Hook and Weiner (1992: 1) identify Nakasone's 1984 pledge to transform Japan into an "international country" (*kokusai kokka nihon*) as a seminal moment in the development of the term *kokusaika*. As government policy, *kokusaika* can be best seen as a defensive reaction to foreign pressure, a process in which Japan attempted to exercise some control over her own fate (Burgess, 2004). For Lincicome (2005: 191), *kokusaika* was a response to outside forces that challenged the preservation of Japanese identity, national unity, and economic power: "Japan must prepare to 'cope' with an increasingly interdependent community of nations that is openly critical of Japan's economic self-centeredness and cultural insularity." In other words, *kokusaika*, at least in its dominant conservative manifestation, was less about transcending cultural barriers and more about protecting them. However, with the bursting of the bubble at the beginning of the 1990s, the *kokusaika* discourse began to lose popularity, and the question of Japan's genuine opening up and engagement with the world became one that had to be squarely faced.

THE SHIFT FROM KOKUSAIKA TO GLOBALIZATION IN THE 1990s

The 1990s opened with further evidence that Japan could no longer depend on economic diplomacy to protect its own interests in a rapidly globalizing world. The Gulf War (August 1990–February 1991) highlighted the shortcoming of Japanese diplomacy amid scathing criticism that Japan was prepared to offer only money: "Japan's failure to dispatch personnel," observes Nakanishi (2011), "strengthened the impression of Japan as a self-centered mercantilist state." Moreover, the failure of Japanese moves to incorporate the U.S entertainment industry—in the form of Sony's acquisition of Columbia Pictures in 1989 and Matsushita's buyout of MCA in 1990—demonstrated that "despite immense wealth and technological and industrial production . . . the Japanese were unable to master the essentially cultural productivity required to secure the globalization process" (Jameson 1998: 67). Japan's economic misfortunes—which saw Japan risk irrelevance as "Japan-bashing" became "Japan-passing" (Morris 2011: Chapter 7) and the "Japanese miracle" became the "Japanese disease"—merely accentuated the need for Japan to become more concerned with its overseas cultural influence. At this stage, however, Japan clearly lacked "global ideological appeal" (Nye 1990: 155); as Schilling (1997: 9) puts it, culturally Japan had "no international face."

The key to raising Japan's cultural presence around the world was to more broadly conceive the process of globalization (Mouer 2004: 166). In the past, globalization had been conceptualized rather narrowly, in

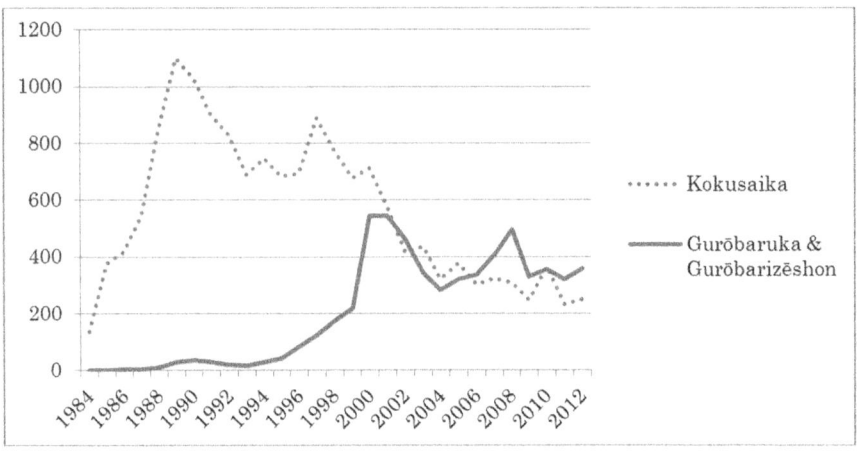

Figure 2.1   Number of Articles Containing "Kokusaika" and "Gurōbaruka" 1984–2012
Source: Asahi Shimbun Database (Kikuzō)

purely economic terms, and was of little interest to most Japanese. In fact, as Figure 2.1 shows, the Japanese term for globalization (*gurōbaruka* or *gurōbarizēshon*) only came into common currency in Japan in the late 1990s; only in the new century did it begin to challenge *kokusaika* as the term used to describe Japan's relations with the rest of the world. This transition from *kokusaika* to *gurōbaruka* was more than simply a shift in word usage; it reflected a shift in broad societal currents and key changes in political ideology taking place in Japan.

Unlike *kokusaika*, which, as discussed earlier, had a rather different meaning from its English counterpart "internationalization," *gurōbaruka* corresponds closely to the English meaning of a growing interconnectedness. As McGrew (1992: 65–66) notes, "events, decisions, and activities in one part of the world can come to have significant consequences for individuals and communities in quite distant parts of the globe." This encapsulates the crucial difference between *kokusaika* and *gurōbaruka*—*gurōbaruka* is an external process over which Japan has little or no influence or control:

> The usage of "global" in the media discourse clearly reads as more passive and less confident, signifying the decay and crisis of Japan. As the term 'global standard' exemplifies, Japanese discourses of globalization have most notably revolved around the necessity for Japan to readjust itself to the new US-led global economic order (Iwabuchi 2005: 104–105).

Of course, *kokusaika* too involved coping and responding to outside challenges and criticism. However, as Iwabuchi notes, *gurōbaruka* demands passive compliance with external norms that Japan is unable to control, whereas *kokusaika* actively pushed back against perceived threats to Japanese identity. Put differently, both *kokusaika* and *gurōbaruka* describe something that surrounds Japan that requires appropriate measures, but *kokusaika*, unlike *gurōbaruka*, also describes an *activity* the Japanese themselves engage in.

As Iwabuchi suggests, the realization that globalization was a broad and inevitable process that Japan must more fully and more openly engage in brought with it an overwhelming loss of national confidence. "[A] decade of recession and political turmoil has made many Japanese seem less secure in some of their fundamental values," notes McGray (2002), ". . . a national uncertainty infused with even more anxiety by the demographic changes that will accompany the graying of Japan's population." On the other hand, McGray, whose article, as the next section shows, triggered the Cool Japan boom, argues that these circumstances, by discrediting Japan's rigid social hierarchy and empowering young entrepreneurs, may have actually helped Japan redefine itself as a cultural superpower in the 2000s as it shifted from economic diplomacy to public diplomacy (on this point see also Daliot-Bul 2009a).

COOL JAPAN AND THE GROWTH OF PUBLIC/ CULTURAL DIPLOMACY IN THE 2000s

Although Iwabuchi (2006: 16; 2011: 263) takes pains to point out that as a former colonial power Japan has had a significant cultural influence in East Asia since "at least" the 1970s, he does acknowledge that the Japanese cultural presence has become much more conspicuous in the 1990s thanks to local industries finding commercial value in promoting popular culture. Although some Japanese cultural products, such as Tetsuwan Atomu (Astro Boy) and Oshin, were consumed outside Japan in the past, it was only in the mid to late 1990s that things Japanese began to occupy a high profile on the global stage (Allen & Sakamoto 2006: 2) and even more recently that they have entered the mainstream (Tsutsui 2010: 16).

In the U.S., the Pokémon boom in the second half of the 1990s coincided with a Japanese-to-English "translation boom" and the rapid spread of comics and animation from the 2000's (Sugiyama 2006: 137, 139). The year 2002 alone saw the debut of *Shōnen Jump* magazine in the U.S. ("Sekai ichiba" 2006) and an Academy Award for Hayao Miyazaki's *Spirited Away*. Closer to home, by the end of the 1990s, writers were commenting on the "Japanization" of Asia as Japanese comics, fashion, and TV dramas became all the rage (Igarashi 1998).

As Iwabuchi touched on earlier, it is the private sector that took the initiative in the promotion of Japanese popular culture. "Until quite recently," writes Tsutsui (2010: 61), ". . . the state was far more comfortable supporting elite cultural forms (such as Noh theatre or the tea ceremony) than mass entertainments." In fact, despite the success of Cool Korea and the U.K.'s Cool Britannia in the 1990s, the Japanese government was rather slow to realize the opportunities offered by Japanese popular culture. Recognizing the need for a national branding strategy, the government did introduce a new national policy—and establish a strategic council—on intellectual property early in 2002. Nevertheless, only with the June publication of McGray's (2002) *Japan's Gross National Cool*, together with similar articles in the *Washington Post* (Faiola 2003) and *Le Monde* (Pons 2003) the following year, did the government finally wake up to the full potential of cultural and public diplomacy. Numata (2008: 53–4), for example, stresses the huge impact McGray's paper had, arguing that until then the government was largely unaware of the richness and potential of what was still regarded as a subculture.

Then Prime Minister Koizumi was one of the first to articulate the government's newfound intention to capitalize on the popularity of Japanese popular culture overseas, announcing Japan's new vision as an "Intellectual Property Nation" in February 2002 (Choo 2012: 89) followed by an address to the diet in 2003:

> Manufacturing is not the only area in which Japan excels. Japanese culture, including film and animation, is also highly praised around the world, and a ripple effect is being witnessed in various areas beyond the area of the economy. We aim to build a richer Japan by utilizing such culture and arts. (Ministry of Foreign Affairs 2003)

Thereafter, the government's efforts were split between the Ministry of Foreign Affairs (MOFA), which was interested in improving Japan's image abroad through public diplomacy, and the Ministry of Economy, Trade, and Industry (METI), which sought to maximize the economic benefits of Japanese culture's popularity overseas (what may be called the "commodification of culture"). The government's development of these two elements— the economic and the political—can be seen in Table 2.1.

The slogan "Cool Japan" itself deserves critical analysis. McGray did not in fact use the term himself, referring instead to Japan's "Gross National Cool." The *Asahi Shimbun* electronic database (Kikuzō) reveals only a smattering of references to "Cool Japan" (aside from a popular column on the popularity of Japanese pop culture in Europe) before the establishment of the Cool Japan Shitsu (Creative Industries Promotion Office) in June 2010, which marked the start of serious government funding. Inclusion in Abe's growth strategy (Seichō Senryaku) in May 2013 saw the slogan's public profile rise further. Obviously inspired by the U.K.'s Cool Britannia slogan, the fact that Cool Japan is written in *katakana* (reserved for foreign names and loanwords) creates a certain sense of distance and exoticness; newspapers often supply the literal Japanese translation *kakkoii nihon*. As Japanese

Table 2.1 Development of the "Cool Japan" Project by the Japanese Government

Date	Event (Source)
2002 Mar	"Strategic Council on Intellectual Property" (Zaisan Senryaku Kaigi) established within Prime Minister's Office (Daliot-Bul 2009b: 250)
2003 Mar	"Intellectual Property Strategy HQ" (Chiteki Zaisan Senryaku Honbu) set up under Intellectual Property Basic Law (Prime Minister of Japan and his Cabinet 2003)
2003 Sep	Prime Minister Koizumi mentions potential of Japanese popular culture in general policy speech (Ministry of Foreign Affairs 2003)
2004	• MOFA establishes Public Diplomacy Department (Kōhō Bunka Kōryū Bu) representing first use of English term (Y. Watanabe 2011: 61) • MOFA uses Captain Tsubasa stickers in Iraq (Ministry of Foreign Affairs 2004) • Content Industry Promotion Law (Choo 2012) (kontentsu sangyō shinkōhō) promulgated.
2005	First use of Cool Japan slogan for promoting industrial content (Bowen-Struyk 2010: 162)
2006 Apr	NHK's "Cool Japan Hakkutsu [excavation]: Kakkoii Nihon" (Discovering Cool Japan) starts broadcasting (www.nhk.or.jp/coolJapan/)
2006 Apr	Foreign Minister Aso makes speech on cultural diplomacy at Digital Hollywood University (Ministry of Foreign Affairs 2006)
2007 July	First International Manga Award presented (Ministry of Foreign Affairs 2007)
2008 Mar	Doraemon appointed first "anime ambassador" (Ministry of Foreign Affairs 2008)
2009	MOFA appoints three female "Kawaii" ambassadors to promote Japanese pop culture ("Cute ambassadors" roam globe to promote Japan's pop culture 2009; Ministry of Foreign Affairs 2009)
2009	• "Cultural/Japan Brand Investigating Committee" (Kontentsu/Nihon Burando Senmon Chōsa Kai) formed inside HQ. • "Japan Branding Strategy" published (Prime Minister of Japan and his Cabinet 2009)
2010 Jun	"Creative Industries Promotion Office" (*Cool Japan Shitsu*) set up under METI. New national growth strategy "to promote a culture-oriented industry" announced (Promoting 2010)
2010 Oct	"Liason Council for Cool Japan Promotion" (Kūru Jyapan Suishin ni Kansuru Kankei Fushō Renraku Kaigi) set up (Prime Minister of Japan and his Cabinet 2011)
2011 Mar (rev. May)	"Action Plan with regard to Promoting Cool Japan" (Kūru Jyapan Suishin ni Kansuru Akushon Puran) published (Prime Minister of Japan and his Cabinet 2011)

(*Continued*)

Table 2.1   (Continued)

Date	Event (Source)
2011 Sep	New Cool Japan logo introduced (New "Cool Japan" 2011)
2012 Feb	METI rolls out Cool Japan spring events to promote food, art, and fashion (METI rolls out 2012)
2012 May	MOFA announces establishment of a new "command post" to unify and reinforce the promotion of the Japan brand (Kūru Jyapan hasshin kyōka 2012)
2012 Dec	Tomomi Inada chosen as first Cool Japan Strategy Minister (*tantō daijin*) (Abe aims 2013)
2013 Feb	"Cool Japan Promotion Council" (Kūru Jyapan Suishin Kaigi) established an expert panel under the Cabinet Office (Seifu, Kūru Jyapan 2013)
2013 Mar	First meeting of Cool Japan Promotion Council opened by Prime Minister Abe (Seifu kaigi 2013)
2013 May	Second batch of economic growth strategy measures include Cool Japan program to promote Japanese pop culture abroad (Abe unveils 2013)
2013 May	"Cool Japan Promotion Council" presents 19-point action plan with focus on food (Cool Japan to focus on food 2013)
2013 Nov	$1 billion "Cool Japan Fund" launched (Cool Japan fund 2013)

Note: Here, and throughout, I use the term "Cool Japan" as a generic term for the promotion of Japanese (pop) culture in general. The slogan itself, as explained above, is of relative recent origin.

pop culture and state policy/ideology become increasingly and explicitly linked, the "Cool Japan" slogan is likely to take on different meanings, risking "killing the cool" (N. Otmazgin & Ben-Ari 2012: 19).

Although Cool Japan itself was originally framed as an economic strategy, specifically the promotion of industrial content branding and support for culture-oriented "creative" industries, in recent years the political side of Cool Japan has risen to prominence (Choo 2012: 88). This was certainly helped by the high profile of manga aficionado Tarō Asō who served as foreign minister from 2005 to 2007 and then prime minister from September 2008 to September 2009.[2] The arrival of Abe as prime minister in December 2012— with Asō as deputy—accelerated this shift, personified by the move of the Cool Japan expert panel from METI to the Cabinet Office in February 2013 ("Seifu kaigi" 2013). Thus the Cool Japan initiative has become increasingly linked to what is known as the "national interest doctrine" (*kokueki-ron*), the idea that performing Cool Japan serves the national interest because it helps reduce anti-Japanese feelings in Asia (Aoki 2004). The pitfalls of an approach based on narrow self-interest—what Iwabuchi (2002b: 52) calls a "growing narcissistic urge to (re)claim Japanese cultural prominence"—and other problems associated with the Cool Japan campaign are discussed in the following section.

PROBLEMS WITH COOL JAPAN: (MIS)MANAGING NATIONAL IMAGES

Mori (2011: 40) describes the government-led Cool Japan project as "both a defensive response against and an adaptation to globalization." This formulation captures the ambiguity inherent in the project: it is both a *kokusaika*-type Japanese-only nationalism that reinforces a "closed" and unique national identity *and* an embrace of globalization that recognizes the need for Japan to open up and rebrand Japanese values as universal values. In terms of the former "closing-in" strand, Daliot-Bul (2009b: 260) sees a number of similarities between 1980s *kokusaika* as promulgated by Nakasone and today's Cool Japan project, especially the goal of removing "misconceptions" and disseminating the "correct" view of Japanese culture. "The similarity between the Japan Brand Strategy and the *kokusaika* project is not coincidental," he writes, "[i]t attests to a long political tradition of . . . 'recurring renovationist nationalism': a government-sponsored national project of state-nation construction and improvement."

As for the second "opening-up" strand of the Cool Japan project, Sugimoto (1999: 87–89), discussing the influence of globalization on *Nihonjinron*, notes that promoting the idea of a "unique national culture" to defend Japan's national interest has become increasingly counterproductive in the face of Japan's rapidly growing involvement in transnational affairs. But by promoting Japanese culture as having universal appeal and stressing the transferability of Japaneseness, the notion of a specific national identity is undermined. Highlighting this contradiction, Daliot-Bul (2009b) notes how problematic it is to appropriate market-made images of Cool Japan for national ends. In particular, he (2009b: 252–253) argues that it is disingenuous for the state to create "new" cultural imagery and then explicitly link this to traditional Japanese culture, aesthetics, and thought. For Daliot-Bul (2009b: 254), a key problem with building the new Japanese brand "around a cultural essence found in Japanese tradition" is that "Japan's cultural tradition is associated with Japan's history of imperial aggressiveness in the region and this bears very little attractiveness." As Iwabuchi (2011: 271) argues, framing Cool Japan as a policy that serves the national interest by helping to reduce anti-Japanese feeling risks failure, especially in Asia:

> While the idea of soft power and cultural diplomacy sounds promising, the current Japanese policy concern with cultural export tends to be confined to a narrow public interest at the expense of a serious

commitment to promoting transborder dialogue. Such policies are too concerned with the convenient uses of media culture for the promotion of national interests.

In other words, if Cool Japan is perceived as a form of cultural imperialism in Japan's former colonies, the outcomes might turn out to be the opposite of those intended ("Anime ninki" 2007; "Nihon anime ni sanpi" 2006). Even when a Japanese cultural product is enthusiastically embraced—such as the popularity of AKB48 in China who recently served as "goodwill ambassadors" to mark the 40th anniversary of normal relations—this is rather fragile and easily overshadowed by historical issues. For example, Osaka Mayor Tōru Hashimoto's "comfort women" comments have been widely broadcast and criticized abroad, the result being that much of the goodwill generated toward Japan post 3/11 has evaporated (Johnston 2013).

Even if Japanese popular culture was not linked to Japan's past, there is scant evidence that interest in Japanese popular culture translates into interest in or trust of Japan (Watanabe 2011: 89). The disjoint between the popularity of cultural products and political influence (as supposed by the soft power doctrine) is highlighted by Graves (2011: 413) in a chapter entitled "Cool is not Enough":

> For nation-building to be effective, the popular culture needs to do more than enlist foreigners in to songs or fashion or even cosplay. It needs to make people think of, understand, seek out, and love the country of origin. The problem with the export of anime and manga . . . is that they may be loved simply for what they are, rather for enlightening anybody about Japan.

For example, the same Chinese youngsters who love Japanese writers, such as Haruki Murakami, hold negative attitudes toward Japan and Japanese people (see also Nakano 2008; Yosuke Watanabe 2005). Iwabuchi notes a similar phenomenon in Korea: "Many Korean fans of Japanese popular music," he (2006: 27) writes, "tend to refuse to conflate their craze for Japanese pop with their frustration toward insincere Japanese attitudes about its war responsibilities." The problem here is that the Japanese government's explicit embrace of soft power as a national diplomatic policy since 2003 may have, ironically, damaged the national image by reviving memories of cultural imperialism ("Nihon anime ni sanpi" 2006). "[S]oft power depends on credibility," writes Nye (2008: xiii), "and when governments are seen as manipulative and information is perceived as propaganda credibility is destroyed." As critics of the "national interest" doctrine point out, a narrow focus on soft power and public diplomacy can be seen as a new form of hegemony (Ogura 2004, 2006).

A further problem with the Cool Japan project relates not to its overseas reception but to the domestic audience. While the primary concern of Cool Japan is Japanese markets and diplomacy overseas—economy and image building abroad—the project has also had half an eye on revitalizing national confidence and recovering national pride. "The Japan Brand Strategy," writes Daliot-Bul (2009b: 249), "is also devised as a mechanism for national mobilization during highly turbulent times." But how representative of Japanese popular culture is the kind of culture promoted by Cool Japan? Put simply, how "Japanese" is Japanese popular culture[3]— and how "popular" is it in Japan? Part of the reason for positive attitudes toward Japan post 3/11 was admiration for (perceived) national traits, such as patience, orderliness, and consideration for others. Indeed, even before 3/11 the Council for the Promotion of Cultural Diplomacy identified Japanese values such as harmony, compassion, and coexistence as soft power resources for Japan (Kondo 2008: 200). However, it has been frequently observed that whereas American culture abroad tends to be linked with specific "American" values, Japanese cultural products in contrast do not promote the "lifestyle" of Japan (Iwabuchi 2002b: 28) and seem "less associated with an implicit appeal to a broader set of values" (Nye 1990: 169). "Its cultural sway is not quite like that of American culture abroad, which, even in its basest forms, tends to reflect certain common values," writes McGray (2002), ". . . [c]ontemporary Japanese culture outside Japan can seem shallow by comparison . . . reflect[ing] the contradictory values of a nation in flux, a superficiality." No doubt aware of this weakness, in November 2006 Foreign Minister Asō announced a new value-oriented diplomacy based on support for universal values ("Japan's 'values-oriented diplomacy'" 2007; see also Lam 2007: 358). Moreover, MOFA's May 2012 announcement that it planned to strengthen the Cool Japan campaign specifically referred to renewed efforts to promote Japanese values such as *reigitadashisa* (politeness, courtesy, civility) and *nintai* (perseverance/endurance) ("Kūru Jyapan hasshin kyōka" 2012). The problem is, though, in contrast to TV dramas such as *Oshin*, contemporary popular cultural products do not, on the whole, demonstrate "Japanese," traits such as diligence and perseverance, which can appeal to people who share these values.[4]

Manga in particular has always been a very hybridized product (Mori 2011). Indeed, the themes readily identifiable in manga and anime seem to have little to do with mainstream Japanese culture or daily life. This may, in fact, help to explain the popularity of Japanese popular cultural products, especially overseas: as Abel (2010: 136–137) argues, perhaps it is their very 'mysteriousness' that generates an emotional pull (*akogare*) that causes them to be considered 'cool.' Iwabuchi (2002b: 33) has gone as far as to describe Japanese popular culture as stateless (*mukokuseki*) and odorless (*mushū*). Tsutsui (2010: 19–22), for example, identifies four central themes—the apocalypse, monsters, technology, and 'cute'—that appear to have little to do with contemporary Japanese society *per se*. Buruma (1984) even theorizes that popular culture captures what is *not* present in Japanese society, the violent and sexual content representing all the repressed desires of the Japanese. A *Japan Times* editorial highlights the dangers of presenting such images as Japan's international face:

> In a matter of years, the overseas image of Japan has become dependent on its pop culture exports. Manga and anime are now Japan's new ambassadors. How did caricatures, fantasy stories and splashy drawings get into the position of such international importance? . . .
>
> That representation is something of a mixed blessing . . . The violence and sexuality in some manga do not correspond precisely to the daily life here. They present almost a dream image of one aspect of the culture, one that is likely to be misinterpreted ("Ambassadors" 2007)

The potential for misunderstanding was highlighted by one Diet member following the government's decision to appoint three "*kawaii*" (cute) ambassadors in 2009 (Table 2.1). At a Lower House Foreign Affairs Committee, New Komeito member Kaori Maruya warned against "unwarranted criticism against overseas tours by 'pretty ambassadors' wearing very short skirts." This raises the question of whether Cool Japan is not essentially a male project, including and representing only those Japanese women who conform to a "narrow model of cute femininity" (Miller 2011).

Of course, some kind of disconnect between the everyday lived reality of a culture and its face on the world stage is inevitable. As Iwabuchi (2002a: 2) points out, no cultural form ever equally stands for all of a culture: it is always a matter of selection and ideology. Nevertheless, the disconnect between the (sometimes vulgar) Akihabara sub-culture and mainstream culture in Japan is rather stark. "Quite frankly, up to now *manga, anime,* and games which *otaku* are fond of, in terms of both individual life course and industry, have not been mainstream," admits Sugiyama (2006: 221), "[i]n fact, we might go as far as saying that they have been treated as the culture of society's marginals and outcasts." Sugiyama goes on to argue that as the government continues to promote and highlight these cultures, people's awareness will undoubtedly change and they will become more mainstream. Certainly, traditional culture which used to be promoted as the face of Japan, such as the tea ceremony or martial arts, could be said to be equally remote from the lives of most Japanese today (Treat, 1996: 1). However, in contrast to the current cultural diplomatic initiative, which fails to "transmit the deeper, more enduring values of Japanese culture" (H. Watanabe 2011c), traditional culture did at least convey some of the distinct 'Japanese values'—that is, the dominant discourses of national character—re-invented, highlighted, and praised abroad following the Tōhoku Earthquake.

Whether, as Watanabe (2011c) suggests, a more thoughtful and creative approach will be enough to turn the "fleeting attractions of *manga* and pop music" into a "vehicle for Japan to build a 'brand' associated around the globe with such qualities as modesty, peace, stability, consideration for others, and stability" is a moot point. At the moment, it is difficult to dis-agree with McGray (2002) when he remarks that there "exists a Japan for Japanese and a Japan for the rest of the world." Or as Abel (2011: 64) puts it, "cool things are also things that mainstream Japanese cannot compre-hend." Of course, this is not to say anime and manga do not have Japanese values—the stories and themes are not ideologically free but products of a particular cultural and economic milieu. Nevertheless, the problem remains the disconnect—the inherent tension—between the policy, goals, and vision that is Cool Japan and the dynamic, free, and alternative nature of pop culture, which leads to the question: Is Japan's soft power doing what it is supposed to be doing?

CONCLUSION: BEYOND INTERNATIONALIZATION?

Undoubtedly, Japan's international image has improved since 1995. The 3/11 disaster in particular generated a groundswell of goodwill that has not altogether disappeared. For example, in a 2012 BBC world survey, Japan came out on top as the most favorably viewed country, although it had dropped to fourth in the 2013 poll ("Poll" 2013). Japanese popular culture has certainly had an impact, as Otmazgin (2008: 73) concludes, in fostering such perceptions, shaping cultural markets, and disseminating new images of Japan; on the other hand, it has not had much of an impact "in exert-ing local influence or creating Japanese-dominated spheres of influence." As Bouissou (2012: 49) notes, an image per se wields no power. One rea-son Japan's soft power remains limited relates to its failure to come to terms with its record of foreign aggression in the 1930s and the result-ing suspicion that constantly undermines relations with China and Korea (Nye 2004: 86–87). The BBC poll mentioned earlier reinforces this point: despite enjoying a positive image across a broad swath of countries, the majority of respondents in China and Korea said Japan has a mainly nega-tive influence on the world. Soft power has to be more than just national advertising; "it means making serious efforts to understand the perspectives, languages, and histories of other countries and to forge institutional and per-sonal linkages among them" (Yasushi Watanabe & McConnell 2008: xxix). As the previous section showed, loving Japanese pop culture does not neces-sarily translate into a love for Japan.

Japan's inability to deal frankly with historical issues clearly limits effec-tive use of soft power, particularly in East Asia, and reflects a much deeper insularity: the inability to get beyond (Japanese-style) internationalization. "The success of Japan's manufacturing sector provides it with an important source of soft power," writes Nye (1990: 169), "but Japan is somewhat limited by the inward orientation of its culture." Thus despite having "more potential soft power resources that any other Asian country" (Nye 2004: 85), Japan's insularity continues to limit its ability "to transform those resources into soft power in the sense of obtaining the policy outcomes it desires" (Nye 2004: 88). Although Nye's comments were made some years ago, Japan remains closed and inward-oriented, especially in terms of its reluctance to accept migrants.

At the root of this insularity is a deep lack of confidence and a strong feeling of anxiety for the future.[5] As discussed earlier, the end of the bubble years saw a more passive and less confident Japan reluctantly resign itself to open up and engage with the process that is globalization. A number of Japan's leaders have promoted this "opening up." For example, then Prime Minister Fukuda (2008), in his opening address to the Diet in January 2008, presented his plan to increase the number of foreign students studying in Japan to 300,000 by 2020 under the heading "an open country Japan" (*hirakareta nihon*). And pressure for Japan to "open-up" has only intensified since 3/11. One of the nominations for buzzword of 2011 was "*Heisei no kaikoku* (opening)" ("Nadeshiko" 2011), a term representing the third "opening" of Japan, particularly in the context of Japan's moves to join the Trans-Pacific Partnership ("Nihon ni yūeki" 2011). More recently, Abe has unveiled a series of growth strategies that include initiatives to foster "global human resources" (Burgess 2013), open university teaching posts to non-Japanese, and encourage Japanese students to study abroad ("Abe unveils" 2013). All of these, however, are more concerned with promoting economic growth, making Japanese families more affluent, and "winning at the world level" than with any genuine kind of opening up.

The danger for post 3/11 Japan is that the sense of togetherness and national pride necessary for recovery risks exacerbating the tendency to close ranks, become self-absorbed, and look inward (H. Watanabe 2011a, b). Certainly, the emergence of "*kizuna*" (human bonds) as the dominant metaphor to describe post 3/11 Japanese society hints at a new style of Japanese-only nationalism. The emergence of public anti-Korean demonstrations—and the entry of the term "hate-speech" into the Japanese lexicon—since early 2013 is one example. However, *kizuna* need not necessarily be a parochial term: it was also used to describe the strengthened bonds of friendship with America following Operation Tomodachi, the post 3/11 US assistance operation (Ruch 2012). Indeed, the government's Japan 21st Century Vision Report was subtitled "A New Era of Dynamism: Closer Ties and a Wider range of Opportunities" and promoted the idea of "an open, culturally creative nation . . . a country without walls" (CEFP 2005). Perhaps a broader interpretation of *kizuna* can act as the trigger for Japan to open its doors to migrants and refugees; welcome foreign trade, products, and innovation; play a more active role internationally; and begin a sincere dialogue with its Asian neighbors. If not—if Japanese fail to, in the words of Nakayama, "open up their hearts"—Japan will remain caught in two minds, forever trapped between the desire to close-in and open-up.

NOTES

1. Nichibunken, the International Research Center for Japanese Studies, is an interuniversity research institute located in Kyōto funded by the government to promote and support the study of Japanese culture and history.
2. According to BBC News ("Manga shares" 2007), manga-linked stocks surged following speculation that Aso would be succeeding Abe as prime minister.
3. Here I leave aside the important issue of localization, of how products from one culture change as they are consumed in another culture, a phenomenon that further problematizes the question of the "Japaneseness" of Japanese popular culture (Allen & Sakamoto, 2006; Iwabuchi, 2002b: Chapter 3; Tsutsui, 2010: Chapter 4).
4. This may, however, be changing. Choo (2012: 102–103), discussing how the content of anime and manga may be transforming due to global market demand, describes "an increased production of narratives and images that employ Japanese traditions as opposed to the popular science fiction narratives that dominated in previous decades."
5. In a June 2010 survey in the *Asahi Shimbun* ("Nukareru Nihon" 2010), more than 90% of respondents said they felt anxiety for the future of Japan.

REFERENCES

Abe aims to boost the power of "Cool Japan" cultural exports. (2013, March 22). *Daily Yomiuri*, p. 2.

Abe unveils more growth tactics. (2013, May 19). *Japan News,* pp. 1–2.

Abel, J. (2010). Kūru jyapanorijii no fukanōsei to kanōsei (On the possibilities and impossibilities of a cool Japanology). In A. Hiroki (Ed.), *Nihon-teki Sōzōryoku no Mirai: Kūru Jyapanorijii no Kanōsei (The Future of Japanese Creativity: The Possibilities of Cool Japanology)* (pp. 135–160). Tokyo: NHK Shuppan.

Abel, J. (2011). Can cool Japan save post-disaster Japan? On the possibilities and impossibilities of a cool Japanology. *International Journal of Japanese Sociology, 20*(1), 59–72.

AKB48 turns to "Idol diplomacy" in China. (2011, September 24). *Majirox News.* Retrieved from http://www.majiroxnews.com.

Allen, M., & Sakamoto, R. (2006). Inside-out Japan? Popular culture and globalizaton in the context of Japan. In M. Allen & R. Sakamoto (Eds.), *Popular Culture, Globalization and Japan* (pp. 1–12). London: Routledge.

Ambassadors, manga and anime [Editorial]. (2007, March 25). *Japan Times.* Retrieved from www.japantimes.co.jp.

Anime ninki to han'nichi to (Love anime, hate Japan). (2007, December 12). *Yomiuri Shimbun,* p. 1.

Aoki, T. (2004). Kūru pawā kokka Nihon no sōzō o (Conceiving Japan as a "cool power" state). *Chūōkōron,* 198–209.

Bouissou, J.-M. (2012). Popular culture as a tool for soft power: Myth or reality? In N. Otmazgin & E. Ben-Ari (Eds.), *Popular Culture and the State in East and Southeast Asia* (pp. 46–64). London: Routledge.

Bowen-Struyk, H. (2010). Puroretaria Bungaku no Kūrusa no Kanōsei (The potential of proletarian literature's coolness). In A. Hiroki (Ed.), *Nihon-teki Sōzōryoku no Mirai: Kūru Jyapanorijii no Kanōsei (The Future of Japanese Creativity: The Possibilities of Cool Japanology)* (pp. 161–168). Tokyo: NHK Shuppan.

Burgess, C. (2004). Maintaining identities: Discourses of homogeneity in a rapidly globalising Japan. *Electronic Journal of Contemporary Japanese Studies.* Retrieved from http://www.japanesestudies.org.uk/

Burgess, C. (2010). The 'illusion' of homogeneous Japan and national character: Discourse as a tool to transcend the 'myth' vs. 'reality' binary. *Japan Focus.* Retrieved from http://japanfocus.org

Burgess, C. (2011). Japanese national character stereotypes in the foreign media in the aftermath of the Great East Japan Earthquake: Myth or reality? *The Tsuda Review*, 56, 23–56.

Burgess, C. (2013, May 21). Ambivalent Japan turns on its 'insular' youth: System discourages overseas study but students get blame. *Japan Times*, p. 12. Retrieved from http://www.japantimes.co.jp

Buruma, I. (1984). *A Japanese mirror: Heroes and villains of Japanese culture.* Blaine, WA: Phoenix.

CEFP. (2005). *Japan's 21st century vision* (The Report of the special board of inquiry for examining "Japan's 21st Century Vision" by the Council on Economic and Fiscal Policy). Retrieved on September 11, 2014, from http://www5.cao.go.jp/keizai-shimon/english/publication/pdf/050419visionsummary_fulltext.pdf

China's view of Japan brighter since quake. (2011, May 17). *Daily Yomiuri*, p. 13.

China: 2020 Olympic success will depend on how Japan faces its history. (2013, September 10). *Japan Today.* Retrieved from http://www.japantoday.com

Choo, K. (2012). Nationalizing "Cool". In N. Otmazgin & E. Ben-Ari (Eds.), *Popular Culture and the State in East and Southeast Asia* (pp. 85–105). London: Routledge.

Choong, W. (2011, March 25). Japan has what it takes to bounce back. *The Straits Times.* Retrieved from LexisNexis *Academic* Database.

Chūgoku shien hyōka sarezu fuman (Dissatisfaction that Chinese support not rated). (2012, March 11). *Yomiuri Shimbun*, p. 6.

Cool Japan fund "to use $1 billion". (2013, November 26). *Japan News*, p. 8.

Cool Japan to focus on food. (2013, May 29). *Japan News*, p. 1.

Crimes plunge in '11; no-entry zone thefts up. (2011, December 17). *Daily Yomiuri*, p. 2.

"Cute ambassadors" roam globe to promote Japan's pop culture. (2009, June 17). *Japan Times.* Retrieved from http://www.japantimes.co.jp/text/nn20090617f1.html

Daliot-Bul, M. (2009a). *Asobi* in action: Contesting the cultural meanings and cultural boundaries of play in urban Japan from the 1970s to present. *Cultural Studies*, 23(2), 1–26.

Daliot-Bul, M. (2009b). Japan brand strategy: The taming of "Cool Japan" and the challenges of cultural planning in a postmodern age. *Social Science Japan Journal*, 12(2), 247–266.

Dower, J. (1986). *War without Mercy: Race and Power in the Pacific War.* New York: Pantheon Books.

Each time they rebuild bigger and better: The Japanese love of order and ability to start anew will help them confront the earthquake crisis. (2011, March 15). *The Daily Telegraph*, p. 21.

Faiola, A. (2003, December 27). Japan's empire of cool: Country's culture becomes its biggest export. *Washington Post*, p. A01.

Goodman, R. (2007). The concept of *Kokusaika* and Japanese educational reform. *Globalisation, Societies and Education*, 5(1), 71–87.

Graves, C. (2011). Cool is not Enough. In McKinsey and Company (Ed.), *Reimagining Japan: The Quest for a Future that Works* (pp. 411–416). San Francisco: VIZ Media, LLC.

Hammond, P. (1997). Introduction: Questioning cultural difference. In P. Hammond (Ed.), *Cultural Difference, Media Memories* (pp. xi–xxv). London: Cassel.

Hook, G. D., & Weiner, M. A. (1992). Introduction. In G. D. Hook & M. A. Weiner (Eds.), *The Internationalization of Japan* (pp. 1–12). London: Routledge.

Igarashi, A. (1998). *Hen'yō suru Ajia to Nihon: Ajia-Shakai ni Shintō Suru Nihon no Popyurā Karuchā (Japan and Asia in Transition: Japanese Popular Culture Seeping into Asian Societies)*. Tokyo: Seishiki Shobō.

Ishihara tochiji "Yappari tenbatsu" "Tsunami de gayoku araiotosu" Higashi Nihon daishinsai (Mayor Ishihara after Tohoku earthquake "This was undoubtedly divine retribution" "Use the tsunami to wash away this egoism"). (2011, March 15). *Asahi Shimbun*, p. 1.

Iwabuchi, K. (2002a). The (im)possibility of understanding 'Japan' through popular culture (part I). *Across the Sea (Japan Cultural Centre, Sydney)*, 43, 1–2.

Iwabuchi, K. (2002b). *Recentering globalization: Popular culture and Japanese transnationalism*. Durham: Duke University Press.

Iwabuchi, K. (2005). Multinationalizing the multicultural: Commodification of "ordinary foreign residents" in a Japanese TV talk show. *Japanese Studies: Bulletin of the Japanese Studies Association of Australia, 25*(2), 103–118.

Iwabuchi, K. (2006). Japanese popular culture and postcolonial desire for "Asia". In M. Allen & R. Sakamoto (Eds.), *Popular Culture, Globalization and Japan* (pp. 15–35). London: Routledge.

Iwabuchi, K. (2011). Cultural flows: Japan and East Asia. In V. L. Bestor, T. C. Bestor, & A. Yamagata (Eds.), *Routledge Handbook of Japanese Culture and Society* (pp. 263–272). London: Routledge.

Jameson, F. (1998). Notes on globalization as a philosophical issue. In F. Jameson & M. Miyoshi (Eds.), *The Cultures of Globalization* (pp. 54–77). Durham: Duke University Press.

Japan's "values-oriented diplomacy". (2007, March 21). *The New York Times*. Retrieved from http://www.nytimes.com

Japanese character shines in the face of disaster: Amid massive destruction in Japan, the Japanese have remained almost unflinchingly respectful, honest, and conscientious. (2011, March 17). *The Christian Science Monitor*. Retrieved from http://www.csmonitor.com

Johnston, E. (2013, June 12). San Francisco spurned Hashimoto amid sex slave outrage. *Japan Times*. Retrieved from http://www.japantimes.co.jp

Kondo, S. (2008). Wielding soft power: The key stages of transmission and reception. In Y. Watanabe & D. L. McConnell (Eds.), *Soft Power Superpowers: Cultural and National Assets of Japan and the United States* (pp. 191–206). Armonk, NY: M.E. Sharpe.

Kūru Jyapan hasshin kyōka: Gaimushō, senryaku soshiki shinsetsu e (Strengthening the Cool Japan campaign: New body to be established). (2012, May 6). *Yomiuri Shimbun*, p. 4.

Lam, P. E. (2007). Japan's quest for "soft power": Attraction and limitation. *East Asia: An International Quarterly, 24*, 349–363.

Lincicome, M. (2005). Globalization, education, and the politics of identity in the Asia-Pacific. *Critical Asian Studies, 37*(2), 179–208.

Manga shares gain on leader hopes. (2007, September 12). *BBC News*. Retrieved from http://news.bbc.co.uk

McGray, D. (2002). Japan's gross national cool. *Foreign Policy*, 44–54.

McGrew, A. (1992). A global society? In S. Hall, D. Held, & T. McGrew (Eds.), *Modernity and Its Futures* (pp. 61–116). Cambridge: Polity Press/ The Open University.

METI rolls out "Cool Japan" spring events to promote food, art and fashion. (2012, February 15). *Japan Times.* Retrieved from http://www.japantimes.co.jp/text/nn20120215f4.html

Miller, L. (2011). Cute masquerade and the pimping of Japan. *International Journal of Japanese Sociology, 20*(1), 18–29.

Ministry of Foreign Affairs. (2003). General policy speech by Prime Minister Junichiro Koizumi to the 157th session of the diet. Retrieved on Septermber 11, 2014, from http://www.mofa.go.jp/announce/pm/koizumi/state0926.html

Ministry of Foreign Affairs. (2004). Samawah "Captain Tsubasa" Dai-sakusen: Kyūsuisha ga Kubaru Yume to Kibō ("Captain Tsubasa" Strategy: Waterwagons deliver dreams and hope). Retrieved on September 11, 2014, from http://www.mofa.go.jp/mofaj/area/iraq/renraku_j_0412b.html

Ministry of Foreign Affairs. (2006). A new look at cultural diplomacy: A call to Japan's cultural practitioners. Retrieved on September 11, 2014, from http://www.mofa.go.jp/announce/fm/aso/speech0604-2.html

Ministry of Foreign Affairs. (2007). "Kokusai Manga shō" no Sōsetsu ni tsuite (About the creation of the "International Manga Award"). Retrieved on September 11, 2014, from http://www.mofa.go.jp/mofaj/press/release/h19/5/1173498_804.html

Ministry of Foreign Affairs. (2008). Anime Bunka Taishi Shūninshiki ni tsuite (About the Anime Ambassador Inauguration Ceremony). Retrieved on September 11, 2014, from http://www.mofa.go.jp/mofaj/press/release/h20/3/rls_0319e.html

Ministry of Foreign Affairs. (2009). Press conference, 26 February 2009. Retrieved on September 11, 2014, from http://www.mofa.go.jp/announce/press/2009/2/0226.html

Mori, Y. (2011). The pitfall facing the Cool Japan project: The transnational development of the anime industry under the condition of post-Fordism. *International Journal of Japanese Sociology, 20*(1), 30–42.

Morris, N. (2011). *Japan-bashing: Anti-Japanism since the 1980s.* London: Routledge.

Mouer, R. (2004). Globalization and Japan after the Bubble. In C. Nyland & G. Davies (Eds.), *Globalization in the Asian Region: Impacts and Consequences* (pp. 164–184). Cheltenham, UK: Edward Elgar.

Nadeshiko, marumori . . . ryūkōgo taishō kōho happyō (Nadeshiko, marumori . . . Buzzword prize candidates announced). (2011, November 11). *Nikkansports. com.* Retrieved from http://www.nikkansports.com

Nakanishi, H. (2011, December 6). The Gulf War and Japanese diplomacy. *nippon. com.* Retrieved from http://nippon.com

Nakano, Y. (2008). Shared memories: Japanese pop culture in China. In Y. Watanabe & D. L. McConnell (Eds.), *Soft Power Superpowers: Cultural and National Assets of Japan and the United States* (pp. 111–127). New York: M. E. Sharpe.

New "Cool Japan" logo: Japan Next. (2011, September). *Japan Probe.* Retrieved from http://www.japanprobe.com/2011/09/14/new-cool-japan-logo-japan-next/

Nihon anime ni sanpi: "Bunka shinryaku, taikō o" "Omoshirokereba ii" (Japan animation pros and cons: 'Oppose cultural invasion' vs 'As long as it's interesting . . .'. (2006, June 8). *Yomiuri Shimbun,* p. 6.

Nihon ni yūeki na "Kaikoku" no ketsudan (The decision to make Japan a profitable "Open Country"). (2011, November 12). *Yomiuri Shimbun,* p. 3.

Nukareru Nihon, reisei na me "Ima to korekara" Asahi Shimbun-sha yoron chōsa (Japan easing up: Looking through clear eyes "Now and in the future" (Asahi Shimbun survey). (2010, June 11). *Asahi Shimbun,* p. 6.

Numata, C. (2008). Kūru Jyapan no shōtai: Urawashiki gokai ni motozuku saininshiki no shōgeki (The true character of Cool Japan: The shock of re-realising based on a beautiful misunderstanding). *Kyoto Women's University Research Studies, 54*, 53–54.

Nye, J. (1990). Soft power. *Foreign Affairs, 80*, 153–171.

Nye, J. (2004). *Soft power: The means to success in world politics.* New York: Public Affairs.

Ogura, K. (2004). Iwayuru "bunka gaikō rieki ron" o haisuru: "Kokusai-zai" no shin no kachi koso sekai ni hasshin shiyō (Rejecting the so-called "national interest" theory: let's export Japanese goods to the world precisely because they have value). *Chūōkōron, 130*(10), 210–217.

Ogura, K. (2006). The limits of soft power. *Japan Echo, 33*(5), 60–65.

Otmazgin, N. K. (2008). Contesting soft power: Japanese popular culture in East and Southeast Asia. *International Relations of the Asia-Pacific, 8*(1), 73–101.

Otmazgin, N. K., & Ben-Ari, E. (2012). Cultural industries and the state in East and Southeast Asia. In N. Otmazgin & E. Ben-Ari (Eds.), *Popular Culture and the State in East and Southeast Asia* (pp. 3–26). London: Routledge.

Poll: 51% think Japan has positive influence. (2013, May 23). *Japan News*, p. 2.

Pons, P. (2003, Dec. 18). "Cool Japan": le Japon superpuissance de la pop ("Cool Japan": Japan, the pop superpower), *Le Monde*, p. 20.

Posturing over senkakus [Editorial]. (2012, September 14). *Japan Times*. Retrieved from http://www.japantimes.co.jp

Prime Minister of Japan and his Cabinet. (2003). Chiteki Zaisan Senryaku Honbu (Intellectual Property Headquarters). Retrieved on September 11, 2014, from www.kantei.go.jp/jp/singi/titeki2/

Prime Minister of Japan and his Cabinet. (2008, January 18). Policy speech by Prime Minister Yasuo Fukuda to the 169th session of the diet. Retrieved on Septermber 11, 2014, from http://japan.kantei.go.jp/hukudaspeech/2008/01/18housin_e.html

Prime Minister of Japan and his Cabinet. (2009). Nihon Burando Senryaku: Sofuto Pawā Sangyō o Seichō no Gendō-ryoku ni (Japanese branding strategy: Making the soft power industries a driving force for growth). Retrieved on September 11, 2014, from http://www.kantei.go.jp/jp/singi/titeki2/houkoku/090310_nihon bland.pdf

Prime Minister of Japan and his Cabinet. (2011). Kūru Jyapan Suishin ni Kansuru Akushon Puran (Action plan for the promotion of Cool Japan). Retrieved on September 11, 2014, from www.kantei.go.jp/jp/singi/titeki2/kettei/cjap.pdf

Promoting "Cool Japan" [Editorial]. (2010, August 15). *Japan Times*. Retrieved on September 11, 2014, from http://www.japantimes.co.jp/text/ed20100815a1.html

Religious conservatives claim Katrina was God's omen, punishment for the United States. (2005, September 13). *Media Matters for America*. Retrieved from http://mediamatters.org

Ruch, G. (2012, March 16). Tomodachi and kizuna: The US-Japan relationship one year after the Great East Japan Earthquake. *Japan Matters for America.* Retrieved from http://www.japanmattersforamerica.org

Schilling, M. (1997). *The encyclopedia of Japanese pop culture.* Trumbull, CT: Weatherhill.

Seifu kaigi shinsō/kaisō datsu minshu kantei shudō uchidasu (Prime Minister's Office takes the lead in breaking with DPJ policies, makeover for government councils). (2013, March 5). *Asahi Shimbun*, p. 4.

Seifu, kūru Jyapan suishin kaigi secchi menbā ni AKB no Akimoto shi (Government establishes Cool Japan Promotion Council, Akimoto of AKB fame a member). (2013, February 26). *Sankei Shimbun.* Retrieved from http://sankei.jp.msn.com/politics/news/130226/plc13022610350005-n1.htm

Sekai ichiba e chōsen aitsugu (Challenging world markets one after another). (2006, March 25). *Yomiuri Shimbun*, p. 12.

Shinraikan Chūkan to ondo sa: Chūgoku, 'Tainichi' daihaba ni kaizen (Feelings of trust—Gap in temperature between China and Korea: Chinese feelings toward Japan show huge improvement). (2011, November 12). *Yomiuri Shimbun*, p. 10.

Shinseiken, zekka ōnami minshu "Aso shushō ni ninmei sekinin" (New government, flood of gaffes, DPJ says "Prime Minister Aso has to take responsibility for his appointees"). (2008, September 27). *Asahi Shimbun*, p. 2.

SMAP concert in Beijing: Thanks, China! (2011, September 18). *Japan Probe*. Retrieved from http://www.japanprobe.com

Sugimoto, Y. (1999). Making sense of Nihonjinron. *Thesis Eleven, 57*, 81–96.

Sugiyama, T. (2006). *Kūru Jyapan sekai ga kaitagaru (The world wants to buy Cool Japan)*. Tokyo: Shoden-sha.

Treat, J. W. (1996). Introduction: Japanese studies into cultural studies. In J. W. Treat (Ed.), *Contemporary Japan and Popular Culture* (pp. 1–14). Honolulu: University of Hawaii.

Tsutsui, W. M. (2010). *Japanese popular culture and globalization*. Ann Arbor, MI: Association for Asian Studies.

Vogel, E. (1979). *Japan as number one: Lessons for America*. Cambridge, MA: Harvard University Press.

Watanabe, H. (2011a, May 9). Doing our part for global security, *JapanEcho.net*. Retrieved from http://japanecho.net

Watanabe, H. (2011b, April 22). A shift in national consciousness. *JapanEcho.net*. Retrieved from http://japanecho.net

Watanabe, H. (2011c, September 15). Toward a new era in cultural diplomacy. *Japan Echo.net*. Retrieved from http://japanecho.net

Watanabe, Y. (2005, November 24). Japan's books find strong favor in China, unlike its politics. *Japan Times*. Retrieved from http://www.japantimes.co.jp

Watanabe, Y. (2011). *Bunka to gaikō: Paburikku dipuromashii no jidai* (Culture and diplomacy: The age of public diplomacy). Tokyo: Chukōshinsho.

Watanabe, Y., & McConnell, D. L. (2008). Introduction. In Y. Watanabe & D. L. McConnell (Eds.), *Soft Power Superpowers: Cultural and National Assets of Japan and the United States* (pp. xvii–xxxii). Armonk, NY: M.E. Sharpe.

Where are the Japanese looters? (2011, March 14). *The Washington Times*. Retrieved from http://communities.washingtontimes.com

Why quakes leave the Japanese unshakeable: They call it "Gaman"—the unflappable stoicism that helps this nation survive whatever nature throws at it. (2011, March 15). *The Times*, p. 25.

3 The Geopolitics of Japanese Soft Power and the Japanese Language and Studies Classroom
Soft Power Pedagogy, Globalization, and the New Technologies

William S. Armour

INTRODUCTION

As a teacher who has used a range of Japanese mass and popular culture products, such as manga and anime, in his Japanese language and studies (hereafter JLS) classrooms for more than a decade, I have been intrigued by my students' seemingly intense and often passionate interest in them. Here I am being influenced by John Fiske who views mass culture as "cultural products that are mass produced (like CDs)" and popular culture as "culture that people themselves have made, rather than culture that is made for them . . . It is, in part, *what we do with the mass media products once we have obtained them*" (Wise 2008: 8–9, emphasis added). Interestingly, The Japan Foundation (2011: 9) reports that under "knowledge-based tendencies," the second most popular purpose of Japanese language study was "learning about manga, anime, etc." To my knowledge, this is one of the first major surveys[1] to empirically document the influence of Japanese mass and popular culture products in JLS education. More recently the Japan Foundation has published its *Survey Report on Japanese-Language Education Abroad 2012*[2] and this again indicates the influence that Japanese popular culture products have had on learners of the Japanese language, ranking it as the third purpose/reason for Japanese language study.

What follows is a conceptual exploration into the relationships between JLS education in Australia, "Japan" as a brand, and its "soft power." As a research project, it can be construed as both illuminating, by making important behaviors or attitudes in a given context evident for contemplation and exploratory, by attempting to show causal connections and relationships between variables. (Hart 1998: 46–47)

Armour (2011: 127) introduced the notion of "soft power pedagogy," which was described as

A way of teaching and learning Japanese language and culture that relies on using and consuming examples of Japan's "soft power" such as manga and anime in and out of the classroom to perpetuate a positive interest in Japanese culture and language in the face of decreasing numbers of learners, competition from other additional languages in the curriculum and other factors related to the choice of Japanese language as an "investment." (Norton Peirce 1995)

This present chapter attempts to broaden the notion of soft power pedagogy, locating it in its geopolitical context by considering the extent to which the products of "soft power," referred to as "soft resources" by Lee (2009), are mediated and then influence JLS education. I base part of the discussion on how Lo Bianco (2000, 2009) and others have constructed a history of Japanese language learning in Australia then build into it other crucial influences, namely globalization, the Internet, "new" media and other (device-related) technologies and argue how they have contributed to disrupting and decentering the "Japanese" language and studies teacher, something that would have been inconceivable in the early 1970s when I began learning Japanese.

UNDERPINNINGS

There are two major influences underpinning this chapter. Firstly, it is uncontroversial to claim that the term "globalization" is a contested one. Bauman (2008: 71) claims that "Whatever else 'globalization' may mean, it means that we are all dependent on each other. Distances matter little now." However, he continues by arguing that while globalization has "thus far produced a network of interdependence . . . It would be grossly premature to speak of even a global society or global culture, not to mention a global polity or global law" (Bauman 2008: 73).

How we have become interdependent is an important aspect of the story of globalization, one that is beyond the scope of this chapter. Suffice it to say, Bauman (2008: 75) notes that "A retreat from the globalization of human dependency, from the global reach of human technology and economic activities is, in all probability, no longer on the cards." Why? Despite the view that Thomas Friedman's take on globalization is "simplistic" (Steger 2009: 1), I believe it is still useful since he bifurcates globalization into "first era" (mid-1800s to the late 1920s) and "Globalization Round II" from 1989 onward (Friedman 2000: xvi–xvii). He argues that the latter is "turbocharged . . . [and] different in kind—both technologically and politically" (ibid: xviii) and based on integration achieved through the World Wide Web (ibid: 8).

Related to this point, Ken Auletta comments[3] that in 1998 there were no iPods, no iPads, no e-book readers, no smartphones, Bill Gates was king, and Google Inc. was just being developed by Larry Page and Sergey Brin. While he casts doubt that the Internet has been the most transformative technology invented, Auletta suggests that the velocity of change is itself remarkable given that in such a relatively short time the Internet and Facebook have had a significant uptake of users compared with the telephone, electricity, and even television. Even in its short life, users of Facebook seem to be abandoning the once popular social media site due in part to, ironically, its popularity—it has already become uncool, especially with the youth who have traditionally been using it.[4] Land (2006: 1) conceptualizes such velocity linked to the sphere of learning technology using a dromological perspective (*dromos* meaning "running"):

> What are often claimed as benefits of networked learning environments, that they can offer productive forms of accessibility, asychronicity, flexible working, interactivity, instaneity, global reach, learner empowerment and inclusivity [locating] the rise of digital information technologies *firmly within the neo-liberal ideology of globalisation*, and see them caught inexorably within a logic of 'fast time,' increasing acceleration and exponential growth of information. (emphasis added)

This is reminiscent of Savoie's (2010) discussion regarding the way that the Internet is shifting power away from its traditional holders. While Savoie is ostensibly talking about the relationships between business organizations, nation-states, and their governments, there are insights layered in his argument relevant for those of us involved in education at whatever level. Savoie (2010: 43) asserts that,

> The Internet, the lowering of trade barriers, and international financial markets that operate in real time, however, are making it increasingly difficult for national governments to control their own economies and to identify who actually wields power, either political or economic. *Whatever else may be said about the Internet, it has promoted more open political systems and encouraged a free flow of information*. (emphasis added)

The notions of speed and free flow link to the second influence in this chapter. I use Bauman's own conceptualization of globalization (Bauman 1998) in relation to speed, as well as his more recent concepts of "liquid modernity" and "liquid life" (Bauman 2005a, b, 2007 and 2011). Bauman (2005a: 1) posits that

> "Liquid life" is a kind of life that tends to be lived in a liquid modern society. "Liquid modern" is a society in which the conditions under which its members act change faster than it takes the ways of acting to consolidate into habits and routines.

Characteristics of liquid life are uncertainty, new beginnings, constant movement, speed not duration, and replacement. Bauman refers to the global world in which liquid life is now being experienced and discusses extensively the "objects of consumption," such as diets, gadgets, wallpaper and the like, in relation to the effect those characteristics and those objects are having, from changing our attitudes to producing vast amounts of waste. Scanlan

(2009: 1) argues that liquid modernity is a "new period of global development" supported through five "departures": 1) familiar institutions and social forms are disintegrating faster than they can be replaced, 2) global business interests hold power that cannot be regulated by the state, 3) social safety nets are disappearing, 4) quick fixes and quick profits trump long-term planning and thinking, and 5) individuals now shoulder the burden of volatile markets.

The significance of Bauman's influence in this chapter resides firstly in what Pollock (2007: 114) refers to as "the shift from solid, defined, localized, territorialized, nation-bound modernity" into the liquid. This notion of "liquid modernity" seems relevant in relation to the time flows, the constant change with no actual finishing points, and the "incessant new beginnings" (Bauman 2007: 121) associated with the many technological milestones in the trans-millennial decades (1990 to 2010—coinciding with Friedman's Globalization Round II mentioned earlier), and specifically the consumption of Japanese mass media products in relation to JLS education. Bauman asserts, "Everything is disposable, nothing is truly necessary, nothing is irreplaceable . . . Everything is offered with a use-by date attached" (ibid: 123–124).

Secondly, and in relation to the notion of the use-by date, in their discussion of one of their contributor's chapters, Bayne and Land (2005: 5) explore the notion of "fluidity" in terms of how the teacher's "considerable control over the learning experiences of their students" has shifted due to online environments, thus undermining the teacher's capacity to control. Related to this, McWilliam (2005) also draws on Bauman's work, in particular, the notion of "de-learning" (or forgetting) in the liquid social setting; that is, "some learning is unhelpful, and thus *in certain circumstances ignorance might be better than knowledge*" (McWilliam 2005: 3–4, italics in the original). Moreover, Bauman (2005b: 312) asks where his conceptualizations of liquid life and liquid modern leave education and educators. The notion of "a stiff curriculum" (Bauman 2005b: 316) is no longer part of the liquid modern setting, that is, "centres of teaching and learning are subjected to a 'de-institutionalizing' pressure and prompted to surrender their loyalty to 'canons of knowledge' . . . thus putting the value of flexibility above the surmised inner logic of scholarly disciplines" (ibid.).

JAPANESE LANGUAGE AND STUDIES IN AUSTRALIA: AN "INHERITED HISTORY"

To provide a context for my discussion about the use of Japanese mass and popular culture products in JLS classrooms, I draw from Lo Bianco's (2000, 2009) characterization of Japanese language education in Australia and refer to it in Table 3.1 as "inherited" since it provides a useful legacy on which to base further discussion.

Lo Bianco (2009) offers us things to celebrate, lament, and contemplate. He employs the metaphor of the "tsunami" when reflecting on the so-called boom times of Japanese language education of the late 1980s to mid-1990s (Lo Bianco 2000) to indicate the positive but overwhelming increase in the number of learners of Japanese language rather than any destructive effect that such waves can have. Marriott, Neustupný, and Spence-Brown (1994: 3) note that "Within the area of Asian languages we can witness a feeling of uneasiness between advocates of Japanese, which at present attracts the vast majority of learners, and representatives of the other languages." It must also be remembered that much of the official government rhetoric regarding the reasons to learn Japanese at the time of the "tsunami" were linked to bolstering Australia-Japan economic ties, arguably a feature of globalization as a neo-liberal discourse. A similar grandiloquence can be seen almost 20 years later in the then Australian Labor Government's (now largely defunct) 2012 white paper, *Australia in the Asian Century*, which employs a comparable discourse though the focus has shifted away from Japan (and, more controversially, South Korea) and toward China and India. Lo Bianco does not include the period 2006–present in his work already cited; however, he calls for "a long-term legitimation and related strategy for Japanese," one related to "building on the stimulus of the national curriculum, the normalisation of its teaching and addressing problems" and suggests that "This should be informed by the *voices of the learners, bottom-up messages*, perhaps serving to 'make real' the top-down proclamations" (Lo Bianco 2009: 334–335, emphasis added).

Table 3.1 The "Inherited" History of Japanese Language Education in Australia (based on Lo Bianco 2000, 2009)

1868–1901*	Australians became fascinated with Japanese exotica after Japan opened its borders in the mid-19th century (see Walker (1999, 2012) and Meaney (2007) for further discussion)
1901–mid-1930s	Exotic, foreign, and rare
mid-1930s–post-WWII	Japanese assumes strategic, geopolitical interest
mid-1960s–mid-1970s	Beginnings of regional consciousness for Australia (Lo Bianco 2000: 15); Incipient regionalism (Lo Bianco 2009: 333)
mid-1970s–late 1980s	Multicultural Asia-literacy policies (Lo Bianco 2000: 16); Multicultural Asia literacy (Lo Bianco 2009: 334)
late 1980s–mid-1990s	Tsunami (Lo Bianco 2000: 16); Enrollment tsunami (Lo Bianco 2009: 334)
mid-1990s–late 1990s*	Not addressed by Lo Bianco
late 1990s–2005	Loss of primacy but normalization (Lo Bianco 2009: 334)

Notes: *indicates my additions.

Reading Lo Bianco's accounts together with Marriott et al. (1994), Akahane and Jonak (1996), de Kretser and Spence-Brown (2010), Lee (2004), and The Japan Foundation (2011, 2013), one begins to understand the good and not so good aspects related particularly to Japanese language education in Australia. Certain motifs resonate throughout the "inherited" history such as the cataloging of numbers of learners, attrition associated with these numbers, teacher quality, students' motivations (vocational and other purposes for learning, reasons for continuing to learn or for discontinuing), funding, and economic ties between the two countries, among others. With hindsight, what seems to be missing in this history, however, is a more thorough engagement with the impact of Globalization Round II, transnational flows between Japan and Australia, for example Japanese soft power/soft resources, the Internet, and new media.

One possible weakness in the "inherited" history is the paucity of reference to the influence of these phenomena. Lo Bianco (2000: 27–28) laments,

> The teaching and learning of Japanese in Australia will need to understand rather better than it has in the past the context of Australian multiculturalism. Australian learners of Japanese will rarely have an identity connection with Japan and Japanese ways of being that their counterparts who study Chinese, Italian or Greek in Australian schools may have. That is, "Japanese" will be construed, for these learners, in relation to Australian culture and its economic and cultural relationship to the economic and cultural contents of Japan-for-Australians. *Since the mediation of this Japan for Australians is by textbook writers, textbooks are of vital importance.* (emphasis added)

Three points emerge from this view. The first is, judging from trends articulated in much of the current literature regarding the impacts that new (digital) literacies and associated technologies are having on both informal and formal experiences in education (e.g., Godwin-Jones 2011; Hicks 2011), discourses surrounding the so-called skills for the 21st century,[5] and the discussion regarding *watashi no Nihongo* (or "my Japanese," see Kobayashi 2011; Sugiura, Onodera, & Beuckman 2011), it is unclear whether such mediation via textbooks, through which knowledge is in some form recontextualized, (a notion gleaned from Basil Bernstein[6]) will continue to remain that central (see Takagi 2011). While Honda (2011: 20) uses the maxim—"*Kyōkasho o oshieru no dewa nai. Kyōkasho de oshieru noda*" (It's not that we teach the textbook. We teach through the textbook)—with the present emphasis on blended learning and M(assive) O(pen) O(nline) C(ourses)[7] within formal education and the proliferation of do-it-yourself type informal learning resources (podcasts, blogs, vlogs) now available, it seems to me that traditional conceptions of the "textbook" and even more broadly, the very spaces where learning occurs[8] are now being redefined in favor of how knowledge (linguistic and content) can be mediated.

On this, McWilliam (2005: 1) makes the point that teachers need to "ply a new trade" since "pedagogy is characterized by *well-rehearsed habits*" (italics in the original) that have been problematized since the 1950s. She echoes Carl Rogers's claim that "it was the learner who ought to be the center and focus of pedagogy" (ibid.). Moreover, identities such as "student" and "teacher," McWilliam (2005: 2) argues, are "becoming somewhat passé. . . . We should all be learners all the time, and those of us who teach students should also understand ourselves to be *facilitators of learning*" (italics in the original). This view appears to have become *the* influential discourse of the present day. For example, Theisen (2013: 7) offers four strategies to "help your students find their voices": 1) let go of control—"Give students ownership of their learning wherever possible," 2) give students creative free time—"It has been said that innovations like Google were developed when creative individuals had time to explore freely," 3) encourage students as decision makers—"Inquire why they want to learn a language and help them set their own goals," and 4) help them be advocates for educational change—"They use technology as a tool to make connections and to expand their own learning opportunities. *With so many open sources available now, they are aware of the power of learning any time, any place*" (Theisen 2013: 7, emphasis added). The August 2013 issue of the American Council of the Teaching of Foreign Languages' *The Language Educator* focuses on the learner and advocates the de-learning of one type of pedagogy (teacher controlled) and learning how to personalize the language learning experience. In short, it appears that there is now a concerted push to implement a type of liberation pedagogy espoused by Paulo Freire in the late 1960s, one that replaces both the teacher-as-narrator and the notion of banking education with a negotiated pedagogy in which learners become the narrators and the classroom a community of inquiry.

The second point derives from another kind of "tsunami," not of learners rushing off to learn Japanese through textbooks but "the penetration of neo-liberalism marketization, and the amplification of international ethno-flows of labor, immigrants and tourists. No less important is the progression of media and cultural globalization" (Iwabuchi 2010: 197–198), a point discussed in the following section.

Furthermore, a third point regarding the identity connection with Japan and Japanese ways of being will be made later in relation to the links that learners have to Japanese mass and popular culture products.

The "inherited" history should also be read together with other documents, for example, the 2012 *Australia in the Asian Century* white paper, the annual *Lowy Institute*[9] *Poll*, and other histories such as Meaney (2007), Wesley (2011), and Walker and Sobocinska (2012) to name just a few. The *Lowy Institute Poll*, for example, attempts to measure public opinion and foreign policy, including how Australia "feels" toward other countries (see Oliver 2013). This measurement may be construed, albeit fairly crudely, as an indication of another country's attractiveness to those Australians who were polled. Using the analogy of a thermometer where 100° is very warm and favorable and 0° is the opposite, Japan has hovered somewhere between 64° and 70° over a period of nine years since the poll was first launched in 2005. In the 2013 *Lowy Institute Poll*, the most favorable country was Great Britain (77°) followed by Ireland (73°), the USA and Germany at 70°, while Singapore at 67° was the most favorable Asian country followed by Japan (65°), a decline of 5° since 2012, however China measured a cooler 54°. Japan's position on the scale somewhat surprises me given the exposure it has had in Australia with the restoration of diplomatic relations in 1952 and the signing of the Basic Treaty of Friendship and Cooperation almost 40 years ago. Despite more recent attempts at implementing its soft power through soft resources, the lower than expected temperature for Japan could indicate a complicated picture for Japanese language pedagogy in Australia.

These kinds of publications together with "inherited" history(ies) of Japanese language teaching and learning in Australia must acknowledge the sociotechnological influences that have also occurred during the transmillennium decades. Consider how an imaginary university student, 21 years old, has experienced these decades. While the historical and technological milestones as well as references related to JLS are too numerous to mention here, my point is to attempt to position this university student into the broader geopolitical and techno-social contexts to better understand what could have impacted him or her. To put the use of the new technologies and media into an Australian context, in the period 2010–2011 the Australian Bureau of Statistics (2011)[10] reports that in relation to the household use of information technology, 18–24 year olds access the Internet 1) to create online content (57%), 2) to download media (60%), 3) for educational purposes (61%), 4) e-mailing (93%), 5) to listen to or watch media (81%), 6) to research or browse (89%), and 7) to network or play games (86%). The Australian Bureau of Statistics (2011) also reports that 49% of persons aged 15–17, 47% of 18–24 year olds and 51% of persons aged 25–34 purchased CDs, music, DVDs, videos, books, and magazines over the Internet for private purposes in the previous 12 months, 2010–2011. From these data, it is not possible, however, to know the nature of these media in terms of countries of origin, type (e.g., for educational use), or language/s used in them.

A (NOT SO) NEW "TSUNAMI": THE INFLUENCES OF THE NEW TECHNOLOGIES AND MEDIA

So what's different from when I began learning Japanese in the 1970s to now? The learning was and is still mediated through a range of materials, social events, and technology. Effort is still required to learn Japanese and learners must learn the so-called basics, though they have most likely changed throughout the years to reflect the times. One major difference is that options afforded to me as a teenager and young adult learning Japanese forty years ago were limited in terms of diversity of materials, teaching methods,[11] types of exposure, and opportunities to visit Japan, among others. However, it is how classrooms, including teachers and their pedagogies, are now constructed and configured that is, for me at least, the most significant difference. This change in the thinking about the classroom and its nature and people links to how Bauman has characterized liquid life.

My initial learning was mediated through Dunn and Yanada's *Teach Yourself Japanese* and Eiichi Kiyōka's *Japanese in Thirty Hours*. I then found *Discovering Japan: A Textbook of the Japanese Language for Secondary Schools Book 1* by Ackroyd, Sayeg, and Beresford (1971) with an approach radically different from those other materials. In 1974, I joined a Japanese language class taught by a Japanese, maybe the first Japanese national I had ever met, and we used Eleanor Harz Jorden's original 1962 *Beginning Japanese Part 1*. I remember the language laboratory sessions very well. I also became involved in a few related social events where I met others interested in Japan and Japanese language learning, such as older high school students who were either going to Japan or had been on exchange, which was something I really wanted to do but was then prohibitively expensive.

In 1975 I sat Level 1 Japanese for the New South Wales Higher School Certificate (HSC), which included studying Japanese history by reading Richard Storry's *A History of Modern Japan* and the Japanese language, which was mediated through Hibbett and Itasaka's *Modern Japanese: A Basic Reader* (named in Japanese as *Nihon Gendai-bun tokuhon*), a textbook that I thought was difficult and dull. I was 17 years old and Lesson V dealing with *on* or moral indebtedness still haunts me. In terms of community, the deputy principal was also studying Japanese (Jorden's *Beginning Japanese Part 2*) so we could reflect on our learning together, and I also had a series of Japanese pen pals who would write to me in both Japanese and English, but it took months to get a reply. I also remember listening to *Nihon Shokai* (sic) broadcast fortnightly on ABC Radio (1975). My parents gave me a Toshiba cassette player in the mid-1970s and as part of my Japanese language learning, I also used the drills in the solidly audio-lingual based *A Language Laboratory Course in Elementary Japanese Book 1* by Garrick and Ono (1973). I still have all these materials so they obviously still mean something to me. I also visited Sydney on a couple of occasions and discovered the *Japanese Bookshop* located just near Circular Quay that sold not just Japanese *objets d'art* and other crafts but more importantly manga, probably my first introduction to authentic materials.

From 1976–1978 I studied from Alfonso's *Japanese Language Patterns* Vols. 1&2 (and more language laboratory sessions), read Hoshi Shin'ichi's *Kimagure Robotto* (1972) and other randomly selected Japanese literary works (modern poetry, plays by Mishima Yukio) at university. I was made to read and translate into English texts that seemed to be more relevant to the teachers' interests than to mine, despite these works being "authentic."

My classmates and I were made to read Japanese newspapers, write compositions, and learn *kanji* by looking them up in a printed dictionary. During this time, for me Japan was "imagined"; however, given that I was inured into Japan at a young age, my brand loyalty was faithful; and in 1985, I arrived there as a 27 year old ready to experience "the real."

Contrast my story to the following. In Semester 1, 2011, six upper-level Japanese language students visited my introductory Japanese language classes as *sempai* (advanced learners). In one class, three *sempai* brought realia to class, including photographs of their trips to Japan (depicting a visit to a maid café and *Komiket* (Comic Market) among others), a map of Tokyo, manga, and the March 2011 issue of *Poporo*, a woman's magazine featuring pictures and interviews of well-known Japanese singers and boy bands. After these *sempai* and my students had interacted in Japanese, I asked them what advice they would give regarding Japanese language learning. The overwhelming advice was for the beginners to watch Japanese television dramas, listen to J-pop, join the campus Japan Club, and go on exchange. After class, one of the *sempai* e-mailed me the links to a Japanese grammar site and an online dictionary and suggested I share them with my students. In Semester 1, 2013 a new group of *sempai* offered similar advice as well as suggesting using Japanese language "teaching" apps on smartphones and online translation sites when the going got tough (my eyes rolled at this advice!).

For the *sempai*, the tools for learning Japanese were two types of authentic mass media (presumably for input), a social space to meet Japanese and to use the language, and supportive online materials. There was no suggestion for students to find a good teacher, attend a class, or consult a Japanese language textbook, the very techniques that I had used in the 1970s. Moreover, Japan itself was no longer "imagined" since the *sempai* (and I am sure my students too) had already been engaging with things Japanese over the Internet in real time. For those students who are, for instance, interacting with their Japanese friends in Japan either through an online chat site, Internet telephony, or some other real-time way, the degree to which Japan is perceived as "imaginary" has decreased.

On this point, an insight was revealed in listening to students in a 2013 course on contemporary Japan—that through the constant exposure to Japan and ostensibly Japanese mass and popular culture that was being broadcast on (children's) Australian television during the mid to late 1990s, these students had built up, in their words, a significant amount of "familiarity" with Japan; that is, Japan was something that they were used to and had grown up with. In my case, instead of Japanese (with the exception of *The Samurai* (Onmitsu Kenshi) and *Kimba the White Lion* (Junguru Taitei) broadcast on Australian television in the late 1960s), I was much more intimate with American and British popular culture of the late 1960s and 1970s. Televised Australian popular culture has been, it seems, less influential.

(JAPANESE) MASS AND POPULAR CULTURE
AND "SOFT POWER"

Therefore, the nexus between the use of information technology and what appears to be a more rhizomatic approach (Usher 2008) to learning mediated through mass and popular culture products cannot be underestimated. Iwabuchi (2010: 197) captures this by claiming that watching, listening, reading, and enjoying a range of "Asian" popular media "are now part of the mundane landscape of East Asian cities," something unthinkable even two decades ago. We know that Japanese mass and popular culture influences many consumers to engage with Japanese language and studies learning, either formally or informally (e.g., Armour & Iida 2014; Northwood & Thomson 2012; Otmazgin 2013; Swenson 2007; The Japan Foundation 2011, 2013; Thomson 2010). Armour and Iida (2014) have called this the "Japanese popular culture effects argument."

To illustrate this, Thomson (2010) found that students taking introductory Japanese language brought with them a variety of vocabulary items and names (of people, places, products) that were specifically linked to Japanese media culture. Using a survey of university students studying Japanese language for the first time at the beginner's level (n=270), Thomson asserts, "gakusei-tachi no *chishiki* wa, tatoeba hon o yonde benkyō shite tsuketa to iu yori, anime, manga, dorama, gēmu nado kara etari . . ." (The student's *knowledge* is acquired through anime, manga, television dramas, and video games rather than through the usual reading of, for example, books and studying alone . . . [Thomson 2010: 167; my translation; emphasis added]). In the English language abstract accompanying her article written in Japanese, Thomson (2010: 157) suggests that "A large number of students are drawn to Japanese by popular culture such as anime, manga, J-pop and drama. The paper argues that they 'consume' Japanese language study just as they 'consume' other popular culture icons such as the Miyazaki anime and Hello Kitty goods."

Joseph Nye has argued that Japan has been involved in globalization long before the transition to Friedman's Globalization Round II and predicted that "information is most likely to be the key source of power" in the 21st century and that Japan "may well confer it significant soft power in the information age" (Nye 2000: 123–124). He reasserts his agent-focused definition of power and suggests that there is a need to "look more closely at the different ways soft power can co-opt, attract, and entice" (Nye 2008: x). More recently, Nye has characterized power through the metaphor of a three-dimensional chess game with the top level representing military power among states, the center level as economic power among states, and the bottom level as "things that cross borders outside the control of governments—nobody's in charge."[12] Furthermore, Nye has bifurcated power into the concepts of "power transition" or a change of power between states and "power diffusion" or the way that power moves from all states to non-state actors.[13] It is this second concept that is relevant here, especially Nye's claim that since computing and communication costs have fallen significantly from the 1970s, access also goes down therefore enabling anybody to "play in the game" and as such the "state" is no longer the single player.[14]

Though the concept of soft power is descriptive, there are normative implications (Nye 2008: xii), that is, ethical considerations. Nye notes that when power is defined behaviorally, it's a relationship ". . . and soft power depends more on the subject's role in that relationship than does hard power. Attraction depends on what is happening in the mind of the subject" (ibid: xiii) and he asks, "How do agents win the hearts and minds of subjects?" (ibid: x)

To answer this question, Lee (2009) offers a useful "theory of soft power" that, among other things, addresses the processes through which "soft resources" exert their influence. These soft resources include, in international arenas, slogans, policy proposals, public diplomacy, theories, concepts, discourses, celebrities, imperial museums, rituals, common languages, traditions, and lifestyles as well as resources for a domestic focus, such as national heroes, typically ones emerging from international sporting competitions (and the competitions themselves), and the countries leaders' outstanding performances on the international stage. Lee (2009: 211) posits that:

> When applying soft resources to the recipients, the applicants wish to change the recipients' preferences, calculations and interpretative frameworks or emotions such that the recipients change their behaviors in the direction which the applicants want . . . When short-term changes are fixed as "common sense" or "habits," then the short-term soft power will have longer-term effects. Institutionalization, global or national standard setting, or the creation of social rhythms through "synchronization and orchestration," are typical examples of producing long-term soft power effects in the form of social habits.

I would suggest that institutionalization includes education, either formal or informal, where the formal implies schools, colleges, and universities (and teachers and students) while the informal covers everything else, such as the private consumption (and prosumption) of soft resources, cosplaying, chatting about products, attending anime conventions, downloading or purchasing some product off the Internet, and so on.

Kelts (2011) has suggested, "By now it's no secret to anyone with *a high-speed Internet connection*: The gap between the popularity of contemporary Japanese culture overseas and its anemic industries at home has become a chasm" (emphasis added). Kelts laments how Japan-based Japanese producers of so-called "Cool Japan" (manga, anime, J-pop music, video games to name a few)—what he refers to as "those beloved products"—who have captured the interests of consumers outside Japan just don't see the international potential keeping their eyes, it seems, solely on the waning domestic Japanese market.[15] That is, these producers do not grasp power diffusion that well.

Can Kelts's lamentation be justified? Akutsu (2008) suggests that Japan-brand-related initiatives began in earnest from 2002, and in 2004 the "Japan Brand Working Group" was established, concentrating on food culture, fashion, and local brands as well as "policy issues concerning ways to build an attractive Japan brand" (Akutsu 2008: 212; also see Burgess (this volume) for a discussion of the Cool Japan policy). More recently, the 2008 Japan National Tourism Organisation (JNTO) sponsored *Yōkoso! Japan* featured "Cool Japan" alongside more traditional and neo-oriental representations. JNTO's new campaign *Japan. Endless Discovery* reduces "Japan" to five elements: cuisine, natural beauty, adventures, cultural heritage, and cool. ANA launched its "Is Japan Cool?"[16] campaign in February 2012. The top five items ranked as "cool" were *omotenashi*[17] (Japanese hospitality), high-tech toilets, hot spring resorts, Mt. Fuji, and ultramodern vending machines. Surprisingly, *manga kissa* (coffee shops where manga can be borrowed and read) were ranked 16 and maid cafés 17, while Japanese *aidoru* (idols) came in at 30 out of 33 categories.

The Japan Foundation launched its Anime Manga no Nihongo (Japanese in Anime & Manga) web site (http://anime-manga.jp/index.html) on February 1, 2010 and has incorporated Spanish (22/10/2010), Korean (31/01/2011), Chinese (23/03/2011), and French (29/06/2011) versions reflecting the international interest in these two Japanese soft power products. Themes include samurai, ninja, love, and school, ones that perhaps reflect expected viewers' age groups.

There are also freely available multilingual publications. The Japan Tourism Agency together with the Association of Japanese Animations[18] published a comprehensive *Japan Anime Tourism Guide* (in English) in 2010 and the Association of Japanese Animations published the *Tōkyō Anime Kenkō Gaido* (*Tokyo Anime Tourism Guide*) in Japanese, English, Chinese and Korean.

Finally, the Ministry of Foreign Affairs of Japan (2013) published a special feature—*Japanese Pop Culture—To the Next Stage*—that simply revisits what is already common knowledge about cosplay, *kawaii* fashion, museums, and vocaloids. Despite all of this active nation branding,[19] Kelts may be correct in pointing out the tardiness with which domestic Japanese producers of those "beloved products" have responded to their uptake outside Japan.

Earlier in the chapter, I made two points in relation to Lo Bianco (2000). I want to elaborate on a third point here regarding the identity connection with Japan and Japanese ways in connection to learners' consumption of Japanese mass culture products. Naturally, many Japanese language learners will not have the same kind of heritage relationship that others have, say in connection to so-called community languages, such as Chinese, Italian and Greek. (see Moloney & Oguro in this volume for discussion of Japanese as a heritage language) However, as Napier (2007) and others have shown, anime and manga enthusiasts or fans appear to have constructed a legitimate identity informed through their relationships with these products. Tsutsui (2010: 46) makes the point that "Fans have also made extensive use of the Internet, creating blogs, chat rooms, and websites (such as the Anime News Network) to interact, build communities, and share information." In fact, I would go as far as to suggest that, these days at least, the mediation between technology and how fans and others learn about Japan (including Japanese language) could be understood as a relationship in which the technology has become *in loco praeceptoris* (in place of the teacher). In the final section of this chapter, I'll briefly discuss the potentials, both positive and negative, that these technologies and media offer.

THE POTENTIALS OF NEW TECHNOLOGIES AND MEDIA

> *The web is their classroom, Facebook is their community . . . if universities won't adapt students will do it without them.*
>
> American e-learning expert, Professor Ashwin Ram

This quote appeared on the cover of *Uniken* (Autumn 2011 edition), an official publication coming out of the University of New South Wales (Sydney, Australia). The article articulates how technology is changing the way not only how teaching and learning are done but also challenging "centuries-old academic structures and practices, the very notion of what it means to be literate and, potentially, the primacy of universities as the world's arbiters and repositories of knowledge" (Williams, 2011: 12). The sentiments embedded in Williams's article need to be measured against other work such as Bennett and Maton's (2010) view, which questions the influence technology is having. They suggest, drawing on Singh (2002), what should be considered is how knowledge gained in a formal educational context has been pedagogized, that is, "knowledge that has been selected, re-arranged into a particular sequence within a curriculum, and recontextualized within specific contexts of teaching and learning" (Bennett & Maton 2010: 327).

Most of my students seem to be distracted by their mobile phones in class these days. Some say they are using them to access dictionaries and other helper apps. I know that others are "doing social media," and I lament their inattention.[20] I acknowledge that my students' familiarity with Japan has been mediated typically through technology; however, I find it difficult to give up the teacher-as-narrator role. The notion of the "Atlas Complex" (Finkel & Monk 1983) comes to mind—I have assumed that my "principal task is one of improving the ways in which [I] express [my] expertise: Clear and precise explanations can always be sharpened; penetrating questions can always be made more penetrating" (Finkel & Monk 1983: 86), while a sense of fixedness lingers. These days, however—

> The role of the twenty-first century teacher . . . is to help young people [sic] know where to find the knowledge, to know what to do with it when they get it, to know "good" knowledge from "bad" knowledge, to know how to use it, to apply it, to synthesize it, to be creative with

it, to add to it even, to know which bits to use and when and how to use them and to know how to remember key parts of it (Gilbert 2011:24)

—and thus making a dull subject seem interesting (ibid.: 30). One suggestion is to "flip" one's classroom by differentiating what is done in and out of the classroom, such as students watching an online (instructional) video at home and then, in class, doing related activities scaffolded by the teacher.[21]

Both the effects and affects of mediated Japanese soft power as examples of how globalization, when applied to (liberation) pedagogy at least, promise various degrees of transformation. What I believe I am witnessing (and experiencing) is the next stage of the "inherited" history beginning to unfold with another kind of "tsunami" hitting, and its consequences are just beginning to become clear. For instance, Rotella (2013) expresses some skepticism in response to the roll out of tablet devices in Guildford County in the USA. One borrowed motif that Rotella brings up in his newspaper article is that education is ripe for disruption. However, this disruption, it seems to me, is being generated not only by learners themselves and the discourses around the customization of learning but also through the role of market forces that inform this customization and blur the line between the consumables that soft and hard power advocate. What and/or who makes all the difference these days—learners?—technology?—the market?—all three?[22] It appears that teachers are now required to forget the past to embrace the now (and the future) and surrender to the liquid life so vividly described by Bauman earlier.

CONCLUDING REMARKS

This chapter has attempted to explore the relationships between Japanese language and studies education in Australia, Brand Japan, and its soft power. It has surveyed an inherited history of Japanese language education in Australia, layering onto it other influences such as geopolitical and sociotechnological impacts that appear to have been significant in the last 20 years. It is known that Japanese soft resources have been influential, even well before official interest in their consequences caught up with their actual consumption by audiences worldwide. Tsutsui (2010: 46) concludes his discussion of why these audiences have embraced these products so wholeheartedly by suggesting that the reasons are "as diverse as the forms of Japanese popular culture and the sources of Japan's pop creativity," and asserts that quality, stylistic and thematic complexity, and difference from Western popular culture attract audiences. I argue in this chapter that the advances in technology that have become commonplace must also be taken into consideration in the discussion of how audiences, such as my students, consume, learn through, access—whatever the verb—those "beloved" products coming out of Japan.

In the *HSC 2012 Study Guide* supplement published by the Sydney Morning Herald (2012, June 12: 32), under "Languages," candidates were advised to "immerse yourself in popular culture . . . to get a handle on the language you're learning." Under "Resources," Cambourne (2012: 33) quotes a classroom teacher—"There are a number of websites, apps and programs that can help students practice everything from listening to writing and even speaking." Furthermore, in 2012 a Japanese colleague of mine attended our university's Courses and Careers Day and was approached by several final-year secondary school students who had been studying Japanese. They spoke in Japanese, telling her they were Japanese popular culture "crazy." What really surprised my colleague most was one of the students wanted to become a *seiyū* (anime voice actor).

If we can read anything into the figures from the Japan Foundation and other research regarding the interest in manga, anime, and the like, as well as more anecdotal observations of Japanese language/studies learners at whatever level, I can tentatively conclude that we need to consider much more carefully the impact that Japanese soft resources as examples of market-driven globalization are having on pedagogy. There is certainly no suggestion of banning or censoring these resources; however, it seems there is an urgent need to offset indiscriminate, unsystematic, and arbitrary uptake with some serious reflection to consider the ethics of using these beloved products in Japanese language and studies classrooms, if such places should continue to exist.

NOTES

1. Other significant surveys are summarized in Otmazgin (2013).
2. I am citing the *Survey Report on Japanese-Language Education Abroad 2012—Summary* (English).
3. See Auletta (2010) for the full discussion.
4. See Miller (2013) for the full discussion.
5. See Partnership for 21st Century Skills (2011) for a full discussion.
6. Apple (2001: 88) explains that Bernstein discussed educational change in terms of three fields: "(1) the field of 'production' where new knowledge is constructed; (2) the field of 'reproduction' where pedagogy and curriculum are actually enacted in schools, and, between these other two, (3) the 'recontextualizing' field where discourses from the field of production are appropriated and then transformed into pedagogic discourse and recommendations."
7. See McMorran's (2013) discussion of MOOCs in relation to the potential delivery of courses (and their problems) in Japanese Studies, particularly those incorporating Japanese popular culture.
8. See Rodriguez (2013) for a discussion of space-as-possibility and the relation to schooling practices.
9. The Lowy Institute is an independent, nonpartisan international policy think tank located in Sydney, Australia (http://www.lowyinstitute.org).
10. See the Australian Bureau of Statistics (2011) for the full report.
11. With hindsight I am able to contextualize my own experiences of being taught Japanese language in the 1970s with its focus on grammar translation and audio-lingual methods, preference for texts that could be construed as reflecting so-called high culture, as well as the authority afforded to the teacher as giver of both language models and feedback in the form of corrections as an example of how Japanese was taught based on the views of that time. This can

be clearly seen reading through the first three chapters of Omaggio Hadley (2000) in which she offers a comprehensive treatment of the past to understand the present in terms of teaching an additional language.

12. Nye (2010).
13. Ibid.
14. Ibid.
15. Kelts (2011). Also see Kelts (2006) for a detailed discussion of Japanese popular culture in the USA.
16. See www.ana-cooljapan.com.
17. This word was among the top-four buzzwords in 2013. See *Japan Today* (2013, December 3).
18. Nihon Dōga Kyōkai can be accessed at http://www.aja.gr.jp/ (in Japanese and English).
19. Anholt (2010: 1) claims he coined the phrase in 1996, though rejects the term as a dangerous myth, preferring instead "competitive identity" (p. 8). Anholt (2010: 2) asserts, however, that "Nations may have brands—the sense that they have reputations, and those reputations are every bit as important to their progress and prosperity in the modern world as brand images are to corporations and their products . . ." He argues that public perceptions of countries tend to be "very stable" and these perceptions are simplistic making alteration rather difficult (p. 98).
20. See Richardson (2013) for a discussion of how teenagers' smartphones disrupt power in the classroom.
21. See Tucker (2012) for a discussion.
22. Otmazgin (2014) makes the point that in the process of transnational penetration, distribution, reproduction, and consumption of cultural commodities (he is discussing anime in the USA), entrepreneurship is key. However, there is a risk, he suggests, in producing disjunctive economic, cultural and political orders. My questions are: (1) what role(s) do learners and teachers play when they are engaged in consuming these cultural commodities as part of both formal and informal education? and (2) to what extent are both learners and teachers reduced to the role of entrepreneur in relation to the commodification of "Japan" as a brand?

REFERENCES

Ackroyd, J.I., Sayeg, T., & Beresford, D. (1971). *Discovering Japan: a textbook of Japanese language for secondary school, Book 1.* Sydney, NSW: Angus and Robertson.

Akahane, M., & Jonak, C. (1996). Language education policy for Australian schools: Implications for Japanese language education. *Current Report on Japanese-Language Education around the Globe (Sekai no Nihongo Kyōiku), 4,* 105–117.

Akutsu, S. (2008). Country case insight—Japan. In K. Dinnie (Eds.), *Nation Branding: Concepts, Issues, Practice* (pp. 211–219). Oxford: Elsevier.

Anholt, S. (2010). *Places, identity, image and reputation.* London: Palgrave.

Apple, M.W. (2001). *Educating the "right" way: Markets, standards, god, and inequality.* New York, NY: Routledge Falmer.

Armour, W.S. (2011). Learning Japanese by reading 'manga': The rise of 'soft power pedagogy.' *RELC Journal, 42*(2), 125–140.

Armour, W. S., & Iida, S. (2014). Are Australian fans of anime and manga motivated to learn Japanese language? *Asia Pacific Journal of Education.* http://dx.doi.org/ 10.1080/02188791.2014.922459

Auletta, K. (2010). *How Google and the internet affect all media* [Presentation]. Retrieved on February 9, 2013, from http://fora.tv/2010/10/02/Ken_Auletta_How_Google_and_the_Internet_Affect_All_Media/Ken_Auletta_Embrace_the_Internets_Velocity_of_Change

Australian Broadcasting Commission. (1975). *NSW Secondary Teachers' Notes: Radio and Television, Term One* (pp. 93–96), *Term Two* (pp. 79–86), *Term Three* (pp. 75–82). Sydney, NSW: Australian Broadcasting Commission.

Australian Bureau of Statistics. (2011). *Household use of information technology, Australia, 2010–11* [Data file]. Retrieved on February 9, 2013, from http://www.abs.gov.au/AUSSTATS/abs@.nsf/Lookup/8146.0Glossary12010-11

Bauman, Z. (1998). *Globalization: The human consequences.* Cambridge: Polity.

Bauman, Z. (2005a). *Liquid life.* Cambridge: Polity.

Bauman, Z. (2005b). Education in liquid modernity. *The Review of Education, Pedagogy, and Cultural Studies, 27*(4), 303–317.

Bauman, Z. (2007). Liquid arts. *Theory, Culture & Society, 24*(1), 117–126.

Bauman, Z. (2008). *Does ethics have a chance in a world of consumers?* Cambridge, MA: Harvard University Press.

Bauman, Z. (2011). *Culture in a liquid modern world* (L. Bauman, Trans.) Cambridge: Polity.

Bayne, S., & Land, R. (2005). Introduction. In R. Land & S. Bayne (Eds.), *Education in Cyberspace* (pp. 1–7). Milton Park: Routledge.

Bennett, S., & Maton, K. (2010). Beyond the 'digital natives' debate: Towards a more nuanced understanding of students' technology experiences. *Journal of Computer Assisted Learning, 26*(5), 321–331.

Cambourne, K. (2012, June 12). Get acquainted—now we're talking. *Sydney Morning Herald* HSC Study Guide supplement, pp. 32, 33.

de Kretser, A., & Spence-Brown, R. (2010). *The current state of Japanese language education in Australian schools.* Carlton South, Victoria: Education Services Australia Ltd.

Finkel, D. L., & Monk, G. S (1983). Teachers and learning groups: Dissolution of the atlas complex. *New Directions for Teaching and Learning, 14,* 83–97.

Friedman, T. L. (2000). *The lexus and the olive tree.* London: HarperCollinsPublishers.

Garrick, A.J., & Ono, K. (1973). *A language laboratory course in elementary Japanese: Book 1.* Sydney, NSW: New South Wales University Press.

Gilbert, I. (2011). *Why do I need a teacher when I've got Google? The essential guide to the big issues for every twenty-first century teacher.* London: Routledge.

Godwin-Jones, R. (2011). Emerging technologies: Mobile apps for language learning. *Language, Learning & Technology, 15*(2), 2–11.

Hart, C. (1998). *Doing a literature review: Releasing the social science research imagination.* Los Angeles, CA: Sage.

Hicks, S. D. (2011). Technology in today's classroom: Are you a tech-savvy teacher? *The Clearing House, 84,* 188–191.

Honda, H. (2011). Kyōkasho wa dare no tame no mono ka? (Who is the textbook for?) *Gekkan Nihongo* (The Monthly Nihongo), 20–23.

Iwabuchi, K. (2010). Globalization, East Asian media cultures and their publics. *Asian Journal of Communication, 20*(2), 197–212.

The Japan Foundation. (2011). *Present condition of overseas Japanese-language education: Survey report on Japanese-language education abroad 2009–Summary.* Tokyo: The Japan Foundation.

The Japan Foundation. (2013). *Survey report on Japanese-language education abroad 2012—Summary* (English). Retrieved on February 1, 2014, from http://www.jpf.go.jp/e/japanese/survey/result/survey12.html#report01

Japan Today. (2013, Dec. 3). 'Jejeje,' 'omotenashi,' 'baigaeshi,' 'madesho' voted top buzzwords for 2013. *Japan Today.* Retrieved from http://www.japantoday.com/category/national/view/jejeje-omotenashi-baigaeshi-imadesho-voted-top-buzzwords-for-2013

Kelts, R. (2006). *Japanamerica: How Japanese pop culture has invaded the U.S.* New York, NY: Palgrave Macmillan.

Kelts, R. (2011, June 10). Soft power hard truths / Japan's pop industries: blind at home, beloved overseas. *Daily Yomiuri Online.* Retrieved from http://www.yomiuri.co.jp/dy/features/arts/T110607003341.htm

Kobayashi, M. (2011). Nihongo wa dare no mono ka—'Watashi no Nihongo' o sasaeru gengo nōryoku (Who Owns Japanese?—The Language Abilities that Support 'My Own Japanese'). *Waseda Nihongo Kyōikugaku (Waseda Studies in Japanese Language Education), 9,* 15–20.

Land, R. (2006). Networked learning and the politics of speed: A dromological perspective. *Proceedings from Networked Learning 2006.* Retrieved on March 9, 2013, from http://www.networkedlearningconference.org.uk/past/nlc2006/info/confpapers.htm

Lee, D. Y. (2004). *Japanese Education in the Australian Context.* In 15th Biennial Conference of the Asian Studies Association of Australia, Canberra (Vol. 29).

Lee, G. (2009). A theory of soft power and Korea's soft power strategy. *The Korean Journal of Defense Analysis, 21*(2), 205–218.

Lo Bianco, J. (2000). *After the tsunami, some dilemmas: Japanese language studies in multicultural Australia.* Melbourne: Language Australia, The National Languages and Literacy Institute of Australia.

Lo Bianco, J. (2009). Return of the good times? Japanese teaching today. *Japanese Studies, 29*(3), 331–336.

Marriott, H., Neustupný, J. V., & and Spence-Brown, R. (1994). *Unlocking Australia's language potential—profiles of 9 key languages in Australia Vol. 7—Japanese.* Canberra: ACT: The National Languages and Literacy Institute of Australia.

McMorran, C. (2013). Teaching Japanese popular culture in the MOOC World. *Electronic Journal of Contemporary Japanese Studies (ejcjs), 13*(2). Retrieved on February 9, 2014, from http://www.japanesestudies.org.uk/ejcjs/vol13/iss2/mcmorran.html

McWilliam, E. (2005). Unlearning pedagogy. *Journal of Learning Design, 1*(1). Retrieved on February 1, 2012, from https://www.jld.edu.au/article/view/2/1

Meaney, N. (2007). *Towards a new vision: Australia and Japan across time.* Sydney: UNSW Press.

Miller, D. (2013, Dec. 20). *Facebook's so uncool, but it's morphing into a different beast.* Retrieved on March 9, 2014, from http://theconversation.com/facebooks-so-uncool-but-its-morphing-into-a-different-beast-21548

Ministry of Foreign Affairs of Japan. (2013). Japanese pop culture—to the next stage. *Niponica, 9.*

Napier, S. J. (2007). *From impressionism to anime: Japan as fantasy and fan cult in the mind of the West.* New York, NY: Palgrave Macmillan.

Norton Peirce, B. (1995). Social identity, investment, and language learning. *TESOL Quarterly 29*(1), 9–31.

Northwood, B., & Kinoshita Thomson, C. (2012). What keeps them going? Investigating Ongoing Learners of Japanese in Australian universities. *Japanese Studies, 32*(3), 335–355.

Nye, J. S. Jr. (2000). Asia's first globalizer. *The Washington Quarterly, 23*(4), 121–124.

Nye, J. S. Jr. (2008). Foreword. In Y. Watanabe & D. L. McConnell (Eds.), *Soft Power Superpowers: Cultural and National Assets of Japan and the United States* (pp. ix–xiv). Armonk, NY: M.E. Sharpe.

Nye, J. (2010). *Global power shifts* [Presentation]. Retrieved on February 1, 2012, from http://www.ted.com/talks/joseph_nye_on_global_power_shifts

Oliver, A. (2013). *Australia and the world public opinion and foreign policy: The Lowy Institute Poll 2013.* Sydney, NSW: Lowy Institute.

Omaggio Hadley, A. (2000). *Teaching language in context* (3rd ed.). Boston, MA: Thomson Heinle.

Otmazgin, N. (2013). Meta-narratives of Japanese popular culture and of Japan in different regional contexts: Perspectives from East Asia, Western Europe, and the Middle East. *Regioninės Studijos (Regional Studies), 7*, 83–94.

Otmazgin, N. (2014). Anime in the US: The Entrepreneurial Dimensions of Globalized Culture. *Pacific Affairs, 87*(1), 53–69.

Partnership for 21st century skills. (2011). *21st century skills map*. Washington, DC: P21.

Pollock, G. (2007). Liquid modernity and cultural analysis: An introduction to a transdisciplinary encounter. *Theory, Culture and Society, 24*(1), 111–116.

Richardson, J. M. (2013). Powerful devices: How teens' smartphones disrupt power in the theatre, classroom and beyond. *Learning, Media and Technology, 39*(3), 368–385.

Rodriguez, S. (2013). "Can we just get rid of the classroom?" thinking space, relationally. *Taboo: The Journal of Culture and Education, 13*(1), 97–111.

Rotella, C. (2013, Sept. 12). No child left untabled. *The New York Times*. Retrieved from http://www.nytimes.com/2013/09/15/magazine/no-child-left-un tabled.html?pagewanted=all

Savoie, D. J. (2010). *Power: Where is it?* Montreal & Kingston: McGill-Queen's University Press.

Scanlan, S. (2009). Book Review. *Journal of American Studies, 43*(1/E19), 1–2.

Singh, P. (2002). Pedagogising knowledge: Bernstein's theory of the pedagogic device. *British Journal of Sociology of Education, 23*, 571–582.

Steger, M. B. (2009). *Globalization: A brief insight*. New York, NY: Sterling.

Sugiura, C., Onodera S., & Beuckman, F. (2011). *Watashi no Nihongo: A beginners level guide to expressing my feelings and thoughts*. Tokyo: Kuroshio Publishers.

Swenson, T. (2007). "What kind of culture could produce these?" appeal of the exotic as entry into Japanese culture. *Ōsaka Jogakuin Daigaku Kiyō (The Working Papers of Osaka Jogakuin University), 4*, 103–122.

Takagi, M. (2011). Kyōkasho ni nai Nihongo nōryoku (Japanese Language Proficiency Unachieved from Textbooks). *Waseda Nihongo Kyōikugaku (Waseda Studies in Japanese Language Education), 9*, 51–57.

Theisen, T. (2013). President's message: What are the possibilities for "student voice" in the 21st Century? *The Language Educator, 8*(4), 7.

Thomson, C. K. (2010). Ōsutoraria no Nihongo gakushūsha-zō o saguru (Understanding Australian learners of Japanese). *The Otemon Journal of Australian Studies, 36*, 158–170.

Tsutsui, W. M. (2010). *Japanese popular culture and globalization*. Ann Arbor, MI: Association of Asian Studies, Inc.

Tucker, B. (2012, Winter). The flipped classroom: Online instruction at home frees class time for learning. *Education Next*, 82–83.

Usher, R. (2008). Consuming learning. *Convergence, XLI*(1), 29–45.

Walker, D. (1999). *Anxious Nation: Australia and the rise of Asia 1850–1939*. St. Lucia, Queensland: University of Queensland Press.

Walker, D. (2012). Rising suns. In D. Walker & A, Sobocinska (Eds.), *Australia's Asia: From yellow peril to Asian century* (pp. 73–95). Crawely: UWA Publishing.

Walker, D., & Sobocinska, A. (Eds.). (2012). *Australia's Asia: From yellow peril to Asian century*. Crawley: UWA PublishingWesley, M. (2011). *There goes the neighbourhood: Australia and the Rise of Asia*. Sydney, NSW: University of New South Wales Press Ltd.

Williams, L. (2011, Autumn). The university of the future. *Uniken*, 12–15.

Wise, J. M. (2008). *Cultural globalization: A user's guide*. Malden, MA: Blackwell Publishing.

Part II
Ideological Transition

4 Paradoxes of Learning English in Multilingual Japan

Envisioning Education for Border-Crossing Communication

Ryūko Kubota

INTRODUCTION

It is often believed that Japan is a monolingual and monocultural society. However, this myth of homogeneity is called into question by the existence of residents from diverse linguistic and ethnic backgrounds, including indigenous peoples (i.e., the Ainu and the Okinawans); multigenerational ethnic minorities of Korean and Chinese descent who came during Japanese colonialism; repatriates from China, including Japanese war orphans (*zanryū koji*), remaining women (*zanryū fujin*), and their family members; "*nikkei*" (Japanese-descent) ethnic return migrants from South America and their families (e.g., Brazilians, Peruvians, Bolivians); guest workers from Asian nations and other parts of the world; and international students predominantly from Asian countries, to name a few (Gottlieb 2012a; Kanno 2008; Kubota 2013a; Tsuneyoshi, Okano, & Boocock 2011).

Despite such diversity, foreign language instruction in schools and universities is predominated by English—an international language par excellence deemed to be critical for work and study in the globalized society. Underlying this predominance is the assumption that English links all people from diverse first language backgrounds across the world. However, the linguistic and ethnic diversity described earlier implies that non-Japanese residents in Japan are not necessarily English speakers and that Japanese, rather than English, functions as a lingua franca in most communicative contexts in Japan. If not to communicate with local non-Japanese residents in Japan, could the purpose of learning English be to interact with people outside of Japan? Does English universally function as an international lingua franca in such situations? If not, what should be taught in English-as-a-foreign-language classrooms? These questions require scholars, educators, and policy makers to rethink the fundamental purpose and ultimate goal of learning a foreign language as part of a school or university curricula and as lifelong learning in the workplace.

In this chapter, I will draw on data from two separate but related qualitative studies—one conducted in a midsize city in Japan in 2007 on Japanese adults' nonformal learning of English (Kubota 2011a, b, c; Kubota & McKay 2009), and another conducted in Japan and China in 2010 and 2011 on language in the workplace (Kubota 2013b)—and demonstrate how research participants' views and experiences of learning English and other languages contradict the sociolinguistic reality and expectation in local and international contexts or the widespread belief and assumption about English as an international language. Calling these contradictions *paradoxes*, I will discuss three paradoxes that are reflected in the research participants' accounts of their experiences and beliefs: (1) a dilemma experienced by two female English learners who wanted to learn and use English but felt obligated as community leaders to support non-English-speaking migrants; (2) a linguistic and national hierarchy implicit in some adult English learners' subjectivities, which perceptually restricts their English use to certain contexts only; and (3) a discordance between the powerful discourse of learning English as a lingua franca for working overseas and the actual experiences and views of Japanese expatriates. Although the research contexts were outside of Japan's formal educational system, all participants mentioned in this chapter had received primary, secondary, and higher education in Japan. Thus, their views and experiences will provide insights into language teaching in general. This chapter will explore how foreign language teaching can be refashioned to foster border-crossing communicative competence that prioritizes dispositions, critical awareness, and strategic competence over a superficial manipulation of skills. Such competence can be developed in any language, including one's mother tongue. First, I will briefly examine the prevalence of English language teaching and learning in Japan.

DOMINANCE OF ENGLISH IN LANGUAGE TEACHING

Prioritizing learning English as a foreign language over other languages is not a new phenomenon in Japan. Since Japan's major encounter with the English-dominant West in the late 19th century, English has been a major language to learn in institutions of secondary and higher education. However, the emphasis on learning English has become quite prominent since the 1980s, when Japan's bubble economy, fueled by international trade and foreign investment, increased economic conflicts between Japan and the Western world, resulting in a perceived need to explain Japan's position to the world and to become an equal international partner (Hashimoto 2000; Kubota 1998, 2002).

More recently, language education policies have been influenced by the *Action Plan to Cultivate "Japanese with English Abilities"* released by Japan's Ministry of Education, Culture, Sports, Science and Technology (MEXT) (MEXT 2003; see Butler & Iino 2005; Hashimoto 2009). MEXT recommended measures such as setting higher achievement goals for English proficiency in secondary education; establishing Super English Language

High Schools (SELHi's—immersion education in English); improving teacher quality by utilizing commercially available tests, such as TOEFL (Test of English as a Foreign Language), TOEIC (Test of English for International Communication), and STEP (Society for Testing English Proficiency Test, better known as the *Eiken* Test of Practical English Proficiency); and introducing a listening test for the Center Test for university entry. Perhaps the most controversial recommendation was introducing English to the elementary school curriculum. Despite heated debates, this initiative has been implemented since 2011 in the form of offering *"gaikokugo katsudō"* (foreign language activities) for grades 5 and 6 as part of the state-mandated curriculum (Butler & Iino 2007; Hashimoto 2011). In higher education, an "English-first mentality" became prevalent following higher education policy reform in the early 1980s that allowed universities to reduce academic credit requirements (Gottlieb 2012b: 82). Learning a second foreign language in addition to English as a primary foreign language at a university has become almost passé. Instead, what is observed is an increased emphasis on both acquiring practical skills in English and providing English-medium instruction (Rivers 2010).

Outside of formal educational institutions, the business sector is enthusiastically promoting English language learning based on an assumption that English is an indispensable tool for international communication for work. Some large businesses such as Rakuten and UNIQLO have announced the implementation of an English-only policy in their Japanese workplaces. In fact, the *Action Plan to Cultivate "Japanese with English Abilities"* mentioned earlier was influenced by recommendations made by two significant business associations—*"Keidanren"* (Japan federation of Economic Organizations) and *"Keizai Dōyūkai"* (Japan Association of Corporate Executives)—both of which urge the teaching of English at the elementary school level and the use of commercially available tests such as TOEFL, TOEIC, and STEP to measure English proficiency for workplace hiring and promotion (Erikawa 2009; Kubota 2011a, b; Mizuno 2008).

Underlying the emphasis on learning English is obviously a discourse of globalization or *gurōbaruka* (a term that provides an alternative to *kokusaika* or internationalization). The assumption is that technology and communication advancements are shrinking the world and increasing demand for global communication. Another ideology behind the promotion of learning English and the use of commercially available tests is a neoliberal belief that skills, such as the ability to manipulate English, constitute an essential component of human capital in the new economy and that people are personally responsible for staying competitive in the unstable employment conditions of the neoliberal society with its reduced social safety nets (Block, Gray, & Holborow 2012; Kubota 2011a; Park 2010; Park & Lo 2012; Urciuoli 2008). In this system, where each individual is accountable for his or her own learning, the ability to learn—or *learning capital* as Kariya (2010) calls it—is regarded as an essential component of human capital.

These beliefs and claims raise many questions: Does acquiring English language skills actually lead to career success? Isn't learning other languages equally important? Is English actually indispensable for global communication, especially in work situations? Answers to these questions emerge from two studies I conducted, to which I shall now turn.

RESEARCH CONTEXTS

As for the first study, I conducted year-long qualitative research in a midsize rural city called Hasu in Morino Prefecture[1] in Japan in 2007 to investigate the views and experiences of adults learning English as a foreign language in nonformal learning settings—i.e., contexts outside of formal educational institutions, such as schools and universities (cf. Benson 2011). These settings included "*eikaiwa*" (English conversation) classes offered by nonprofit organizations or the private sector or organized informally by groups of people with common interests. The learning locations in this study included community centers and other public spaces, private homes, and a workplace. I focused on nonformal learning of English for adults because it was where a great amount of learning of English was taking place, and yet limited knowledge existed about what purposes these adults were learning English, what significance such learning had in their lives, and what macro-level ideological forces were linked to their views and experiences.

The data came mainly from informal interviews with approximately 30 adult women and men learning English, supplemented by ethnographic observations in order to understand the interview data in larger sociocultural and educational contexts. Although learning *eikaiwa* is typically seen as a gendered practice involving mostly women (Bailey 2006, 2007; Kelsky 2001; Takahashi 2013), men turned out to be active participants as well. I was particularly interested in the meaning of learning *eikaiwa* in the multicultural rural city of Hasu, which hosted very few English-speaking, non-Japanese residents but many non-English-speaking South American and Asian workers in the manufacturing sector. Overall, non-Japanese residents constituted 3.7% of Hasu's population in 2007, a much larger percentage than the national average of 1.6% (see Kubota & McKay 2009).

Although most interviewees were learning English for leisure or for the *consumption* of pleasure associated with socializing and a sense of self-fulfillment (Kubota 2011c), learning English for work or career purposes also became a theme for me to explore when several research opportunities arose. While some of the interviewees were indeed learning English in order to increase their economic capital, my everyday experience in Hasu, which required little English for direct intercultural communication (Kubota 2011b), made me skeptical about the discourse of linguistic instrumentalism (Wee 2008), which posits that proficiency in a language of power brings forth tangible socioeconomic benefits and career success. In fact, interviews with managers at four local manufacturing companies in the Hasu area revealed a disconnect between linguistic instrumentalism and their view that English proficiency per se is secondary to one's professional knowledge and skills (Kubota 2011a).

This observation led to another research project, focusing this time on major Japanese manufacturing companies with larger global operations and the actual experiences of Japanese expatriates in China (Kubota 2013b). In this case study, I investigated Japanese managers' views about their employees' competencies required for living and working overseas, as well as the experiences and perspectives of former and current Japanese expatriates working in China, which hosts more Japanese subsidiaries than any other country. I interviewed managers at six companies and six former expatriates in Tokyo as well as four current expatriates and six Chinese staff members at three subsidiaries in China. My discussion of the third paradox is based on the aforementioned interviews at smaller companies in Hasu as well as at larger companies in this study.

Drawing on these two studies, I shall discuss three paradoxes that raise questions about the meaning of learning English in diverse local and global communities.

PARADOX #1: DESIRE TO VOLUNTEER IN ENGLISH AND THE LOCAL LINGUISTIC REALITY

Some of the research participants I got to know through tutoring Japanese as a second language (JSL) to non-Japanese residents turned out to be avid learners of English (see Kubota & McKay 2009). My interviews with two older female community leaders—Mrs. Nakai (aged 65) and Mrs. Honma (aged 61)—revealed a dilemma between their long-term commitment to learning English, which is closely linked to white Western culture, and their having to adapt to the demographic shift in the local community.

As community volunteers, both Mrs. Nakai and Mrs. Honma played various leadership roles, including JSL tutorial support for newcomers. When I first introduced myself to them in order to become a volunteer JSL tutor, they both wanted me not to expect to interact with English-speaking people. Later, my interviews with them revealed that this initial warning came from their own experience. Both women were college graduates, majored in English, and grew up with *"akogare"* (yearning) for Western cultures and people associated with Inner Circle Englishes (Kachru, Kachru, & Nelson 2006), especially North American English. For instance, Mrs. Honma said, "I must admit that I felt *akogare* for American culture,"[2] when mentioning American TV drama series aired between the 1950s and '60s, such as *I Love Lucy*, *Father Knows Best*, *Ben Casey*, and *The Fugitive*. Mrs. Nakai, who grew up during the postwar U.S. occupation of Japan, formed an impression of America as an advanced country when she saw such food items as chocolate, white bread, and peanut butter brought by U.S. soldiers and civilians. An uncle who spoke English fluently aroused "*akogare* for being able to talk to those people and learn about their everyday life." Both Mrs. Nakai and Mrs. Honma had been tutoring English to children at their homes while learning *eikaiwa* from native speakers of English in small groups. In the early 1990s, they also participated in a community program to train English-Japanese interpreters for a large international event that was to be held in the late 1990s. Around the same time, some community groups of mostly women learners of English like Mrs. Nakai and Mrs. Honma created volunteer groups to tutor JSL. Mrs. Nakai remembered that JSL tutors originally targeted business people from English-speaking countries. For Mrs. Honma, teaching Japanese was supposed to benefit her because she had expected to use English as a medium of instruction. Both women eventually got involved in tutoring JSL. Mrs. Nakai began to play a leadership role in Hasu's International Exchange Council, which organized a JSL tutorial for newcomers and the city's annual international festival.

As the demand for unskilled labor increased in Hasu's manufacturing sector, newcomers to Hasu began to be predominated by *nikkei* adults and their family members, mainly from South America or interns from China who came under the Industrial Training and Technical Internship Program implemented in the early 1990s. Since few of these individuals spoke English, teaching JSL via English—an imagined communicative activity envisioned by many learners of English like Mrs. Honma—became moot. As a prominent community leader who had chaired the Hasu Board of Education and other community organizations, Mrs. Honma was unable to give up her commitment to a JSL tutorial program partially funded by the central government. In her words, "you can't quit just because there is no merit, right? If they need us . . ." Mrs. Nakai also continued to participate in a leadership role in the same JSL tutorial program; however, she also created a JSL support group specifically for international students at a local university who were "graduates from national universities (of their home countries) and so they can speak English."

Both Mrs. Nakai and Mrs. Honma were actively learning English by creating opportunities to use it through learning, teaching, and volunteering. Yet, unlike immigrants who strive to obtain cultural and economic capital (Bourdieu 1982) via the investment of learning the language of the host society (Norton 2000), their learning of English provides them with pleasure, self-fulfillment, and status—or symbolic capital (Bourdieu 1982)—as a speaker of an international language of prestige. Learning English was "a hobby, actually for enjoyment" for Mrs. Honma, while Mrs. Nakai was learning English "so that I won't lose it 'cause I made so much effort to learn it." Like other men and women I interviewed, learning *eikaiwa* for these two women may be more aptly understood as *consumption* of pleasure and enjoyment than efforts to develop language skills (Kubota 2011c). At the same time, their involvement in "international" activities in the local community positions them as leaders with a global outlook. Yet, their learning of English came to be at odds with a shift in local linguistic diversity that excluded English. They struggled with this gap in their private consciousness while continuing to negotiate it in their public roles. Their warning to me—that volunteering to tutor JSL would not generate English learning opportunities—perhaps reflected not only their observation of their peers who discontinued JSL tutoring but also their own inner dilemma. Specifically, the dilemma was the one between their desire to use English in the local community and the need to abandon their fantasy of interacting with Inner Circle English speakers in the community. Despite such ambivalence, these two women's positive attitudes toward diversity were publicly visible through their community support for all newcomers, which are contrasted by the subjectivities of other learners of English described in the next section.

PARADOX #2: "LEARNING ENGLISH IS COOL" BUT "GOING TO CHINA TO WORK? NO THANKS"

Two male English learners whom I interviewed in and near Hasu felt reluctant to work in China. One of them was Kazuo, a 37-year-old employee of a local manufacturing company with a bachelor's degree in science. We interacted often through informal interviews and regular participant observations of small-group, secular English lessons organized by a local Christian organization. Kazuo was learning English not only to explore better career options but also to meet a marriage partner via an expanded social circle. Learning English was among his leisure activities, which included taking a cooking class, playing tennis, and taking wedding photographs. Learning English also facilitated his foreign travel to conduct astronomical observations, another of his hobbies.

During my first interview, it took me a while to realize that Kazuo was an assembly-line worker; he had been demoted from product designer due to health issues (Kubota 2011a). Before fully understanding his circumstances, I asked about the overseas operation of his company. He said factories were located in the Philippines, Taiwan, and China and provided some detailed technical explanations of his company's products. I asked where he would like to be dispatched if an opportunity became available. He replied, "China? No thanks." He had heard that the factory in China was in an industrial complex where public safety was ensured but said, "I heard the outside is dangerous." To my question why he would not go to China, he responded, "First of all, I can't speak Mandarin.[3] Also I see anti-Japanese sentiment in the news and it's scary." He said he felt more comfortable about the other two countries since he had heard that people there understood English. Ironically, Kazuo revealed in a subsequent interview that he studies Mandarin at his university as a required second foreign language since the chair of trustees was from China.

Kazuo apparently had a certain linguistic/racial/national hierarchy in his consciousness. In our conversation about international marriage, he thought that an English-speaking woman would be a better candidate than a Chinese or Korean woman because of the negative sentiment held by the general public toward China and Korea. He then mentioned how acquaintances of his parents' generation would look down on a Chinese or Filipina wife and stated: "Between an American partner and a Filipina partner, if you choose a Filipina, there is a perception that 'Oh you couldn't even find a Japanese partner!'" In Kazuo's narrative, the United States ranks higher than Asian countries and English has a higher social status or symbolic power than other languages.

A feeling somewhat similar to Kazuo's was held by Sōichi, a 30-year-old single man who was an assembly-line worker at another manufacturing company near Hasu. He had an associate's degree in economics and this was his second job. I conducted a joint interview with Sōichi and his colleague, Osamu, a 25-year-old with an undergraduate degree in business. Their company has a policy in which most male employees work on the assembly line for the first few years of employment regardless of their previous educational background. The company also encourages its employees to engage in *"jiko keihatsu"* (self-development) of any kind. One's level of engagement in *jiko keihatsu* influences annual evaluations for salary increases. The company outsources English lessons and subsidizes the tuition. For both Sōichi and Osamu, learning English would open doors to higher paying office work and overseas assignments, including a two-year training arrangement at the company's service center in the United States. Sōichi described his initial motivation to learn English as: "I thought it'd be *"kakko ii"* (cool) to learn English," whereas Osamu was a fan of American movies and hip-hop artists such as 50 Cent and Snoop Dogg. However, Sōichi's feelings toward China contrasted sharply with Osamu's. After hearing that their company had just opened a factory in China, I posed a question that initiated the following exchange:

RYŪKO: Would you like to go to China?
SŌICHI: No, 'cause that country can't be trusted.
OSAMU: I want to go.
SŌICHI: No thanks for me.
OSAMU: It'll be a good experience, I think.
SŌICHI: If it's for three months or so, I don't mind, but I don't want to stay long term.
OSAMU: I want to go. I want to talk with different people.
SŌICHI: Oh.
RYŪKO: Do you want to learn Mandarin too?
OSAMU: I won't go that far but if I go to China, I think there are places where English is useful.
SŌICHI: You want to see the world.
OSAMU: Yes, I do.

Sōichi's response to my question implies that he would not be enthusiastic about communicating with Chinese workers in English. The current emphasis on English language learning in Japan is predicated on the assumption that English is a vital international language, which implies that it will enable people to communicate with each other regardless of their race, ethnicity, or nationality. Nevertheless, Sōichi's comment indicates that English skills alone may not connect diverse groups of people; willingness to communicate seems to be indispensable for communication across difference.

Compared to Sōichi, Osamu had had more exposure to English in his childhood through a family trip overseas, hosting an exchange student from New Zealand, and his sister's studying in the United States, in addition to watching American films and listening to hip-hop music. It is not certain whether it was his earlier experience that made him more open-minded, but this exchange demonstrates that learning English even for career purposes may still be influenced by the "cool" image of English as a language of the West—or the symbolic capital attached to English—which is at odds with the notion of English as purely a tool for international communication that transcends national borders.

While Osamu displayed a more open attitude than Sōichi did, he did not express a desire to learn Mandarin. This might be related to the fact that for him, international exposure had been mostly through English. However, as discussed in the next section, Mandarin is actually a key language for business purposes for Japanese expatriates in China.

Osamu's motivation to learn English was linked to his earlier exposure to English and, similar to the case of Mrs. Honma, his fascination for American pop culture. However, it is important to note that the subjectivities of English learners in this study were diverse; some interviewees expressed a more cosmopolitan outlook toward linguistic and ethnic diversity and were critical of the commonly perceived superiority of Western culture or English speakers (Kubota 2011b, c; Kubota & McKay 2009). For instance, Misaki, a 28-year-old woman who was learning English in order to be certified to teach English to children, married a Caucasian American English teacher. She admitted that she felt *akogare* for English and American culture as an English learner but also stated that she made friends with Chinese and Brazilian colleagues in her former workplace and interacted with people from Vietnam, where her father was assigned to work by his company. Before visiting her father in Vietnam, she informally learned some Vietnamese phrases. She commented, "If you use the language of the people (in a foreign country), they are pleased. The ideal is to speak the language of the country you are visiting." Likewise, Seiji, a 42-year-old male local government worker, who was learning Portuguese in order to assist the local Brazilian residents, was an avid learner of English as well. Yet, as a world traveler, he had "a desire to speak various languages even at the very basic level" (Kubota & McKay 2009: 610). These learners obviously exhibited open and proactive attitudes toward multilingual learning and interaction with people from diverse linguistic and racial backgrounds. This disposition overlaps with the communicative dispositions that emerged from my interviews with Japanese expatriates and managers.

PARADOX #3: IS ENGLISH A UNIVERSAL LINGUA FRANCA IN THE WORKPLACE?

In Hasu, an acquaintance who had connections with local businesses introduced me to three of the four company managers I interviewed. My acquaintance also attended these interviews. After the final interview, he shared with me his reflection: "Everyone says similar things, don't they?" Here are some major commonalities: What is essential for working overseas is not English skills per se but rather knowledge and skills in one's specialization, as well as an ability to communicate in general, not necessarily in English but in Japanese as a mother tongue. The managers believe that as long as employees have basic communicative competency (i.e., willingness to communicate with others and the ability to do so effectively), they can develop proficiency in the language of the host country after they start work. This is consistent with the observation by Piekkari (2008) that the main corporate criterion for assigning staff members abroad is professional competence rather than language competence per se. Another perception shared by the managers was that being able to use the language of the host country was necessary and the demand for Mandarin especially was growing.

These comments led me to conduct another case study, as mentioned earlier. I investigated which languages Japanese expatriates working in China for major Japanese manufacturing companies used, what challenges expatriates experienced, and what competencies managers deemed important for working overseas. Consistent with other research (Nebashi 2007), Japanese and Mandarin were widely used by the former and current Japanese expatriates I interviewed. Contrary to the common belief about the major status of English for international business communication, only three of the ten expatriates mentioned English as the major language for work in China. The use of language—the kind and the level of proficiency required—naturally depends on the nature of the tasks in the workplace. The expatriates who mainly dealt with clients outside of China tended to use English more. A manager in Tokyo in charge of global human resources strategies mentioned that management-level personnel working abroad need a sophisticated level of English proficiency to interact with international partners at meetings. Conversely, technical specialists who interact with local clients need a less sophisticated level, enough for expressing and understanding basic terms related to the products. Furthermore, the interviewees shared this view: "The closer you get to the worksite where our machines operate, the more necessary the local language becomes." This implied that Japanese expatriates who traveled within China to troubleshoot technical issues, for instance, needed proficiency in Mandarin.

Although all the former and current expatriates reported that they used Mandarin, their self-reported proficiency and frequency of use varied. Three expatriates had gained higher levels of proficiency through formal instruction at Chinese universities (i.e., study abroad or yearlong, company-sponsored training). Others learned through self-study, face-to-face tutorials, or classes. While some used Mandarin in the workplace extensively, others used it sporadically because Japanese was a lingua franca.

The widespread use of Japanese by Japanese expatriates in China implies that some Chinese colleagues can speak Japanese. Because I lacked Mandarin proficiency, I made a request in recruiting Chinese interviewees that I interview in either Japanese or English. It turned out that all the Chinese interviewees spoke fluent Japanese, which they had acquired either studying in Japan or studying at a university in China. It was also reported that as many as 50% of the Chinese office workers at these subsidiaries speak some level of Japanese and many Chinese employees were encouraged to learn Japanese.

Regarding challenges experienced by expatriates, the interviewees pointed out issues of communication and cultural understanding. The communication challenges were not necessarily related to a lack of English proficiency. As mentioned earlier, English was not a lingua franca in many local work contexts. Thus, workers tried to find ways to communicate using available linguistic resources. In order to compensate for linguistic limitations, expatriates used various strategies, including *hitsudan* (brush talk— writing down *kanji*), rephrasing, simplifying, repeating, exemplifying, and using hand and body gestures, which parallel strategic competence (Canale 1983; Nakatani 2005). In short, the most important ability is summarized by one participant, "to communicate in a straightforward, simple, and clear manner—*sutorēto ni, shinpuru ni, kuria ni tsutaeru*—and yet politely." With regard to cultural challenges, being unaware of the cultural underpinnings of everyday work practices (e.g., saving face, business practices) could cause misunderstandings.

With respect to the competencies deemed necessary for overseas work, what was highlighted was not language proficiency per se but the *ability to communicate*, as described earlier, or "to convey meaning even without grammar." This ability is supported by what can be termed *communicative dispositions*, including a persistent willingness to communicate and the understanding that communication is made possible through mutual accommodation (Lippi-Green 2012; McNamara 2011; Nieto & Bode 2008). Such dispositions are further reinforced by *foundational dispositions and cultural knowledge*, which enable mutual respect and collaboration through antiprejudiced and nondiscriminatory attitudes. One ex-expatriate found problematic some expatriates' condescending attitude to "teach" their knowledge and techniques to the local people. Another ex-expatriate mentioned the importance of building trusting relationships with a collaborative mind-set of making contributions to the host society. A sense of superiority or a denial of the partners' integrity would quickly result in a failure. Expatriates also mentioned that working effectively in China requires historical knowledge of Japanese colonialism and current issues between China and Japan.

The predominance of Japanese and Mandarin rather than English as means of workplace communication is rather exceptional from a global perspective, according to the expatriates who had worked in other countries. Nonetheless, using the host country's dominant language and the expatriates' native languages in a transcultural workplace is not totally uncommon as indicated by Amelina's (2010) study on highly educated Russian workers in Germany. Even in English-dominant countries, the language for workplace interaction is not necessarily English (e.g., Block 2007; Goldstein 1997; Kramsch & Whiteside 2007). Although English does play a major role in international business as the interviewees perceived, it is by no means universally functional. What is deemed even more important than language proficiency is the ability to *communicate* by using available resources "even without grammar" and possessing appropriate dispositions and cultural knowledge. Furthermore, the priority in the workplace is "to accomplish one's tasks" and "one's expert knowledge." Therefore, as one manager stated, language skills are seen "as just one of the tools." Business people's awareness of this reality seems to underlie their reluctance to prioritize preexisting language skills over professional competence. Contrary to common assumptions, English is clearly not a universal lingua franca, nor do linguistic skills alone constitute the essential competency for transcultural work. The interviewees' accounts indicate that the practice of using tests like TOEIC to measure workers' linguistic competence does not necessarily reflect the actual communication demands for international work but rather functions to assess the learning capital of neoliberal workers, ultimately leading to symbolic capital.

ENVISIONING EDUCATION FOR BORDER-CROSSING COMMUNICATION

As evident in the three paradoxes discussed in this chapter, learning English in Japan is entangled with various facets of symbolic power or "a power of constructing reality" (Bourdieu 1982: 166) and a power of constructing agreed-upon relations among such objects and concepts as languages (e.g., English, Japanese, Mandarin), language competencies, cultures, racialized groups, work, and so on. Reflecting symbolic colonialism that perpetuates an unequal relation of power between English and Japanese (Kubota & McKay 2009), learning English is closely linked to *akogare* for Western or American culture and Inner Circle varieties of English, which are regarded as *cool* objects of desire, as revealed in many of the interview accounts. This is contrasted by the undesirable images of China and Mandarin as expressed by English learners like Kazuo and Sōichi. However, the cases of Misaki and Seiji indicate that English learners have diverse subjectivities in relation to English; not all of them expressed exclusive attraction to English but rather displayed interest in multilingual communication with people outside of the Inner Circle countries.

In general, the neoliberal notion that acquiring skills of English as an international language is essential for one's life success is entrenched in tandem with the symbolic power attached to English. However, the two powerful assumptions—i.e., English as a universal lingua franca and the promise of English—are indeed ideological constructs. The falsity of these assumptions is evidenced by the increased local ethnolinguistic diversity in Japan, language use in the workplace in China, and Japanese business people's views that prioritize professional competency over language proficiency per se.

The ethnolinguistic diversity in Hasu, in other parts of Japan, and in the world, as well as English learners' divergent engagements with the symbolic power of English pose the following important questions about the meaning and purpose of learning and using English: If English is not a universal lingua franca, what are the implications of teaching and learning English? What type of imagined self is shaped in the process of learning English? In what ways do learners of English want to engage in global communication? What barriers exist in encouraging learners to affirm differences and overcome prejudices? How can we transform the status quo? Inferring from interpretations of the interviewees' accounts in the first study, a fundamental problem seems to be that learning English (or possibly any other languages) is often detached from genuine, respectful, and tolerant exchange of ideas with any group of people in the global community, which underlies the fundamental purpose of *communication*. Neoliberal language teaching in Japan increasingly focuses on the practical dimension of language skills that are to be objectively measured by standardized tests. Yet what is rarely addressed is how to initiate and engage in meaningful communication with diverse people in the world in an effective and respectful manner. Perhaps due to this oversight, linguistic skills and knowledge tend to become an object of learning rather than a medium through which the ultimate purpose of communication is achieved. This object of learning is measured by language tests and the results lead to symbolic capital—a credential, prestige, and status for competent neoliberal subjects. What is lacking in this framework is the vision of using linguistic skills as a means of border-crossing communication.

Border-crossing communication is "active, critical, and reflective engagement in communication across diverse ethnic, racial, linguistic, and socioeconomic differences" (Kubota 2012: 63). This broad definition appears to overlap with the general vision of any framework of language education.

For instance, the Common European Framework of Reference for Languages (CEFR)—the Council of Europe's language education policy—promotes the need "to facilitate communication and interaction among Europeans of different mother tongues in order to promote European mobility, mutual understanding and co-operation, and overcome prejudice and discrimination" (Council of Europe 2001: 2). In recent recommendations made by a MEXT committee, foreign language (i.e., English) competency required for globalized society is defined as "the ability to communicate efficiently through a medium of a foreign language," which further includes "the attitude to try to actively communicate with people from different countries or cultures" (MEXT 2011: 1; original in Japanese). However, these national or transnational policies place primary emphasis on the development of linguistic skills, leading to the objectification of communication ability as reflected in the reduction of proficiency levels to simple numbers or test scores (McNamara 2011).

In contrast, *border-crossing communication* gives priority to dispositions, critical awareness, and strategic skills that are required for communication. As such, it can be accomplished in any language including *"kokugo"* (national language = Japanese as a mother tongue), allowing an interdisciplinary approach to teaching. Paralleling pluralist approaches to English as seen in world Englishes (Kachru et al. 2006) and English as a lingua franca (Jenkins, Cogo, & Dewey 2011; Seidlhofer 2011), *border-crossing communication* problematizes the norm of the standard language and the native speaker and instead affirms linguistic diversity.

The dispositions to be developed include communicative and foundational dispositions mentioned earlier. Communicative dispositions include a willingness to communicate by using available linguistic resources and to learn multiple languages. Foundational dispositions include developing interests in learning about the culture and history of Self and Other, and nonprejudiced and antiracist attitudes.

The critical awareness enables learners to understand how our common beliefs—such as the universal usefulness of English, the uniqueness of a certain language and culture, and the superiority of the Western culture, whiteness, and the native speaker—privilege a certain language, culture, and group of people while marginalizing others, perpetuating unequal relations of power (Motha 2014). By becoming aware that multiple points of view exist about controversial political and historical issues and that commonly accepted knowledge reflects and reinforces symbolic power, learners can enhance their understanding of Self and Other. Critically acknowledging one's own privilege (Vandrick 2009) in terms of socioeconomic status, ethnicity, gender, sexual identity, physical ableness, and so on is also essential in this critical engagement.

Strategic skills include linguistic competency as traditionally conceptualized, but it places more emphasis on the effort to communicate by using available linguistic or nonlinguistic resources to supplement one's linguistic skills, making messages comprehensible by using strategic competence (Canale 1983) and sharing communicative responsibility (Lippi-Green 2012).

Language education across the curriculum provides learners with the opportunity to engage in *border-crossing communication*. One example is an activity called *"Kyōshitsu marugoto gakkō hōmon"* (the whole-class visit to a school), which took place in Tokyo (Noyama 2011). In this activity, a community JSL class visits an elementary or junior high school with the aim of enhancing cultural understanding and intercultural communication involving all participants. Noyama (2011) presents an example in which a third-grade class hosted a group of JSL learners in the community and engaged in activities using recently learned map-reading skills. The task given to each child was to take a guest to a favorite place in the school by showing a school map. After engaging in other group tasks, students and guests ate a school lunch together, during which they reflected on the activities with facilitators. According to Noyama (2011), the lingua franca was mostly Japanese, but the JSL learners' native languages were intermixed. Despite the limited amount of shared linguistic resources, both parties achieved remarkable levels of communication through strategies such as repeating, slowing down, and using foreigner talk. This exemplified how learners can engage in border-crossing communication even in their native language. I argue that such an educational activity that creates immediate interactions with those who are often positioned as the Other in the community offers communicative experiences that are way more meaningful and critical than the recent initiative announced by the Tokyo Board of Education. In preparation for Tokyo Summer Olympics of 2020, the initiative involves 200 English teachers' participating in annual mandatory study abroad in English-dominant countries to improve English-language teaching (Wada 2013, November 25). Clearly, the former fosters the ability and dispositions to *communicate* across linguistic, ethnic, and cultural differences, while the latter unrealistically and uncritically assume that speaking solely in English as the default language will solve all communicative challenges.

CONCLUSION

Language education in Japan in the 21st century is situated in a paradox between a powerful discourse that emphasizes teaching English as a common global lingua franca and growing linguistic and ethnic diversity at home. The local diversity as well as the complexity of communicative demands in transcultural workplaces clearly indicate the fallacy of the assumption that English is a universal lingua franca. An overemphasis on learning English through developing measurable linguistic skills overlooks the vision that language education should ultimately aim to enable learners to *communicate* across borders. As our society is facing imminent economic, environmental, and political challenges, it is necessary to reconceptualize language education as a means to foster border-crossing communicative competence. Such a vision will enable learners to become willing and able to collaborate with people from diverse backgrounds in order to create a more equitable and sustainable society.

NOTES

1. All names presented in this chapter are pseudonyms.
2. All interviews were conducted in Japanese and audio recorded. Quotes are translated from Japanese transcriptions.
3. In this chapter, "Mandarin" is used as the translation of *chūgokugo* [Chinese language].

REFERENCES

Amelina, M. (2010). Do other languages than English matter? International career development of highly-qualified professionals. In B. Meyer & B. Apfelbaum (Eds.), *Multilingualism at Work: From Policies to Practices in Public, Medical and Business Settings* (pp. 235–252). Amsterdam: John Benjamins Publishing Company.

Bailey, K. (2006). Marketing the *eikaiwa* wonderland: Ideology, *akogare*, and gender alterity in English conversation school advertising in Japan. *Environment and Planning D: Society and Space, 24*, 105–130.

Bailey, K. (2007). *Akogare*, ideology, and 'Charisma Man' mythology: Reflections on ethnographic research in English language schools in Japan. *Gender, Place and Culture, 15*, 585–608.

Benson, P. (2011). Language learning and teaching beyond the classroom: An introduction to the field. In P. Benson & H. Reinders (Eds.), *Beyond the Language Classroom* (pp. 7–16). Basingstoke, UK: Palgrave Macmillan.

Bourdieu, P. (1982). *Language and Symbolic Power*. Cambridge, MA: Harvard University Press.

Block, D. (2007). Niche lingual francas: An ignored phenomenon. *TESOL Quarterly, 41*, 561–566.

Block, D., Gray, J., & Holborow, M. (2012). *Neoliberalism and applied linguistics*. Abingdon, UK: Routledge.

Butler, Y.G. (2007). Foreign language education at elementary schools in Japan: Searching for solutions amidst growing diversification. *Current Issues in Language Planning, 8*, 129–47.

Butler, Y. G., & Iino, M. (2005). Current Japanese reforms in English language education: The 2003 "Action Plan." *Language Policy, 4*, 25–45.

Canale, M. (1983). From communicative competence to communicative language pedagogy. In J.C. Richards & R.W. Schmidt (Eds.), *Language and Communication* (pp. 2–27). London: Longman.

Council of Europe (2001). *Common European framework of reference for languages: Learning, teaching, assessment*. Cambridge: Cambridge University Press.

Erikawa, H. (2009). *Eigo kyōiku no politics: Kyōsō kara kyōdō e* [The politics of English language education: From competition to collaboration]. Tokyo: Sanyûsha Shuppan.

Goldstein, T. (1997). *Two languages at work: Bilingual life on the production floor*. Berlin: Mouton de Gruyter.

Gottlieb, N. (Ed.) (2012a). *Language and citizenship in Japan*. New York, NY: Routledge.

Gottlieb, N. (2012b). *Language policy in Japan: The challenge of change*. Cambridge, UK: Cambridge University Press.

Hashimoto, K. (2000). 'Internationalisation' is 'Japanisation': Japan's foreign language education and national identity. *Journal of Intercultural Studies*, *21*, 39–51.

Hashimoto, K. (2009). Cultivating "Japanese who can use English": Problems and contradictions in government policy. *Asian Studies Review, 33,* 21–42.

Hashimoto, K. (2011). Compulsory 'foreign language activities' in Japanese primary schools. *Current Issues in Language Planning*, *12*, 167–184.

Jenkins, J., Cogo, A., & Dewey, M. (2011). Review of developments in research into English as a lingua franca. *Language Teaching*, *44*, 281–315.

Kachru, B. B., Kachru, Y., & Nelson, C. L. (Ed.) (2006). *The handbook of world Englishes*. Malden, MA: Blackwell.

Kanno, Y. (2008). *Language education in Japan: Unequal access to bilingualism*. New York, NY: Palgrave Macmillan.

Kariya, T. (2010). From credential society to "learning capital" society: A rearticulation of class formation in Japanese education and society. In H. Ishida & D. H. Slater (Eds.), *Social class in contemporary Japan: Structures, sorting and strategies* (pp. 87–113). Abingdon, UK: Routledge.

Kelsky, K. (2001). *Women on the verge: Japanese women, Western dreams*. Durham, NC: Duke University Press.

Kramsch, C., & Whiteside, A. (2007). Three fundamental concepts in second language acquisition and their relevance in multilingual contexts. *The Modern Language Journal*, *91*, 907–922.

Kubota, R. (1998). Ideologies of English in Japan. *World Englishes*, *17*(3), 295–306.

Kubota, R. (2002). Impact of globalization on language teaching in Japan. In D. Block & D. Cameron (Eds.), *Globalization and language teaching* (pp. 13–28). London, UK: Routledge.

Kubota, R. (2011a). Immigration, diversity, and language education in Japan: Toward a global approach to teaching English. In P. Seargeant (Ed.), *English in Japan in the Era of Globalization* (pp. 101–122). Basingstoke, UK: Palgrave MacMillan.

Kubota, R. (2011b). Learning a foreign language as leisure and consumption: Enjoyment, desire, and the business of *eikaiwa*. *International Journal of Bilingual Education and Bilingualism*, *14*, 473–488.

Kubota, R. (2011c). Questioning linguistic instrumentalism: English, neoliberalism, and language tests in Japan. *Linguistics and Education*, *22*, 248–260.

Kubota, R. (2012). The politics of EIL: Toward border-crossing communication in and beyond English. In A. Matsuda (Ed.), *Principles and Practices of Teaching English as an International Language* (pp. 55–69). Bristol, UK: Multilingual Matters.

Kubota, R. (2013a). Language and education for returnees. In C. Chapelle (Ed.), *Encyclopedia of Applied Linguistics*. Wiley. Retrieved from http://onlinelibrary. wiley.com/book/10.1002/9781405198431 DOI: 10.1002/9781405198431.wbeal 0652

Kubota, R. (2013b). "Language is only a tool": Japanese expatriates working in China and implications for language teaching. *Multilingual Education*. Retrieved from http://www.multilingual-education.com/content/3/1/4. doi:10.1186/2191-5059-3-4

Kubota, R., & McKay, S. (2009). Globalization and language learning in rural Japan: The role of English in the local linguistic ecology. *TESOL Quarterly*, *43*, 593–619.

Lippi-Green, R. (2012). *English with an accent: Language, ideology and discrimination in the United States* (2nd ed.). New York, NY: Routledge.

McNamara, T. (2011). Managing learning: Authority and language assessment. *Language Teaching, 44*(4), 500–515.

MEXT (Ministry of Education, Culture, Sports, Science and Technology). (2003). *Action plan to cultivate "Japanese with English abilities."* Retrieved from http://www.mext.go.jp/b_menu/shingi/chukyo/chukyo4/007/gijiroku/03032401/009.pdf

MEXT (Ministry of Education, Culture, Sports, Science and Technology). (2011). *Kokusai kyōtsūgo to shite no eigo ryoku kōjō no tame no itsutsu no teigen to gutaiteki shisaku* [Five recommendations and concrete measures for improving competence in English as an international lingua franca]. Retrieved from http://www.mext.go.jp/b_menu/houdou/23/07/1308888.htm

Mizuno, Y. (2008). *Keidanren to "eigo ga tsukaeru" nihonjin* [Keidanren and the Japanese who can use English]. *Eigo Kōiku* [The English Teachers' Magazine], *57*(1), 65–67.

Motha, S. (2014). *Race, empire, and English language teaching.* New York: Teachers College Press.

Nakatani, Y. (2005). The effects of awareness-raising training on oral communication strategy use. *The Modern Language Journal, 89,* 76–91.

Nebashi, R. (2007). Chūgoku shinshutsu nikkei kigyō ni oite jūgyōin ga konnan o kanjite ita kōdō: Mensetsu chōsa no jiyū kaitō bunseki kara [Behaviors perceived challenging by employees at Japanese companies in China: Analysis of open-ended responses in structured interviews]. In H. Nishida (Ed.), *Beikoku Chūgoku shinshutsu nikkei kigyō ni okeru ibunkakan comyunikêshon masatsu* [Intercultural communication conflicts at Japanese companies in the United States and China] (pp. 439–461). Tokyo: Kazama Shobō.

Nieto, S., & Bode, P. (2008). *Affirming diversity: The sociopolitical context of multicultural education* (5th ed.). Boston: Allyn & Bacon.

Norton, B. (2000). *Identity and language learning: Gender, ethnicity, and educational change.* London: Longman/Pearson Education.

Noyama, H. (2011). Chiiki nihongo kyōiku no tenkai to fukugengo fukubunka shugi [The development of community Japanese language education and pluralingualism/pluriculturalism]. In Y. Kitawaki (Ed.), *"Hirakareta nihon" no kōsō: Imin ukeire to shakai tōgō* [Planning for the "open society" of Japan: Immigrant policies and social inclusion] (pp. 148–181). Tokyo: Koko Shuppan.

Park, J. S.-Y. (2010). Naturalization of competence and the neoliberal subject: Success stories of English language learning in the Korean conservative press. *Journal of Linguistic Anthropology, 20,* 22–38.

Park, J. S.-Y., & Lo, A. (2012). Transnational South Korea as a site for a sociolinguistics of globalization: Markets, timescales, neoliberalism. *Journal of Sociolinguistics, 16,* 147–164.

Piekkari, R. (2008). Language and careers in multinational corporations. In S. Tietze (Ed.), *International Management and Language* (pp. 128–137). London: Routledge.

Rivers, D. J. (2010). Ideologies of internationalization and the treatment of diversity within Japanese higher education. *Journal of Higher Education Policy and Management, 32,* 441–454.

Seidlhofer, B. (2011). *Understanding English as a lingua franca.* Oxford, UK: Oxford University Press.

Takahashi, K. (2013). *Language desire: Gender, sexuality and second language learning.* Bristol, UK: Multilingual Matters.

Tsuneyoshi, R., Okano, K. H., & Boocock, S. (Eds.). (2011). *Minorities and education in multicultural Japan: An interactive perspective.* Abingdon, UK: Routledge.

Urciuoli, B. (2008). Skills and selves in the new workplace. *American Ethnologist, 35,* 211–228.

Vandrick, S. (2009). *Interrogating privilege: Reflections of a second language educator.* Ann Arbor: University of Michigan Press.

Wada, H. (2013, November 25). Tokyōikui: Eigo no sensei, Ryūgaku hisshū rainendo shidō kyōka e [Tokyo Board of Education requires English language teachers to study abroad next year to boost their teaching skills]. *Mainichi Shinbun.* Retrieved from http://mainichi.jp/select/news/20131125k0000e040181000c.html

Wee, L. (2008). Linguistic instrumentalism in Singapore. In P. K. W. Tan & R. Rubdy (Eds.), *Language as Commodity: Global Structures, Local Market Places* (pp. 31–43). London: Continuum.

5 "Internal Internationalization" and Language Ideologies in Japanese Criminal Courts

Ikuko Nakane

INTRODUCTION

Japan's criminal justice system has seen a dramatic increase in the number of so-called *gaikokujin jiken* (foreigner cases) since the 1980s. The increased number of non-Japanese-speaking background (hereafter NJSB) defendants has often been associated with the need for 'internal' internationalization (*uchinaru kokusaika*), a term used to represent one of the two dimensions of Japan's internationalization, the other being 'external' internationalization (Sugiyama 1992). External internationalization entails the education of Japanese citizens in order that they become competent in communicating and negotiating in international contexts as global citizens (ibid.). In contrast, internal internationalization refers to "the influx of foreign workers, known as 'newcomers,' but also the existence of underrepresented ethnic groups in Japan," while also referring to a movement toward "a society that encourages diversity and equity among both Japanese and non-Japanese" (Nukaga 2003: 92). In this sense, 'internationalization' is considered as embracing "human rights and a multicultural coexistence society," although it is sometimes used "in relation to English and to populations that come from abroad" (Tsuneyoshi 2011: 123).

One prominent aspect of internationalization in the Japanese legal system has been the adequate provision of court interpreters (Taki 2005; Tsuda 1997). The quality of court interpreting has also been discussed extensively by the media with the introduction of the "*saiban-in*" (lay judge) system into the Japanese criminal justice system in 2009, in which major felony cases are brought to a panel of judges, including lay judges selected from the electoral roll. While these developments are positive, there has been little attention drawn to context-specific issues of language proficiency in courtroom communication. As non-Japanese-background residents of Japan have increased in number, so too have speakers of Japanese as a second language. Many multilingual court proceedings now consist of interpreter-mediated stages, partially interpreted stages, and/or Japanese only stages. Thus there is a need to scrutinize the realities of multilingual courtroom practices associated with the 'internal internationalization' of Japan's criminal justice system. This chapter therefore attempts to approach language in the legal process from a perspective that accounts for issues of language proficiency and communication skills in the courtroom context. In doing so, the chapter discusses how certain ideologies about language in the legal process might bring about disadvantage to defendants regardless of their language backgrounds.

'INTERNAL INTERNATIONALIZATION' AND INTERPRETER-MEDIATED CASES

The influx of foreign nationals into Japan has increased dramatically since the 1980s. The number of registered foreign nationals residing in Japan in 2011 was 2.44 times as many as in 1985, growing from 850,612 to 2,078,508 (Ministry of Justice 2012). A large proportion of this growth was due to the increase in flow of labor migrants from South East Asia and South America, who are often called "newcomers" (Nukaga 2003; Taki 2005). This shifted the demography of immigrants from mainly Korean background population to a more diverse population. Thus there has been an increasing need for a larger supply of quality interpreter assistance in criminal justice procedures. Taki (2005) states that in the late 1990s, the Japanese government acknowledged the two main objectives of formal implementation of judicial interpreting, that is: "effective crime control and to guarantee the rights of foreigners in the criminal justice process" (p. 71). The number of interpreter-mediated cases saw a sixfold increase between 1989 and 2009 (Supreme Court of Japan 2011). In 2010, the nationalities of the defendants who received interpreter assistance included 75 countries compared to 35 in 1989, and one in 21 defendants who were sentenced in Japanese district or summary courts was a foreign national who received interpreter assistance (Supreme Court of Japan 2012). There seems to be a general view that problems due to language barriers in the context of the Japanese legal system have been substantially addressed (Taki 2005). However, there have also been claims that the quality control of court interpreters is inadequate (Mizuno 2006a).

While these developments are likely to have a positive effect on the legal process, discussions of court interpreting have, with very few exceptions, approached the matter with an assumption that foreign defendants are always given full interpreter assistance. However, there are now many trials in which foreign defendants give evidence by answering questions directly in Japanese or listen to the proceedings without interpreter mediation. The number of foreign residents who speak Japanese has probably increased (Shiramizu & Kaburagi 1999) but despite this, communication in Japanese as a second language in courtroom proceedings has been underinvestigated. As Japan goes through a transition from its internationalization to globalization, with increasing mobility of its residents, issues in courtroom communication need to be discussed beyond the prevalent equation of "providing interpreter mediation to foreigners" as internal internationalization of the Japanese criminal justice system.

LANGUAGE IDEOLOGIES IN LEGAL CONTEXTS

In exploring language and internal internationalization of the Japanese justice system, this chapter draws on the notion of language ideologies, which are, according to Blommaert (2005: 253), "socially, culturally and historically conditioned ideas, images and perceptions about language and communication." Furthermore, Woolard (1998: 27) argues that focusing on language ideologies "allows us to relate the microculture of communicative action to political economic considerations of power and social inequality." Language ideologies affect how we interact in various social settings, but they are also reproduced and reinforced in our social interactions.

In regard to ideologies at least, Eades (2010) provides a number of dominant instances found in legal processes, of which some are relevant to the current chapter. One such ideology is 'monolingualism-as-a-norm,' that is, there is a reluctance in Japan to accept the concept of multilingualism (Gottlieb 2012), although minority communities have long had bilingual speakers of Japanese and languages such as Korean and Chinese and the so-called newcomers include a large number of Spanish and Portuguese speakers who speak Japanese as their second language. The ideology that "foreigners do not speak Japanese" is common in the public discourses of *"yōtsūyakunin jiken"* (interpreter-required cases), despite the fact that around 20% of the non-Japanese defendants in Japanese district court level criminal cases do not require interpreters (Nakane 2012). Eades (2010), drawing on Angermeyer's (2008) study analyzing the court's lack of accommodation of bilingual speakers' code switching, argues that the ideology that people either speak language competently or not at all does not reflect the reality of multilingualism and that such ideology may deprive laypeople in court of expressing themselves in the language that they prefer to use in the evolving context of court proceedings.

Such an 'all-or-nothing' view of language proficiency also assumes that so-called native speakers would all be capable of participating in the legal process without problems. Eades (2010) also challenges an assumption held by legal professionals that accurately produced legal language leads to accurate understanding. However, the way in which court interpreting is provided in Japan, as will be shown later in this chapter, points to an ideology that formal legal language is difficult for second-language speakers and that language issues in the courtroom only apply to second-language speakers.

A STUDY OF MULTILINGUAL COURTROOMS IN JAPAN

To examine how language diversity is addressed in criminal trials, a study of a multilingual courtroom was undertaken in Japan. Courtroom proceedings of a total of 21 cases were observed in two district courts in 2007 and 2009. These cases were selected from the court list by identifying defendant names that did not appear to be conventionally Japanese. One case was excluded from the data set for this study since only the questioning of a witness (not defendant) was observed. Two other trials were excluded from the data set, as no interpreter was assigned to their trial and the defendants' Japanese was deemed to be of native-speaker-level proficiency. The rest of the trials had an interpreter present in court. The languages used included Mandarin Chinese (8), Cantonese (1), Tagalog (2), Portuguese (2), English (2), Swahili (1), Farsi (1), and Mongolian (1). As it was not possible to note down all the details of the observed discourse, the field notes are not entirely an accurate representation of the language used in the courtroom. The note taking focused on Japanese utterances due to the lack of capacity to keep up with the speed of interaction in court. However, where possible, notes were taken of utterances in other languages. In Japan, it has not been possible for researchers to obtain recordings of court proceedings. Therefore, in view of the lack of access to official court transcripts or recordings, the need for empirical studies of real multilingual courtroom discourse means that, although less than ideal, extensive field notes from the real trials are regarded as the best data source available.

Courtroom observation found that interpreting was not provided at all stages of courtroom proceedings in a number of trials. Interviews with the interpreters and the judges also confirmed that it is a common practice to partially remove interpreter mediation from courtroom proceedings if the defendant's Japanese language proficiency is regarded as sufficient for certain types of courtroom interaction. The questions then arose as to what are the principles and criteria upon which the court bases decisions regarding use and nonuse of interpreter mediation, as well as the extent to which this dual mode practice serves to protect the right of the NJSB defendants to participate in the legal process in a way equal to the defendants who have Japanese as a first language.

GENRE, REGISTER, AND MULTILINGUAL COURTROOM DISCOURSE

To understand the relationships between the chosen patterns of interpreting and the various phases of trials, the analysis of courtroom discourse in this chapter draws on the notions of register and genre developed by Halliday (1978; 1989) and Martin (1992) respectively. Genre can be described as a discourse type or the configuration of meaning in socially situated language use (Maley 1994). Martin (1992: 505) defines it as "a staged, goal oriented social process." Maley (1994) and Gibbons (2003) identified a number of trial genres, such as opening statements, cross-examination, and jury instructions. Since genres are structured for a goal, it is useful in considering the choice of interpreting mode in the courtroom in relation to the genres found in the courtroom. Genres can be characterized by relating them to the context of their use, and the register framework originally developed by Halliday and Hasan (1985) is drawn upon in this study. Three components of register have been identified by Halliday and Hasan (1985): *field*, which is what the discourse is about, e.g., schedule of court hearings; *tenor*, which is about the relationship between the sender and the recipient of the discourse, e.g., the judge addressing the defense counsel; and *mode*, which is the role that language plays in the text, e.g., spoken and face-to-face. The register framework can describe characteristics of trial genres that may affect the decisions on language choice or mode of interpreting in the courtroom. Since such decisions are influenced by the evaluation of NJSB defendants' language proficiency and types of genre they would be able to cope with, the genre and register frameworks are able to provide a link between the interpreting pattern and the various phases of trials.

When the courtroom data were examined, an overall pattern was found in the mode of interpreting and the trial genre. Table 5.1 summarizes the overall patterns of register and courtroom genres based on the interpreting patterns found in the study.

There were trial genres that were almost always interpreted. These genres were originally in written forms but 'read aloud' in court. From the register perspective, these genres tend to have technical legal details (field), be monologic and formal as they are presented by lawyers to the court (tenor), and are written with careful planning and editing to be read aloud to the court (mode). Examples are indictments, opening statements, summaries of evidence, and judgments. Apart from judgment, the interpreting was usually conducted simultaneously through a wireless system that connects the interpreter's microphone with the defendant's headset.

The second type of trial genre was either partially interpreted or not interpreted at all. These genres tend to have more 'oral' and 'interactive' characteristics, and the language is less planned. The content tends to be recounts of events related to the charge (field). The communication is dialogic

Table 5.1   Register, Interpreting Modes, and Courtroom Genres

Interpreting pattern *Register*	Fully interpreted	Partially or not interpreted	Summary-only interpreting
Field	Technical Legal	Recount of Events	Technical Legal
Tenor	Monologic Formal Lawyer-Court/ Judge	Dialogic Semiformal Lawyer-Defendant	Dialogic Formal/Semiformal Lawyer-Lawyer
Mode	Written (and read aloud) Planned	Spoken (spontaneous) Semiplanned Interactive	Spoken Unplanned Interactive

between a lawyer and the defendant, and it is semicolloquial (tenor). It is also more spontaneous and interactive than the 'fully interpreted' genres (mode), although there is usually some planning involved before the court appearance. Examples of these are identification of the defendant, examination and cross-examination, and final statement.

The third category of genre includes courtroom discourse that was summarized and then interpreted. Examples found in this study were discussions among legal professionals; for example, discussion regarding submission and presentation of evidence and discussion regarding the scheduling of hearings. While the discussion takes place, the interpreter sits quietly; and once the discussion is over, it is summarized by the judge, and this summary is rendered into the defendant's language by the interpreter. Such discussions involve technical legal details (field), while they are formal dialogic communication among lawyers (tenor), which is spontaneous and unplanned interaction (mode).

As we can see, the decisions regarding the pattern of interpreting appear to be based on the type of register that characterizes trial genres, although the court probably relies on the norms established unofficially over years of handling the participation of NJSB defendants. Guidelines compiled by the Supreme Court[1] refer to the possible partial removal of interpreting in the examination of the defendants who speak Japanese, as well as to the common practice of rendering the judge's summary of lawyers' discussions instead of turn-by-turn consecutive interpreting of the discussion. However, these are not officially implemented rules. A question then arises as to the legal protection of the language rights of NJSB defendants in Japan. Article 74 of the Code of Criminal Procedure (Keisohō 2014) states:

> When the court has a person who is not proficient in the national language make a statement, it shall have an interpreter interpret it. (Translation from *Japanese Law Translation* site[2])

The 1976 International Covenant on Civil and Political Rights (OHCHR 2014), to which Japan is a signatory, unlike the aforementioned rule, includes the right to access the content of the court proceedings in the language that the defendant can *understand*:

> Article 14 *All persons shall be equal before the courts and tribunals.*
> . . .
> 3. *In the determination of any criminal charge against him, everyone shall be entitled to the following minimum guarantees, in full equality:*
>
>   (a) *To be informed promptly and in detail in a language which he understands of the nature and cause of the charge against him.*
>   . . .
>   (f) *To have the free assistance of an interpreter if he cannot understand or speak the language used in court . . .*

As has been discussed by scholars in language and law (Angermeyer 2008; Eades 2003, 2010; Gibbons 2003; Laster & Taylor 1994), the criteria for identifying the need for an interpreter are often open to a wide range of interpretation—for example, what exactly does "proficient in the national language" mean? The statutes noted earlier do not, however, have provisions specifying the situations in which the court can exercise discretion to have interpreter mediation removed or a summarized version interpreted. Thus, as Taki (2005) suggests, it is necessary to empirically examine exactly how language barriers are addressed in separate trials. The following sections attempt to do so by analyzing some examples of the genres categorized in Table 5.1.

FULLY INTERPRETED GENRES

The technical and originally 'written' courtroom discourse genres tend to be interpreted in full, as long as an interpreter is assigned to the trial by the court. This implies an assumption that second-language speakers cannot cope with the technicality and complexity of such genres. One example is indictment, which often contains long sentences with multiple layered clauses characteristic of a written mode of discourse. Indictment also contains technical legal terms and marks grammatical referents explicitly, as it has to describe the 'facts' for which the defendant is indicted using the language that fits the framework of the law (as a 'field' in the register framework). These characteristics are also consequences of the need to adhere to the precision that the law requires (Bhatia 1994; Tiersma 1999). Indictment and other genres, such as opening statements and judgment, are read aloud in court as carefully planned monologic discourse. They are available as written texts and are often provided to the interpreter so he or she can be prepared for accurate rendition. Mōri (2006) gives an example of an indictment and discusses the challenges of translating indictments from Japanese into English. The example (adapted from a real case) is presented as one sentence containing dozens of clauses and expressions unusual to laypeople. Mōri (2006) argues that "indictments read aloud in the courtroom are difficult to understand even for people whose mother tongue is Japanese" (p. 394, translation by the author) and proposes an approach to translation in which extremely complex and long sentences are broken down into shorter ones, more priority is given to meaning equivalence, and the discourse strategies needed to make the English version easier to understand are used. A form-based literal translation of an indictment given as an example by Mōri (2006: 396) is shown in the text that follows (see Appendix for the Japanese original):

Example 1

Facts of [sic] constituting the offense charged:
    The defendant, in the absence of legal grounds for exceptional treatment and with profit-making purpose, conspired with unidentified

others, intending to import cannabis, checked in this carrying bag as check-in luggage to FF International Airport in EE (Japan), when boarding CC Airlines flight number DD at BB Airport, in AA on bb/cc/20xx, concealing about 3,000 grams of cannabis leaves, in the twofold bottom of the dark blue carrying bag, and transited to the same airline flight number JJ at HH International Airport in GG and had this carrying bag delivered to FF Airport by the above airplane around ff:gg a.m. on bb/ee and made the airport staff member, who did not know the circumstance, carry out this carrying bag from the above airplane to bring the above cannabis into this country and tried to import cannabis and again tried to import cannabis, contraband goods listed on Customs Tariff Law, without telling that he had cannabis with him to customs officers at the custom clearance section at FF Airport around hh:jj on the same day, but failed to import cannabis, because the custom officer found the cannabis.

The indictment is one continuous sentence with the subject "defendant" and clauses presenting a chain of his/her actions. Inserted among the list of defendant's actions are subordinate clauses and phrases that provide circumstances. This inevitably makes it difficult for listeners to absorb the information. The technical expressions such as "in the absence of legal grounds for exceptional treatment" (*midarini* "having a different meaning from the everyday one 'recklessly'" (Mizuno 2006b)), "unidentified others" (*shimei fushōsha*) and "contraband goods listed on Customs Tariff Law" (*kanzētēritsuhō jō no yunyūkinsēhin*) make this a 'specialist' genre. The Japanese original of this indictment also utilizes far more archaic expressions than the English translation mentioned earlier, for example *jō o hishite* (without telling that) instead of the Japanese equivalent of "without telling that" (*iwanaide/iwazuni*). For a layperson, *jō o hishite* is likely to mean "concealing the sentiment" in their everyday understanding of these words (Mizuno 2006b). There are also explicit cohesive devices such as "the above airplane" and "on the same day" which indicate formality. These devices are often used in newspaper reports and television news reports, but in the text mentioned earlier, they appear within a single long sentence with considerable distance from the deictic reference, which makes it challenging to understand by just hearing the text.

Considering these challenges, it appears that there is an assumption that NJSB defendants would not be able to understand these genres without interpreter mediation. Consequently, this assumption informs the decision to fully interpret these genres. What is worrying, however, is that the legal Japanese found in these genres is difficult for Japanese native speakers (cf. Mizuno 2006b; Ōkawara 2008). The translation process may make the genre accessible for the defendant (in fact, Mōri (2006) proposes a more comprehensible version of the translation), while Japanese native speakers without legal training or a high level of literacy may not achieve the same level of understanding if the original version remains cognitively challenging and linguistically complex. This is especially the case for the large proportion of defendants whose literacy skills are low: 22.6% of prisoners incarcerated in 2010 had an IQ of 69 or lower (Ministry of Justice 2010a), and those who plead guilty are also required to be put on trial in Japan. Aside from that dealing with interpreter-mediated cases, there has hardly been any academic or public discussion of courtroom language issues in relation to defendants' literacy levels. The prevalent ideology that language problems in the justice system are only about foreigners may need to be challenged.

PARTIALLY OR NOT-INTERPRETED GENRES

The trial genres that are interactive and less planned tend to be conducted in Japanese without interpreter mediation or with an interpreter on "standby interpreting" (Angermeyer 2008: 391) if the defendant speaks Japanese to a certain extent. In standby interpreting, the interpreter is present but only renders translation when there is a need for it. It is mentioned in the Supreme Court guidelines as a possibility:

> 5. Questioning of defendant
> (2) Defendants who can manage in Japanese to a certain extent
> Even when the defendant claims that interpreting is not necessary, caution should be exercised in managing such a situation, taking account of the nature of the case, the defendant's Japanese language proficiency, and the attitude of the defendant. When the defendant responds in Japanese to questions asked in Japanese, upon his/her request, then interpreting might be removed for such a section, but it may be reasonable to interpret the questions in Japanese causing comprehension difficulty, and have the defendant make a statement in a foreign language when it is difficult to express him/herself in Japanese, and have only such statements interpreted.
> (Supreme Court of Japan 2003: 81,
> translation by the author)

It is interesting that the earlier noted guidelines put the onus of the language choice on the defendant, as the aforementioned passage mandates, for removing interpreting, the defendant's claim that the interpreter is unnecessary, and the defendant's request not to have interpreter assistance during questioning. There are cases in which the defendants themselves wish to participate in the questioning without interpreter mediation, according to interpreters and judges. However, the question remains as to how to determine "the defendant's Japanese language proficiency" and whether the defendant "can manage in Japanese to a certain extent."

The language ideology behind the guidelines for removing interpreter assistance is likely to be that the interactive genre of face-to-face questioning does not require a sophisticated language proficiency like other types of trial genres, and, therefore, second-language speakers with reasonable fluency can manage it without problems. However, problematic exchanges were found in one of the trials observed in the present study. In Example 2, a defendant of Chinese speaking background is cross-examined in Japanese[3] with an interpreter on standby. The prosecutor is probing the defendant regarding the role he played in a series of robberies for which a group of people are charged. The questions are concerned with distribution of money.

Example 2

Questioning by a prosecutor of a Chinese defendant who was accused of burglary (uninterpreted, in Japanese only) (PC = prosecution counsel; DF = defendant; [ ] = elements omitted by ellipsis in Japanese)

1 PC: *Un, de kekkyoku anata wa sonō sonō Han ga mottekita okane no Han no houni itta okane no naka kara yachin to sorekara jibunno toribun o moratta wake ne.*
'Yes, so in the end you uh uh you received rent and your own share of the money Han brought, or the money that went to Han, right?'

2   ((pause))

3 PC: *De, sono ato, toiu koto desho?*
'Then, [it was] after that, [that you distributed the money] wasn't it?'

4 DF: *Hai?*
'Sorry?'

5 PC: *Ii?*
'Okay?'

6 DF: *Hai.*
'Yes.'

7 PC: *Ja Han ga mottekita okane no naka kara*
'So, from the money that Han brought,'

8 DF: *Hai*
'Yes'

9 PC: *yachin to,*
'rent and'

10 DF: *Hai.*
'Yes.'

11 PC: *sorekara anatano toribun no hō, saisho totta wake ne*
'and your share, [you] took it first, is that right?'

12   ((pause))

13 DF: *Toribun? Hai, un.*
'[My] share? Yes, yeah.'

14 PC: *De, soshitara Han no hō ga hokano hitotachi ni mo wakete*
kure tte anata ni itta wake ne
'And then it is the case that Han asked you to also distribute the money to other people.'

15   ((pause))

16 PC: *Konomae sō itta desho.*
'[You] said so before, right?'

17 DF: *Iya waketeta no wa jibun da to omou.*
'No, [I] think it was me who distributed [the money].'

This questioning sequence does not contain technical legal language or complex sentence structures, and everyday words are used throughout. However, the defendant indicates a problem in turn 4, and when the prosecutor breaks down the question into smaller chunks, the defendant still seems to be having a problem as there is silence in turn 15. The question in line 3 has many omitted elements, and the omitted elements appeared a few turns prior to this question. For a second-language speaker, this may have made the question extremely ambiguous, especially in terms of what the subject of the sentence was and the omitted action was. Ellipsis is one of the characteristics of Japanese that often becomes a source of miscommunication among learners of Japanese (Nariyama 2009). The frustrated prosecutor tells the defendant that he had "said so" (turn 16). However, the response in turn 17 attempts to correct the prosecutor's version, giving an account that is more incriminating for the defendant. The defendant misunderstood the reported speech structure and may have confused the focus of the question that was Han's action of asking him to distribute the money.

While it is possible that the defendant was being evasive in his responses, he may also have been confused by the numerous ellipses and the subject-predicate relationship in the complex sentence structure. If the latter is the case, his inconsistent responses may give the court (unfairly) an impression of him as an unreliable defendant. The interactive mode may allow for a more inexplicit construction of discourse than more formal and written trial genres, and this example indicates that there are risks involved in removing interpreter mediation even when the defendant is seemingly fluent in Japanese. The Supreme Court guidelines actually recommend that lawyers "mark subjects, predicates and tenses explicitly" (Supreme Court of Japan 2003: 81) when questioning through an interpreter. Direct questioning in Japanese, then, cannot assume that NJSB defendants would be able to understand questions with ellipses.

There are also cases in which the interpreters step out of the standby mode to provide mediation in two languages. Below, a Portuguese-speaking-background defendant is cross-examined.

Example 3

Defendant questioned in a mixture of Japanese only and standby interpreting options (Brazilian Portuguese speaker, accused of possession and use of marijuana) (J = judge; DF = defendant; PC = prosecution counsel; IR = interpreter)

1 PC: *Anata wa hokano hito ni ne, taima o uttari agetari shita koto wa arimasu ka.*
'Have you either sold or given marijuana to other people before?'

2 DF: *//Nai desu.*
//'No, I haven't.'

3 IR: // ((Portuguese, overlapping DF))

4 PC: *Sorekara, meeru yaritori shiteita tomodachi tono kankē toka kono ato dōsuru tsumori desu ka.*
'And what do [you] intend to do with regards to things like your relationship with the friend you exchanged e-mails with?'

5 IR: ((Portuguese))

6 DF: *Mō warui hito ni wa tsukiawanai you ni shimasu.* ((looking at PC))
'[I] will not be seeing the bad person anymore.'

7 PC: *Mō tsukiawanaindesu ka sono hito to wa.*
'So [you] won't be seeing that person anymore?'

8 DF: *Hai.*
'No.'[4]

9 PC: *Hokani taima, aruiwa hokano ihōyakubutsu tsukatteiru yōna tomodachi tte mawarini imasen ka.*
'Aren't there any other friends who may be using marijuana or other illegal drugs?'

10 DF: ((Portuguese))

11 IR: *Ēto sono warui tomodachi tteiu no wa mēru no kōkan shiteita hito de, hoka wa imasen.*
'Uh that bad friend, it's the person with whom [I] exchanged e-mails, and there is no one else.'

12 PC: *Kono F tteiu tomodachi desu ka.*
'Is [that] this friend called F?'

13 DF: *Hai.*
'Yes.'

14 PC: *Ima dōnatte irundesu ka ne.*
'What has become of [him/your relationship with him]?'

15 DF: ((Portuguese))

16 IR: *Wakarimasen.*
'[I] don't know.'

17 PC: *Owarimasu.*
'That's all from me.'

The exchange shows irregularity in interpreting patterns. The first question from the prosecutor (turn 1) is not interpreted but directly responded to by the defendant, whose reply in Japanese overlaps with the interpreter's attempt for rendition. The prosecutor's question in turn 4 is interpreted into Portuguese, but the defendant responds to this interpreted question in Japanese (line 6). The defendant also responds in Portuguese twice in the second half of the excerpt, but the questions he responds to are not interpreted into Portuguese. Such irregular pattern of interpreting was observed throughout the questioning of the defendant, including the questioning by the defense counsel. As the defendant was facing the judge and the interpreter, who was seated below and in front of the judge slightly to his left, the interpreter provided interpreting when the defendant turned his gaze from the judge to her or when he remained silent after questions were asked. There was a silent, nonverbal negotiation between the defendant and the interpreter over whether or not interpreting was to be provided. There was no intervention given by the counsel or the judge, and decisions regarding language choice were left with the defendant and the interpreter.

While there was no obvious communication breakdown in the questioning of this defendant, there are some features of the interaction that suggest problems in the way he communicated that may have put the defendant in a negative light. Regarding his relationship with the friend with whom he exchanged e-mails about drugs, the defendant says, "I will not be seeing the bad person anymore." Due to grammatical differences between Japanese and English, it is not possible to see any problems as far as the back translation is concerned, but the word "*tomodachi*" (friend) in the prosecutor's question (turn 4) can be singular or plural in Japanese. While it is not possible to find out what was said in Portuguese, which would have marked plural with "s," the word "*warui hito*" (bad person) is used in the defendant's response as the topic of the sentence. This noun phrase would normally be taken as a singular form (for animate nouns, there is a typical plural marker *tachi*) and therefore can be interpreted as referring to "friend" (singular) in the question. Nevertheless, if the defendant was referring to one friend with whom he exchanged e-mails about drugs, it would have been more natural to specify "bad person" with "*sonna/sōiu*" (such) or "*sono*" (the/that) as he was introducing a new noun phrase as a topic. However, the topic of the question was in fact "*things like your relationship with the friend you exchanged e-mails*" with "*toka*" (like) preceding "your relationship." Thus, one could regard the original question as referring to his friendship circle related to drugs in general, and if that is the case, the response in turn 6 would be textually cohesive, although this also would suggest that the defendant had an unspecified number of friends who may have been "bad." The problem is that the prosecutor, in turn 7, asks a question to narrow down the focus to "that person," clarifying whether the defendant meant that he would not see "a specific friend" when he said "bad person." The prosecutor recycles the defendant's expression "*mō tsukiawa-nai*" (will not see [a person]) in the preceding turn. This interactional feature, which "generally involves participants' strategic use of phonological, syntactic, and semantic surface structure features of prior turns at talk" (Goodwin 1990: 177) can be used by conversational participants to challenge the previous speaker (Church 2009). This move by the prosecutor projects the defendant response in turn 6 as vague and failing to be cohesive.

Once the defendant confirms that he would not see the friend specified in the question, the prosecutor's question in turn 9 challenges the defendant by raising a possibility of other friends who might be a bad influence on him. This appears to be done by capitalizing on the defendant's declaration that he would not see the specific friend and contrasting it with the possible existence of "other friends" using drugs. Such a contrasting strategy is often deployed by counsel in cross-examination to undermine the credibility of witnesses (Drew 1990; Gibbons 2003). In responding to this challenge, in Portuguese, the defendant first repairs his earlier turn (turn 6) by saying that "*warui hito*" was meant to refer to a particular friend, and he has no other friends who are using drugs. We now see that, after being challenged by the prosecutor because of the noncohesive response, which he gave in Japanese, the defendant chose to speak in Portuguese, the language he feels more comfortable with in expressing himself, to repair the damage. The interpreter also confirmed in an interview that this defendant seemed to be better at listening comprehension than expressing himself in Japanese.

SUMMARY-ONLY INTERPRETING

Lawyer-only discussion was found not to be interpreted immediately but only later in summarized form. In relation to this, the Supreme Court guidelines say:

> When a discussion takes place among the court, the defense counsel and the prosecutor, for example due to an objection being raised, usually the utterances in such a discussion are not interpreted word for word, but a summary, provided by the judge after the discussion has been resolved, is interpreted. (Supreme Court of Japan 2003: 74, translation by the author)

The common practice of interpreting a summary of discussion rather than turn-by-turn is also mentioned in Yoshida (2014). One court interpreter in the author's fieldwork also mentioned in an interview that when she

tried to provide turn-by-turn interpreting of a discussion among legal professionals, she was told to wait until the discussion was over. Below is an example
of interpreting the judge's summary of lawyer discussion. The first part shows
a discussion between the judge and the prosecutor regarding the defendant's
possible additional charge for attempted possession of marijuana. The underlined parts indicate some of the essential information that is not mentioned in
the summary version (Part 2) which is rendered in English for the defendant.

Example 4 (Part 1)

Lawyers' Discussion in Japanese

(Nigerian English speaker, accused of Violation of Immigration Control
and Refugee Recognition Act, attempted possession of marijuana)

1 J: *Ima yōyaku sarenakattandesu kedo san pēji no ue kara*
yongyōme atari ni aru kono <u>kontorōrudo deribarī sōsa</u>
<u>toshite okonawareta mono de aru tame,</u> yūbinkyokuin ga
gyōmujikan ni ninmutoshite atatteita toieru toiu bubun
nitsuite wa koremade no shōko seikyū no naka de nanika
<u>arundesu ka.</u>
'You haven't summarized it but from around the fourth line
of page three there is a section which reads "<u>because it was</u>
<u>conducted as a controlled delivery investigation,</u> it can be
said that the postal worker was deployed on duty during
his/her shift," but regarding this, <u>do you have anything</u> in
your request for examination of evidence so far?'

2 PC: *Kontorōrudo deribarī ga okonawareta tteiu koto wa*
tōzenn dete masushi, sono sōsa no kono dankai dake de
(   ) masunode, ma, nanika aru ka to iwareru to
'<u>It is obvious there that an investigation by controlled deliv-</u>
<u>ery was conducted,</u> and with only this stage of the investiga-
tion (   ), <u>so, if you ask me if there is anything, well . . .</u>'

3 J: *Kontorōrudo deribarī ga okonawareta tteiu koto made wa*
jijitsu
'It is a fact that a <u>controlled delivery ([investigation]) was</u>
<u>carried out.</u>'

4 PC: *Hai*
'Yes.'

5 J: *Sōsuruto ja watashi no tokoro niwa*
'In that case, for me'

6 PC: *Sōdesune*
'Right'

7 J: *Toiuka, mada nanika*
          'I mean is there still anything'

8 PC: *Tsūjō ( ) deno kototo ukagattemasu kedo, moshi are*
          deshitara mōichido keisatsu no kata ni ( ), <u>soko made wa</u>
          <u>*hitsuyōnai no ka to omoimashite*</u>
          'I hear that normally ( ), but if that is the case ( ) to people
          with the police, . . . <u>I didn't think we needed to go that far</u>.'

9 J: *Kore yūbin kyokuiin ga jissaini haitatsu ni itta tteiu yōna*
          mune no shōko tteiu no wa <u>nain desu ka</u>
          'For this, <u>isn't there any evidence</u> like something that
          shows a postal worker actually went to deliver?'

10 PC: *Sore wa <u>ano</u>, kono ( ) shite itadakimashite. <u>Ma</u>, konkai*
          no jiken tōji no shokuin no, yūbinkyoku no hō, yakusho ya
          nyūkannado mo shirabete mitanndesu ga, somosomo shōko
          no hō kara dekinakattandesu. De konkai no otasshi ukete,
          kēsatsu no kata ni onegai shite, <u>chotto</u> kono yūbinkyoku
          no kata ni gokyōryoku itadaitedesu ne, ( ) ga mata tokutē
          ( ) no haitatsu datta tteiu no to, ato mata <u>yūbinkyoku no</u>
          <u>*kata wa hanashiwa surukedo amarinimo jikan ga tattan*</u>
          <u>*de, shōgen to shite wa ( ) masen, toiu kotode atte*</u>, ima
          <u>*chotto*</u> *soko wa shōko to shite wa <u>nai jōtai nandesu.</u>*
          'That is <u>um</u>, this we requested to have ( ) done. <u>Well</u>, we
          tried to find the worker at the time of this incident, checked
          with the post office, the ward office, and the Immigration,
          but in the first place we could not trace evidence. In receiv-
          ing the instruction, we have asked people from the police,
          so we can <u>sort of</u> get cooperation from people from the post
          office, ( ), since it was a special ( ) delivery, and also <u>the</u>
          <u>post office also says it's been too long since then and they</u>
          <u>don't/can't ( ) as testimony</u>, so at the moment <u>the situation</u>
          <u>is that</u> evidence for that is <u>not really</u> available.' (Discussion
          continues, with DC's participation)

In the discussion, the judge probes the prosecutor regarding the evidence for an attempted possession of marijuana. In particular, there is a mention of "controlled delivery," which is used by the police in their investigation into drug offenses. The prosecutor's response in turn 2 is produced with hesitation and without an explicit admission that the concrete evidence the judge is asking for does not exist. The judge probes further (turns 5 and 7), to which the prosecutor offers an excuse in turn 8. The judge's probing continues in turn 9, but the prosecutor's response in turn 10 contains expla-nations and excuses, including the fact that the postal worker would not be prepared to testify. This response also contains hesitations and mitigating devices ("sort of," "not really," "the situation is . . ."). Overall, this part of the discussion can be described as the judge placing the prosecutor under direct scrutiny and pressuring him to explain a lack of evidence.

The aforementioned part of the discussion was summarized by the judge:

Example 4 (Part 2)

Judge's Summary

1 J: *Sōsuruto konokoto o yakusa nakerebaikenaindesu keredo,*
       'So then we have to translate this matter,'

2 J: *Ō taima no shojimisui no kankei de, jissaini haitatsu ni omomuita yūbinkyokuin no shōko ga aru kadouka saibansho no hō kara tazuneta. Kansatsukan ni tazuneta.*
       'Uh in relation to attempted possession of cannabis, the court asked, asked the prosecutor, whether there was any evidence from the postal worker who actually delivered.'

3 IR: ((English))

4 J: *Kensatsukan ga shirabeta keredomo sōsa de shirabeta shorui no nakani wa sono shōko ga nakatta to.*
       'The prosecutor checked, but he says that they did not find that evidence among the documents that they examined in their investigation.'

5 IR: ((English))

6 J: *Arata ni kēsatsu ni onegaishite yūbinkyokuin nit suite sōsa shite moratteiru keredomo genjiten dewa shōko ni natteiru mono wa nai to.*
       'He says that he asked the police to find out about the postal worker again, but at this point there is nothing that serves as evidence.'

7 IR: ((English))

8 J: *Sono ten ni kanshite sarani kensatsukan ga kentō suru to.*
       'The prosecutor says that he will consider this matter.'

When the original discussion (Part 1) and the summarized version (Part 2) are compared, numerous items are found to have been excluded from the latter. In terms of the textual structure (or *mode* in the register framework), the summary is coherent, cohesive, and easy to understand, although the social meaning derived from the pattern of participation in the original discussion is lost as numerous turn exchanges are compressed into a smaller number of turns. In terms of content (or *field*), the summarized version does not mention "controlled delivery" (which is mentioned three times in the original), the fact that the postal worker does not wish to provide testimony, or the prosecutor's excuse that he "didn't think [they] needed to go that far" with providing the evidence. This is important information for the defendant in order to grasp matters relevant to the charge, the strength of evidence and positions of the counsel. Furthermore, because the summary naturally takes the form of a reported speech, the interpersonal aspect of the original discussion is lost. In other words, the tenor of the discourse changes.

Thus not only is the defendant given limited access to the content of courtroom proceedings but also is not given the same level of access as Japanese-speaking-background defendants. There are many elements in the earlier interaction that native speakers would be able to pick up on but that the NJSB defendant may miss.[5] Since everything else was interpreted during the questioning of the defendant in this trial, it can be assumed that he would not have been able to pick up much information in the original lawyer-only discussion. An important question arising from the common use of summary-only interpreting is whether there is an ideology that, native speaker or not, defendants are not expected to fully understand discussions among lawyers involving technical legal concepts.

LANGUAGE IDEOLOGIES IN THE JUSTICE SYSTEM: TOWARD A GLOBAL APPROACH

The analysis noted earlier suggests that the Japanese judiciary exercises some flexibility in applying different modes of interpreter mediation to various genres of court proceedings. The technical and written-based genres, such as indictments, are considered too difficult for NJSB defendants without the interpreter mediation. The decision to use interpreting, however, is also motivated by the ideology that these genres need to be accurately presented to ensure the legality of the trial processes. The need for precision and the ideology about the level of literacy required for these genres thus protect NJSB defendants' rights. However, as mentioned earlier, meaning-based translation of these genres may make them more accessible to NJSB defendants than to Japanese speakers who hear the Japanese version, especially given the proportion of intellectually challenged defendants in Japan.

The removal of interpreter mediation during the questioning of those defendants with a certain level of Japanese language proficiency appears to be based on the ideology that this genre does not involve specialist legal terms, strict precision, or grammatical complexity. On one hand, this reflects a realistic view of multilingualism that is not based on "the all-or-nothing view of language learning and use" (Eades 2010: 69). In this sense, the Japanese judiciary applies a more realistic approach to multilingualism.

While standby interpreting and the removal of interpreter mediation benefit the court by avoiding the duplication of questioning time, it also allows NJSB defendants to choose the language in which they wish to make their story heard (cf. Angermeyer 2008; Cooke 1996). Media reports based on the comments given by lay judges in *saiban-in* trials suggest that they find it difficult to capture the attitudes and emotions of the defendants through interpreters (e.g., Asahi Shinbun 2009a, b). Eades (2010: 70) also discusses some concerns that lawyers may have, such as "Will it be harder to gauge the credibility of the witness?" and "Will the interpreter provide a 'buffer' between lawyer and witness?" However, removing interpreter mediation involves risks. The seemingly less demanding genre of face-to-face questioning may not challenge defendants in terms of the field aspect of register, but communication problems may occur because textual cohesion is not as explicit as in the formal and written-based trial genres. It is worrying that the examples presented in this chapter were observed in the questioning of the defendants by the prosecution counsel. As questioner, legal professional, and first-language speaker of Japanese, power asymmetry favors the prosecutor, although the potential for lay answerers to resist the power does exist (cf. Drew 1990, 1991). In theory, if an interpreter is in court, it would be possible for any of the counsel, the judge, or the defendant to request that the interpreter step in. However, the participants themselves may be unaware of problems caused by language barriers unless they cause obvious miscommunication or lack of understanding. The other potential source of problems is the expectation that defendants would ask for interpreting assistance if they felt the need. This is not always the case, considering the pressure and nervousness that a second-language speaker might feel when facing legal authority and being on the spot in the courtroom.

The analysis of the interpreting of a summarized discussion demonstrated that some aspects of communication are lost and may disadvantage NJSB defendants. This practice has also been questioned by Watanabe (1998) who suggests that while it is efficient because of the time saved and of the removal of the technical details (and therefore challenges of translation), it may potentially lead to the breakdown of communication and trust between defendants and their defense counsel. The summarizing practice also appears to be underpinned by the ideology that people without a legal background, whatever their first language, cannot fully understand discussions among lawyers. In fact, one of the criteria given in the Supreme Court guidelines for not assigning an interpreter is "mostly able to understand the points of the interaction which takes place in court proceedings" (The Supreme Court of Japan 2003: 61, translation by the author).

The difficulty of the courtroom language for Japanese mother-tongue speakers has been discussed by forensic linguistics in Japan (Hotta 2012; Ōkawara 2008). This means that rather than focusing only on citizenship and native language, we need to focus on the language barriers facing a range of courtroom participants who lack the required language, literacy, or cognitive capabilities. In other words, the internationalization discourse of appreciating differences across ethnicity, cultures, and languages and bridging the gaps between 'us and them' may prevent the Japanese judiciary from addressing language and communication issues that defendants may face in court regardless of their language backgrounds. There have been positive initiatives taken by lawyers (e.g., Gotō 2008) and scholars (e.g., Hotta 2012; Ōkawara 2008) to improve legal communication involving lay judges in the *saiban-in* system. However, initiatives that address language issues from the defendant's (or witness's) perspective have not been taken.

Intelligibility of language used in courtroom proceedings involving Japanese-dialect speakers has also begun to draw attention as an important issue (e.g., Fudano 2012). It will be necessary for the Japanese judiciary to go beyond the 'internationalization' approach and take a more 'global' approach to communication issues in the courtroom using language proficiency and intelligibility as the key factors affecting them.

CONCLUSION

This chapter has discussed how language barriers are addressed in Japan's multilingual courtrooms as part of Japan's internationalization initiatives. Trial genre categories were identified to which different interpreting patterns are applied according to the language proficiency of the defendant. Although having these options may suggest Japan's effort to internationalize its justice system, there are risks in using standby interpreting and summarizing lawyer-only discussions for interpreter rendition, for depriving NJSB defendants of equal opportunities for communication in the courtroom. It was also suggested that the issues of language barriers go beyond so-called foreigner cases or interpreter-mediated cases that are directly associated with 'internationalization.' Further research into NJSB participation without interpreter mediation as well as communication issues in trials of Japanese-as-the-first-language defendants and Japanese citizens who require interpreter assistance, is necessary. In other words, an alternative 'global' perspective that captures issues of language in the legal process beyond the dichotomy of foreign-Japanese categories will be required.

Appendix
Japanese Original of the Indictment
(from Mōri 2006: 393)

公訴事実

　被告人は、みだりに、営利の目的で、大麻を輸入しようと企て、氏名不詳者と共謀の上、大麻である大麻草約3,000グラムを2重底の紺色キャリーバックに隠匿した上、平成aa年bb月cc日、AA国BB空港において、CC航空DD便に搭乗するに際し、上記キャリーバッグをEEのFF国際空港までの機内預託手荷物として同航空会社に運送委託し、GG国HH国際空港において、同航空JJ便に乗り継ぎ、同月ee日午前ff時gg分ころ、同便により、上記キャリーバッグを上記FF空港に運送させた上、情を知らない同空港作業員をしてこれを同航空機から機外に搬出させて上記大麻を本邦内に取り降ろさせ、もって大麻を輸入するとともに、同日午前hh時jj分ころ、同空港内FF空港税関検査場において、同税関職員に対し、上記大麻を携帯している事実を秘して申告しないまま通関手続きを終了させて関税定率法上の輸入禁制品である大麻を輸入しようとしたが、同税関職員に上記大麻を発見されたため、その目的を遂げなかったものである。

　罪名
　大麻取締法違反、関税法違反

NOTES

1. The Supreme Court guidelines mentioned hereafter are for dealing with *gaikokujin jiken* (foreigner cases).
2. Translation from *Japanese Law Translation* site. http://www.japanese lawtranslation.go.jp/dict/?re=02
3. Pseudonyms are used in all examples.
4. The affirmative response 'Hai' indicates agreement to the proposition of the utterance as a whole in turn 7.
5. There is also a possibility that turn-by-turn interpreting of the original discussion may not guarantee accurate rendition.

REFERENCES

Angermeyer, P. (2008). Creating monolingualism in the multilingual courtroom. *Sociolinguistic Studies*, 2(3), 385–403.

Bhatia, V. K. (1994). Cognitive structuring in legislative provisions. In J. Gibbons (Ed.), *Language and the Law* (pp. 136–155). London: Longman.

Blommaert, J. (2005). *Discourse*. Cambridge: Cambridge University Press.

Church, A. (2009). *Preference organisation and peer disputes: How young children resolve conflict*. Aldershot: Ashgate.

Cooke, M. (1996). A different story: narrative versus 'question and answer' in Aboriginal evidence. *Forensic Linguistics, 3*(2), 273–288.

Drew, P. (1990). Strategies in the contest between lawyer and witness in cross-examination. In J. N. Levi & A. G. Walker (Eds.), *Language in the Judicial Process* (pp. 39–64). New York: Plenum Press.

Drew, P. (1991). Asymmetries of knowledge in conversational interactions. In I. Marková & K. Foppa (Eds.), *Asymmetries in Dialogue* (pp. 21–48). Hemel Hampstead: Harvester Wheatsheaf.

Eades, D. (2003). Participation of second language and second dialect speakers in the legal system. *Annual Review of Applied Linguistics, 23*, 113–133.

Eades, D. (2010). *Sociolinguistics and the legal process*. Bristol: Multilingual Matters.

Fudano, K. (2012). *Hōtei ni okeru Hōgen: rinshō kotobagaku no tachiba kara* [Dialects in the Courtroom: from the perspective of empirical linguistics]. Osaka: Izumi Shoin.

'Gaikokujin hikoku no hatsugen' [Foreign Defendants' Statements]. (2009a, September 7). *Asahi shimbun*. 26.

Gibbons, J. (2003). *Forensic linguistics* (1st ed. Vol. 32). Oxford: Blackwell.

Goodwin, M. H. (1990). *He-Said-She-Said: Talk as social organization among Black children*. Bloomington: Indiana University Press.

Gotō, A. (2008). *Saiban-in Jidai no Hōtei Yōgo: hōtei yōgo no nichijō ka ni kansuru PT saishū hōkokusho*. Tokyo: Sansēdō.

Gottlieb, N. (2012). *Language policy in Japan: The challenge of change*. Cambridge: Cambridge University Press.

Halliday, M. A. K. (1978). *Language as social semiotic: The social interpretation of language and meaning*. London: Edward Arnold.

Halliday, M. A. K. (1989). *Spoken and written language*. Oxford: Oxford University Press.

Halliday, M. A. K., & Hasan, R. (1985). *Language, context and text: Aspects of language in social-semiotic perspective*. Oxford: Oxford University Press.

Hotta, Syūgo. (2012). Saiban-in no kotoba: saibankan to saiban-in no komyu nikēshon. In T. Hashiuchi & S. Hotta (Eds.), *Hō to Gengo: hōgengogaku e no izanai* (pp. 53–64). Tokyo: Kurosio Publishers.

Keisohō (2014). *Keiji soshōhō* [Japanese code of civil procedure as at 2014].

Laster, K., & Taylor, V. L. (1994). *Interpreters and the legal system*. Sydney: The Federation Press.

Maley, Y. (1994). The language of the law. In J. Gibbons (Ed.), *Language and the Law* (pp. 159–173). London: Longman.

Martin, J. R. (1992). *English text: System and structure*. Amsterdam: John Benjamins.

Ministry of Justice. (2010). *Statistics for Corrective Services*. Retrieved on May 10, 2012, http://www.e-stat.go.jp/SG1/estat/List.do?lid=000001076421

Ministry of Justice. (2012). *Immigration Control in Recent Years, 2011*. Retrieved on September 25, 2013, from http://www.moj.go.jp/content/000105769.pdf

Mizuno, M. (2006a). Hanketsubun no tsūyaku ni okeru tōkasei hoji no kanōsei to genkai [Possibilties and limitations for legal equivalent interpreting of written jedgements]. *Speech Communication Kyouiku, 19*, 113–131.

Mizuno, M. (2006b). Nick Baker jiken no eigo tsūyaku o meguru shomondai. *Quarterly Keiji Bengo, 46*, 108–111.

Mōri, M. (2006). Shihō tsūyaku ni okeru gengo tōkasei iji no kanōsei: kisojō eigoyaku no kokoromi [Language equivalency in judicial interpretation: the challenge of translating Japanese indictments into English.] *Nihon Daigaku Sōgō Shakai Jōhō Kenyūka Kiyō, 7*, 391–397.

Nakane, I. (2012). Language rights of non-Japanese defendants in Japanese criminal courts. In N. Gottlieb (Ed.), *Language and Citizenship in Japan* (pp. 155–174). London: Routledge.

Nariyama, S. (2009). *How can we know who did what to whom in Japanese?* Tokyo: Meiji Shoin.

Nukaga, M. (2003). Japanese education in an era of internationalization: A case study of an emerging multicultural coexistence model. *International Journal of Japanese Sociology, 12*(1), 79–94.

OHCHR (2014). *Office of the High Commissioner for Human Rights.* Retrieved February 15, 2014, from: http://www.ohchr.org/EN/ProfessionalInterest/Pages/CCPR.aspx

Okawara, M. (2008). *Shimin kara mita saiban-in saiban* [Lay Judge Trials from the citizens' perspective]. Tokyo: Akashi Shoten.

Shiramizu, S., & Kaburagi, H. (1999). Zainichi gaikokujin to nihonjin tono komyunikēshon: chiiki ni okeru kōryū, shien katsudō no jittai. *Hiroshima Daigaku Ryūgakusei Kyōiku, 4*, 47–67.

Sugiyama, Y. (1992). Internal and external aspects of internationalization. In G.D. Hook & M.A. Weiner (Eds.), *The Internationalization of Japan* (pp. 72–103). London: Routledge.

Supreme Court of Japan. (2003). *Tokushu keiji jiken no kiso chishiki.* Tokyo: Hōsōkai.

Supreme Court of Japan. (2011). *Gozonji Desuka: Hōtei Tsūyaku Heisei 23nendo Ban.* Retrieved on September 5, 2011, from http://www.courts.go.jp/about/pamphlet/pdf/houtei_tuuyaku.pdf

Supreme Court of Japan. (2012). *Gozonji Desuka: Hōtei Tsūyaku Heisei 24 nendo Ban.* Retrieved on May 5, 2012, from http://www.courts.go.jp/vcms_lf/210021.pdf

Taki, T. (2005). Labor migration and the language barrier in contemporary Japan: the formation of a domestic language regime of a globalizing state. *International Journal of the Sociology of Language, 2005* (175–176), 55–81.

Tiersma, P. M. (1999). *Legal language.* Chicago: The University of Chicago Press.

Tsuda, M. (1997). Human rights problems of foreigners in Japan's criminal justice system. *Migrationworld, 25*(1/2), 22–25.

Tsuneyoshi, R. (2011). The 'internationalizaion' of Japanese education and new comers: Uncovering the paradoxes. In D.B. Willis & J. Rappleye (Eds.), *Reimagining Japanese Education: Borders, Transfers, Circulations, and the Comparative* (pp. 107–126). Oxford, UK: Symposium Books Ltd.

'Tsūyaku kaizai yomenu kanjō' [Interpreter Mediation: Unable To Interpret Feelings]. (2009b, October 8). *Asahi shimbun*, 29.

Watanabe, O. (1998). Tsūyakunin no 'ibasho'. In O. Watanabe & H. Nagao (Eds.), *Gaikokujin to Keiji Tetsuzuki: tekisei na tsūyaku no tameni* (pp. 10–15). Tokyo, Seibundō.

Woolard, K.A. (1998). Language ideology as a field of enquiry. In B.B. Schieffelin, K.A. Woolard, & P.V. Kroskrity (Eds.), *Language Ideologies: Practice and Theory* (pp. 3–47). Oxford: Oxford University Press.

Yoshida, R. (2014). *Court interpreting and linguistic ideology: anthropological linguistic analysis of court discourse mediated by an interpreter.* Unpublished doctoral dissertation, Rikkyō University, Tokyo, Japan.

6 Metrolingual Tokyo
"C'est un Peu Difficile, mais it's very Fan desu yo"

Emi Otsuji

A SOCIOLINGUISTICS OF MOBILITY: FROM 'LANGUAGE-IN-PLACE' TO 'LANGUAGE-IN-MOTION'

Due to the increasing mobility of people, artifacts, languages, and ideas across borders, people are bringing different cultural, social, and language ideologies and practices to their everyday interactions. Within the domain of sociolinguistics, a significant number of studies deal with this phenomenon under the name of 'multilingualism.' While these studies attempt to capture the manifold and dynamic nature of language through a celebration of multiplicity, their models of diversity tend to pluralize languages and cultures. These models align with one of the dominant underlying ideologies of multilingualism and multiculturalism, which sees them as being composed of multiple discrete languages and cultural practices.

A recent movement in bi- and multilingual studies has moved beyond these understandings. (Auer & Wei 2007; Bailey 2007; Blommaert 2010; Heller 2007a, c; Jørgensen 2008; Møller 2008; García and Li Wei 2014). It sees national and cultural boundaries as the result of particular language ideologies, emphasizes the limitations of thinking in terms of discrete languages, and suggests a focus on the linguistic features, items, styles, and codes of mixed-language use; for example, the use of 'multilingual' resources in the everyday. 'Everyday culturalism'—"a grounded approach to looking at everyday practice and lived experience of diversity in specific situations and spaces of encounter" (Wise & Velayutham 2009: 3)—is the main concern of this chapter, which focuses on the everyday practices and co-constitutions of people, space (city), and language in Tokyo.

The move towards thinking in terms of an everyday linguistic practice is associated with a rethinking of space. Like cultural geographers such as Massey (1991), who problematize the identification of place in terms of bounded and coherent social groups, sociolinguists have recognized that their "traditional attention to fixed places and moments, or to fixed groups, no longer provides the tools to investigate the kinds of questions we are now asking" (Heller & Duchêne, 2011: 14). In light of this awareness, Blommaert (2010) proposes that linguistic phenomena should be investigated in terms of a 'sociolinguistics of mobility' and 'sociolinguistics of globalization.' Linguistic mobility has thus become one of the main concerns in the field of (socio) linguistics (Blommaert 2010; Pennycook 2012). This epistemological turn claims that a society or a place should no longer be conceived of as a bounded flat surface in which a particular language is used, but instead it should be seen as practices that are open to change, negotiation, and new possibilities through mobile language use. This shift away from deterministic associations between language/community/society and space is one ramification of mobility within globalization.

The broad theme in this chapter concerns mobility and the city: that is, the intense diversity that occurs as people are brought together in urban spaces. The primary objective of this chapter is to link language practices more intimately to the city by elucidating and deploying the notion of metrolingualism, a term describing the use of multilingual resources in urban contexts (Otsuji & Pennycook 2010, 2011). Metrolingualism opens up a new way of thinking about multilingualism centered on the everyday use of mobile linguistic resources in relation to urban space. Urban linguistic practices entail the conversion of "peculiarly large, intense and heterogeneous constellations of trajectories" (Massey 2005: 154) of people, places, and languages. Inspired by a conception of space (Massey 2005; Thrift 2007) as dynamic, social, and open to practices of becoming, metrolingualism is concerned with how the city refashions urban language (users) and how this in turn remakes the city, i.e., how the city and everyday language practices and users co-constitute each other. Its interest is not so much on mapping and fixing the languages of a city (looking at the distribution of languages) or on a people (listing the languages individuals can speak) but on the connectivity and mobility of people and their language practices (Otsuji & Pennycook 2014, Pennycook & Otsuji 2014a). Therefore, rather than viewing hybrid language use as a constellation of discrete languages A, B, and C (additive monolingualism), the basic concept of metrolingualism begins with mobile and hybrid linguistic practices to examine ways in which linguistic space is produced. Using Tokyo as a research site, this chapter scrutinizes a number of basic assumptions about multiple language use by rethinking what it means to mobilize particular linguistic resources—'Japanese,' 'English,' 'Italian,' 'French'—in an urban 'multilingual' context within globalization[1] by explicating metrolingualism.

In order to capture the mobility of language and people across urban space, unlike previous metrolingual research that has focused on the linguistic traffic of a particular location (Pennycook & Otsuji 2014a, b), the data here instead focus on the linguistic practice of individuals to show how they deploy different spatial and linguistic repertoires and practices in an urban context. Audio data (conversation and semistructured interview) are drawn from over 30 hours of recorded and transcribed data collected in Tokyo. In addition to the audio recordings, the researcher accompanied the participants in their daily activities on a number of occasions and asked them to keep diaries focusing on language-related activities for a period of up to one month. There are also data from participants' later reflections on the recorded conversations. Data used for this chapter are collected from Takeshi and Satoko, both of whom are ethnically Japanese; except for their short visits as tourists, neither have ever lived overseas but have extensive involvement in a foreign language and culture in their everyday lives. These data were chosen because they illustrate that linguistic mobility is not exclusively an artifact of human mobility and migration across borders, but it is a mind-set and lifestyle available to people in an urban context.

QUALE VA BENE (*EITHER LANGUAGE IS GOOD*)

外国人のイベントなどで、わざわざ海外へ出て行かなくて も、日本に居ながら外国にいるような雰囲気を味わうことも できる (*Even if I do not go overseas, it is possible to enjoy the feeling of being overseas by attending events organised by foreigners*[2])

This remark was made by Takeshi, an ethnic Japanese in his late thirties. Takeshi, apart from a few short holidays in Europe (each approximately two weeks), has never lived outside of Japan. His fascination with foreign languages and cultures can be traced back to his secondary-school days; growing up in Kyoto, he had Italian pen pals, watched foreign films (mainly American and European), and listened to Italian and French pop music on the radio. Takeshi studied English through formal Japanese school education for six years, German through elective subjects at university for two semesters, and Italian through a language school in the central part of Tokyo for two years (one evening a week). His language diary showed his curiosity and engagement with various languages and cultural practices on a daily basis. Although his proficiency levels varied among the languages, he wrote e-mails to American, German, Italian, and Japanese friends (in English, Italian, and Japanese), used the English language for his computer software setup, posted comments on Facebook (in English, French, Italian, and Japanese), and went out with English- and Italian-speaking friends in Tokyo.

As a business owner, Takeshi develops and sells mobile phone applications and provides IT support to both Japanese and non-Japanese clients, making use of both his linguistic and technical knowledge. In Excerpt 1, Takeshi is giving advice to his client, Rosabella, who is developing Japanese grammar dictionary software for Italian speakers. Rosabella is ethnically Italian, in her early forties, and lives in Tokyo. She had been introduced to Takeshi through a mutual Italian contact. The conversation was held in Rosabella's house at her dining table during the first meeting between Takeshi and Rosabella.

Excerpt 1[3]

(Italian: underlined words; Japanese: Japanese characters; English: plain. Italian and Japanese translations are provided in parentheses in italics.)

1. T: <u>Sì sì sì</u> (*yes yes yes*)
2. R: <u>In quel caso, per il</u> copyright <u>non devrebbero esserci problemi</u> (*Now we should not have any copyright problems*)
3. T: To avoid the problem of copyright OK [spoken in Italian-like intonation]
4. R: <u>Penso</u> (*I think*) I think if it is a closed and only educational site, then, with the password of the students, uhh, then I think there is no problem with the copyright
5. T: <u>Sì ho capito</u> (yes I got it)
6. R: Thus, that's uhh our big problems. But, but . . . 英語でいいの？どっちでも . . . (*is English ok? Whichever one.*)
7. T: hahaha . . . <u>Quale va bene</u> (*either one is good*)
8. R: うん、うん　まあ (*yes, yes, but*)
9. T: <u>Ti piace. Quella che preferisci</u> (*as you like, you can chose the one you like*)

In this excerpt, not only are the interlocutors ambivalent about language choice, but the ascription of languages to these resources appears more complex than the underline and italic transcriptions suggest. The excerpt starts with Takeshi's utterance "si si si" in Italian in response to Rosabella's explanation of copyright issues in a previous turn. Rosabella, in Line 2, continues: "In quel caso, per il copyright non devrebbero esserci problemi" (*Now we should not have any copyright problems*). While the word 'copyright' is ostensibly 'English,' the word does not seem to sit easily with language labels; it is a well-adapted loan word both in 'Japanese' and in 'Italian.' Rosabella commented, in her later reflections on the conversation, "Copyright is 'diritti d'autore' but we use 'copyright' too. In this conversation I used it as Italian." The fact that the word 'copyright' exits in all Italian, English, and Japanese languages renders its status ambiguous. The conversation continues and in Line 3, Takeshi confirms in 'English' what Maria has said. In this utterance, although syntactically and lexically he was speaking in 'English,' his intonation pattern, influenced by 'Italian,' is almost identical to that of Rosabella's in the preceding turn. While Takeshi is ostensibly speaking in 'English,' Takeshi's utterance in Line 3 represents a form of language mix: 'English' vocabulary and syntax with an 'Italian' phonological pattern, showing the arbitrary and indeterminate border between languages. 'English' and 'Italian' are heavily mixed, and this pattern continues until Line 6 when Rosabella asks, this time in 'Japanese,' if it is okay to use English. After stating that either language is okay, they continue to mix 'English,' 'Japanese,' and 'Italian' within and between sentences throughout the five-hour meeting. The examination of Excerpt 1 shows that while some utterances more readily align with particular languages, an identificatory orientation takes us only so far (Otsuji & Pennycook 2010).

The next two related excerpts also demonstrate the complexity of language choice observed in the conversation between Takeshi and Rosabella. Excerpt 2A is an utterance from Takeshi during the meeting. Excerpt 2B includes some of the reflection comments on this utterance after Takeshi and Rosabella had listened to the audio data. Takeshi's comments ('*t' in parentheses) were inserted in the transcript when he initially transcribed the data and Rosabella added hers ('*r' in parentheses) when she checked the transcription.

Excerpt 2A

> T: Ahh, io non con.tatto con questo PC, perché, ehh, non c'è, ahh, non instollato, ehh. (*Well, I did not connect this PC, because it [the software] is not there I did not install it on this PC.*)

Excerpt 2B

> T: Ahh, io non (*t* 'ho' should have been inserted here) con. . . . tatto (*r* Maybe he wanted to say <u>connesso?</u>) con questo PC, perché, ehh, non c'è, ahh, non (*t* 'ho' should have been inserted here) instollato (*t* I tried to say 'install' in English in an Italian sounding way. The correct expression would have been 'installato'), ehh.

Takeshi's comment "I tried to say 'install' in English in an Italian sounding way" at the end of Excerpt 2B shows his capacity for linguistic improvisation, making use of his English resources to create an 'Italian' word. Rosabella commented that she notices Takeshi sometimes creates Italianate words by drawing on his 'English' knowledge and that this neither bothers her nor prevents her from understanding him. This shows a relaxed understanding of the different ways of reinventing 'Italian.' Here the language use between Rosabella and Takeshi shows ad hoc and fluid characteristics.

The conversation between Rosabella and Takeshi in Excerpt 1 does not appear to have a preferred language choice; 'Italian,' 'Japanese,' and 'English' were mixed throughout the meeting. Although Takeshi has a sense of a 'correct Italian' language reflected in his Excerpt 2B remarks such as "'ho' should have been inserted here" and "the correct expression would have been 'installato,'" I question what constitutes correctness and what it means to be correct in this hybrid space. Rather than examining such language practices through the predominant linguistic ideologies of a static structure representing a 'correct' grammar, an exchange like this can be read as a registration of the various ways in which cultural and linguistic practices (of 'Japanese,' 'Italian,' and 'English') are being relocated and reinvented in local, everyday practices in Tokyo.

Makoni and Pennycook (2007) argue that language is a social, political, and historical construct, and they propose the need for its disinvention and reconstitution. Furthermore, Pennycook (2010) addresses the importance of looking at local linguistic practices in terms of what language does as a form of action at a specific place and time. Taking on these theoretical strands, what sort of local and global linguistic practices are exemplified by "Quale va bene (*either one is good*)"? For Rosabella and Takeshi, language choice is secondary to a multitude of practical paths to communication, a priority illustrated by the subsequent difficulty in labeling a term such as 'copyright' as either 'English' or 'Japanese,' as well as by the intonation applied by Takeshi and his lexical inventions such as 'instollato.' In this space, it is not so much about 'which language' is spoken but about getting things done by bringing in various linguistic resources. The speakers 'improvise' using various linguistic resources to create new meaning and linguistic space. This, in turn, may contribute to disinventing and reinventing language ideologies.

The focus of metrolingualism, as was stated earlier, is the everyday language use in urban context. Although language mix exemplified in the interactions between Takeshi and Rosabella, could occur in nonurban interactions, for example, between a Japanese and Japanese Brazilian speaking in so-called 'truncated language,' (Blommaert 2010) i.e., a bit of Japanese and a bit of Portuguese, the 'metro' element present here is linked to lifestyle and the intensity and accessibility of linguistic diversity where the intersection of a variety of languages, people, and activities is prominent. Takeshi had the opportunity to access face-to-face Italian classes, foreign friends, and foreign customers for his business. In this regard, metrolingualism is characterized by the integration of diverse linguistic resources and activities in the city and the harmonizing (or conflicting) moments of adjustment of these linguistic resources. Its concern lies in the ways in which linguistic resources, activities, and urban space are bound together (Pennycook & Otsuji 2014a, b).

'C'EST UN PEU DIFFICILE, MAIS IT'S VERY FANDESUYO' (*IT'S A BIT DIFFICULT BUT IT'S VERY FUN*)

Satoko is another example of someone who has never lived abroad but is keen to be involved in various linguistic and cultural practices on a daily basis in Tokyo. At the time of data collection, Satoko was in her midforties, married, and had a teenage daughter. Several years after her university graduation and one year after she had had a child, she went back to study French at a French language school in Tokyo, an escape from her everyday routine of looking after her baby facilitated by leaving the child with her mother-in-law, who was then living with her. She has since studied French over the last fifteen years. She works part-time for a national research institution in Tokyo three days a week. She also holds English and French tour guide licenses that she obtained while she was raising her child.

Excerpt 3 is a Skype text chat between Satoko, Mari, her university friend from Tokyo who lives in Australia, and Anna, Mari's colleague. Mari is originally from Japan but had been living in Australia for fifteen years at the time of data collection. Mari speaks English and Japanese. Anna is an Australian with a Greek ethnic background and is married to a Frenchman. She speaks English, Greek, and French. Although Satoko and Anna have never met in person, they were introduced to each other by Mari when Anna's brother-in-law Mathis was looking for an interpreter for his business trip to Tokyo about one year prior to this Skype text chat.

In Excerpt 3, Mari and Anna are chatting in Mari's office when Satoko contacts Mari via Skype.

Excerpt 3

(The text is an exact copy of the original chat, including original typographical and spelling errors. French and Japanese translations are provided in parentheses in italics.⁴)

1. [16:18:18] Satoko: おーい (*heey*)
2. [17:10:50] Mari: オフィスで仕事中！アナがいるよ。ちょっとまって。チャットする？(*I am working in the office right now! Anna is here. Wait a min. Do you want to chat?*)
3. [17:11:36] Anna: bonjour satoko (*hi Satoko*)
4. [17:11:41] Anna: c'est Anna (*this is Anna*)
   (a few exchanges)
5. [17:12:49] Satoko: aujourd'hui, c'set un conge national (*Today is a national holiday*)
6. [17:12:57] Satoko: au japon (*in Japan*)
7. [17:13:03] Anna: pour nous la journee est presque fini donc c'est la pause chocolat et conversation (*for us, the day is almost finished, so we are having a chocolate and conversation break*)
8. [17:13:27] Anna: Mari ne sait pas pourquoi c'est un conge national (*Mari does not know why it is national holiday today*)
9. [17:13:32] Satoko: pause chocolat!? (*chocolate break!?*)
10. [17:13:54] Anna: oui on aime beaucoup le chocolat (*yes, we like chocolate very much*)
11. [17:14:23] Satoko: dit lui, c'est National Foudation Day kenkoku kinennbi (*tell her it is a national foundation day kenkoku kinennbi*)
12. [17:14:50] Anna: ohhhhhh Mari n'etait pas au courant! mauvaise Japonaise (*ohhh Mari was not aware! Bad Japanese*)
13. [17:15:20] Satoko: oui, oui, c'es ca (*yes, she is*)

14. [17:15:46] Anna: a bientot je dois donner a manger a mes enfants car il est tard maintenant (*bye, I have to feed my children and it is late now*)
15. [17:16:29] Satoko: a bien tot! dites bonjour a Mathis (*bye, say hi to Mathis*)
16. [17:17:28] Mari: cool!
17. [17:18:06] Mari: i want to learn french
18. [17:19:06] Satoko: c'est un peu difficile, mais it's very fandesuyo (*it's a bit difficult but it's very fun*)
19. [17:19:25] Mari: (rofl[5])

In the Skype text chat, the 'French,' 'Japanese,' and 'English' languages are used (hereafter, single quotation will not be used around the names of language since the problem associated with language labeling has already been established in the aforementioned section). After the initial contact made by Satoko when she saw Mari online, the chat starts with Satoko and Anna communicating with each other (Lines 1–15) until Mari returns in Line 16. Whereas at the beginning of the chat, Lines 1 and 2, Mari communicates in Japanese, in Lines 16 and 17, she writes in English: 'cool' and 'i want to learn French' to which Satoko responds playfully, "c'est un peu difficile, mais it's very fandesuyo." The sentence starts with a French clause "c'est un peu difficile (it's a bit difficult)" and the French connective "mais" (but) is a transition to the English "it's very," followed by the ambivalent phrase "fandesuyo." "(F)an" is supposedly 'fun' in English but is written in Japanese *romaji* (alphabetical orthography system). "Fan" is then followed by the Japanese predicate "desu" and sentence-ending particle "yo," that functions to assert the statement to the listener. In a similar way to Takeshi improvising language with his linguistic resources, Satoko seems to have spontaneously deployed her linguistic resources to improvise the utterance. This again is an example of the integration of linguistic resources available to people and of the ludic harmonizing moments of linguistic resources.

The focal point here is not so much on the ways and patterns in which languages are switched and mixed (Auer 1995, 1999; Milroy & Muysken, 1995; Wei 1998) or on 'correctness' but rather what this linguistic practice "c'est un peu difficile, mais it's very fandesuyo" and other language practices by Anna, Mari, and Satoko are doing from a spatial perspective. In this text chat, 'mistakes' in spelling and grammar were also observed due to the spontaneity and speed of the chat process; for example, when Satoko wrote 'c'set' in Line 5 and 'dit lui' rather than 'dis-lui' in Line 11. However 'correctness,' again, is a construct and not the focus here. The interest here is the context in which the sentence "c'est un peu difficile, mais it's very fandesuyo" emerged, as well as the processes in which this type of linguistic practice localizes global practice.

Any given conversation entails a complex traffic and interaction of multiple trajectories, temporalities, and mobilities of people and space

(Blommaert 2010). The participants in the earlier Skype conversation have distinct linguistic and cultural trajectories and are engaged in the chat by mobilizing the linguistic and cultural resources they have accumulated. By manipulating their resources, each person reproduces, resists, or transgresses linguistic, ethnic, and cultural borders in their local practices. Neither Satoko nor Anna is ethnically French, but they associate with each other through French language and culture. Satoko and Mari, similarly, do not seem to have opted for the language associated with their ethnicity. Mari's English language choices (Lines 17 and 18) may have been triggered by the English space Mari was in, or by the trace of the presence of Anna. Or English may have been deployed as a mode of global capital. When Satoko says "c'est un peu difficile, mais it's very fandesuyo" in Line 18, it is harder to determine a motivation for this move from one linguistic resource to another from the point of view of a conventional language ideology associated with nation-state and ethnicity. Later on, when Satoko was asked about her language use, she could not rationalize the reason for her mixed choices in 'c'est un peu difficile, mais it's very fandesuyo'; her choices seemed rather spontaneous and emergent from the local interaction. This is in line with metrolingualism that "describes the ways in which people of different and mixed backgrounds use, play with and negotiate identities through language [. . .] its focus is not on language systems but on languages as emergent from contexts of interaction" (Otsuji & Pennycook 2010: 246).

While metrolingualism admits ludic possibility in inventing new language practices and identities in the late modern context, there are also serious matters of identity politics at work here in metrolingualism. Akin to students' playful and mocking manipulation of heritage languages to refashion their identities (Blackledge & Creese 2010), an important characteristic of metrolingualism is its capacity to view linguistic practices in terms of their capacity to present possibilities for the change of practices and identities. In this space, discourses such as what it means to speak French or what it means to be Japanese are called into question. Anna, in Line 13, teases Mari as a bad Japanese for not knowing about the Japanese national holiday, and Satoko lightly and teasingly agrees "oui, oui, c'es ca," knowing that Mari is watching over their chat. Anna and Satoko's play with cultural essentialism to tease Mari shows the complex, fluid, and temporal associations between language, territory, and ethnicity, where people with varied ethnic and linguistic background and trajectories, here, an ethnic Greek migrant (although, again, identification of people with a cultural or ethnic background may be problematic in a mobile society) and two 'Japanese' are creating a new space by transgressing linguistic, cultural, and ethnic boundaries. As will be shown in the next section, this is done through the push and pull of linguistic and cultural boundaries between states of fixity and fluidity, and the concomitant capacity to both mobilize and mock essentialized identity ascriptions.

While making multiplicity or instability a central aspect of its discursive framework, it is not possible for metrolingualism to ignore the continued deployment of fixed categories of linguistic and cultural identity. In emphasizing fluid language ideologies, therefore, the conventional language ideologies of correlations between nation, language, and ethnicity should not be completely dismissed, but rather how such relations are produced, resisted, defied, or rearranged needs to be explored (Otsuji & Pennycook 2010).

PUSHING AND PULLING IDENTITY ASCRIPTIONS

Although Takeshi and Satoko showed fluid linguistic practices by improvising with the linguistic resources available to them, the linguistic creativity demonstrated was not completely free from a fixed identification with language and culture. Canut (2009: 99) reminds us "[w]e tease out a so-called 'identity' from the polyphonic discourse, and, ultimately, we guarantee the categories which permit the politics of classifying, creating hierarchies, and monitoring the population." That is, we also live in a world of fixities; and as we seek to identify identities, we all too often reinscribe particular modes of categorization. This raises epistemological questions as to what constitutes 'creativity' in relationship with what is regarded as a conventional practice.

In her performativity theory, Butler (1993; 1997a; 1999a, b) argues for the limits and possibilities of performative acts. The main argument of her notion of performativity is that gender is not pre-given but is the sedimentation of iterative performances; gender is "a set of repeated acts within a highly rigid regulatory frame" (Butler 1999a: 43). Ethnic and cultural identities can similarly be considered constructed through discursive performances including the way we talk, rather than as given (Otsuji 2010). That is, identities, in general, can be understood to emerge in the process and sedimentation of communicative and performative acts of culture and ethnicity. While these performative understandings of culture and ethnicity give us room to become different, they may also regulate our daily practices. As Butler points out "performativity is neither free play nor theatrical self-presentation; nor can it simply be equated with performance" (Butler 1993: 95). Creativity, therefore, is by no means a question of free-willed choice to take up one or another identity, but rather emerges within a "highly rigid regulatory frame" (Butler 1999a: 43) and within an interaction between fixity and the fluidity (Harrisi, Otsuji, & Pennycook 2012; Otsuji & Pennycook 2011). Thus in focusing on the creative, hybrid, and complex urban linguistic practice of metrolingualism, Otsuji and Pennycook (2010, 2014) argue for ways to acknowledge fixed categories as being able to be mobilized as an aspect of hybridity and creativity. As Blackledge and Creese (2008: 535) put it,

If languages are invented, and languages and identities are socially constructed, we nevertheless need to account for the fact that at least some
languages users, at least some of the time, hold passionate beliefs about
the importance and significance of a particular language to their sense
of "identity."

The following statements made by Takeshi and Satoko demonstrate how
their improvisations of linguistic repertoires are performative acts between
fixity and fluidity and part of a metrolinguistic spatial production. We can
glimpse both playfulness and serious matters of identity politics at work.

Takeshi's hobby is "to do things using foreign language. To go and attend
events organized by foreigners"; and, he says, "I have Italian and British
friends in Japan." For Takeshi, speaking other languages is a way to rein-
vent his identity. He notes "I had *akogare* (desire) for Western society," and
"Italian and French are romantic languages and cool." He likes hanging
around with foreigners because "when I am with them, I feel as if I have
become a hero in a film or drama" and "when I speak English, I became a
different Takeshi and when I speak Italian, then again, I become a different Italian Takeshi. My personality and my behavior change. Interesting.
It fills my transformation desire." While he essentializes Japanese and Italian
culture, language, and people, he suggests that this essentialist practice liber-
ates him from an undesirable Japanese 'Takeshi.' This demonstrates on the
one hand that there is a creative, transgressive process of constructing new
linguistic and spatial identities. On the other hand, there is a confirmation
that this creativity and difference is realized in and through the mobilization
of ascriptions of identity along static lines. This is precisely the argument
regarding performative power, drawing on Butler (1997b), that the deple-
tion of a category or term cannot be achieved without applying and therefore
affirming the very term or category that we wish to modify (Harrisi et al.
2012; Otsuji & Pennycook 2010). The complex relationship between a
static understanding of language, nation, and cultural identity and that of a
fluid and hybrid one can be seen here. By breaking with his fixed Japanese
identity in performing an Italian Takeshi, Takeshi is showing the creative
link between the language and ethnic identity and he is transgressing 'Japaneseness.' In doing so, however, he is also essentializing 'Japanese' Takeshi
and the Japanese language as well as Italian culture and people. Takeshi's
practice shows a sense of freedom and creative possibility, but that freedom
and creativity is a result of the interaction between static and fluid cultural
and linguistic identities. In this space, fixing and unfixing is constantly in
motion: by mixing language, choosing a language, improvising language, or
being engaged in "Quale va bene" practice.

In his work on metroethnicity, in which a young Japanese ethnic minority
(*Ainu*) man rewrites his own ethnicities without being able to speak *Ainu*
language by associating himself with Italian culture and language, Maher
(2005: 98) challenges the orthodox notion of ethnicity and writes "you are

a residual ethnic code that is becoming a new, emergent code" and defines metroethnicity as "an exercise in emancipatory politics. It is an individual's self-assertion on his own terms and that will inevitably challenge the ortho- doxy of 'language loyalty.'" Metroethnicity allows the reconstitution of language and an alternative way of being in and through other possibilities of the everyday. Although he had to disguise his *Ainu* background when working in Hokkaido, the *Ainu* protagonist in Maher's study was received as cool in Tokyo, where minorities, diversity, and other subcultures were valued. In Tokyo, 'Ainu-ness,' especially with the creative association with Italian linguistic and cultural knowledge, is not only tolerated but also con- tributes to the diversified subcultural landscape of Tokyo. Takeshi's access to diverse networks and subcultural connections, similarly, enabled him to pursue his transformative desire, and his performance in turn became part of the repertoire of Tokyo.

Satoko, on the other hand, has said that although she likes herself speak- ing in French, she does not particularly have a desire to be a French person or to go to France. Unlike Takeshi, she does not speak French because she thinks it is cool but because she likes 'L'actualité' (news):

> あのね、フランス・・・を知るっていうことは、世界を違う角度か
> ら見るんだなっていうことに、だんだん勉強しながら、思い立っ
> た。(. . .)アメリカのニュース見てても、アフリカのことなんて、ほ
> とんど取り上げられることはないけど、フランスはアフリカとすごく
> 近いし、植民地もあったし、だから、アフリカのことが入ってくる。
>
> (*I learned as I study, knowing France means to look at the world
> from different perspectives (. . .). When I watch American news, they
> hardly take up news about Africa but France is very close to Africa and
> they had colonies so I hear a lot about Africa.*)

Although she does not have a strong desire to be physically mobile and go to Paris, she likes to be 'mobile' by having different perspectives gained from American or Japanese news. She claimed "what I think is important is peace" and "what I aim for is mutual understandings and respect." For Satoko, it is not so much about reinventing herself as a French person, but about reinventing herself as a global citizen. Nevertheless, even for Satoko, someone with a culturally and linguistically open-minded disposition, mobi- lization of a relatively fixed mode of cultural identification was identified in her practice. For example, on the title page of her French blog site, she writes "Je décris ici des histoires quotidiennes et aussi mes impressions sur eux. Découvrez l'acutualité au Japon à travers la vie d'une femme japonais (e)"[6] (*Here I describe daily stories and also my impressions of them. Dis- cover the acutualité in Japan through the life of a Japanese woman*) and explained during the interview that the rationale behind her blog-keeping is "日本が好きだから。日本を好きだから。だから、日本の本当の姿を 外国人に正しく伝えたいと思ったから。" (*Because I like Japan. Because*

I want to tell the real appearance of Japan to foreigners correctly). Her aspiration to bridge cultural differences and to promote world peace is engendered by her global awareness and sensitivity toward national and cultural borders. However, her awareness and sensitivity seems to be supported by essentialist views. For example, she believes that there is a "real appearance of Japan" that can be "discovered." Additionally, her everyday engagements (see more in the text that follows) also show the creative processes in which cultural and linguistic (performative) practices are produced, reproduced, resisted, or rearranged through her associations with English and French. Satoko, therefore, manages—in Tokyo and beyond—the linguistic and cultural resources available to her in and through an interaction between fixity and fluidity. As such, the historically sedimented discourses and practices Satoko engages in both regulate and make possible the performative acts she mobilizes to become different.

For Heller (2007b: 342), bilingualism is a "kind of fault line, a space particularly sensitive to and revealing of social change." Her attention to 'a space' that is created by practices around an ideologically constructed 'fault line' is noteworthy. This 'fault line' engenders a fixed and fluid interplay. It undermines conventional statist correlations between nation, language, and ethnicity while regulating and leading social change. Pennycook (2010:140) writes "the locatedness of language is not just about being in a place at a time, but also about producing that place." If we conceive language as performative, through the interactions between fixed and fluid modes of linguistic and cultural practices, what we are observing here in Takeshi and Satoko's data is their engagement in creating urban linguistic and identity practices and spaces in Tokyo by producing, defining, and, at other times, eliminating, 'fault lines.'

FROM MULTILINGUALISM TO METROLINGUALISM IN TOKYO

Metrolingualism is about the connectivity, diversity, and mobility of people, language, activities, and artifacts in the city (Pennycook & Otsuji 2014b). Satoko's two-week language diary shows her highly culturally and linguistically diverse lifestyle. Her continuous endeavors to enhance her language skills as well as her diverse engagements in multilingual practices in different capacities are apparent. Table 6.1 shows a typical day.

While this is just a snippet of her day, her other entries were not very different in terms of the diversity of linguistic and cultural exposure she experienced. She read novels in Japanese, English, and French and during the month-long, diary-keeping period, she was reading three novels, mainly on the commuting trains: (1) the French novel *La Trace*, (2) *The Edo Inheritance*, originally written in Japanese and translated into

Table 6.1   Satoko's Language Diary

9/6/2011 (Tue)	-Work (RWSL:Japanese, RW:English)	-I am in charge of corresponding with foreign students invited academics about their stay in Japan and taking care of them when they are here.
	-Reading an American Novel "Nights in Rodante" on the train to work (R:English)	-映画の原作になった簡単なもの．会話の参考にしようと思って拾い読みしている．[*an easy read that is the original novel of the film. I am browsing through the book to learn some conversations.*]
	-Read *Le Monde* online (R:French)	-to improve my level of French, I subscribe to online version.
	-Write blogs (W:English, W:French)	- I have 2 sites (English and French) for the purpose of presenting Japanese culture to the world.　記述フランス語難しいと思う．[*I found writing in French is difficult*]
	-アンデスの"星と雪の聖地"への巡礼についてのテレビ番組を観た．(L:Japanese) [*I watched a TV program about a pilgrimage to the 'Holy land of stars and snow' in the Andes*]	-アンデスの人々の純真さに心打たれる．[*I was touched by the genuine heart of people in the Andes*]
	-家族で会話(SL:Japanese) [*conversation with a family*]	-家に侵入したアリの大群の行動パターンとアリの退治方について．子どもが良く観察しているのに感心した．[*a large group of ants entered the house. I was impressed by the close observation made by my child regarding their behavioral patterns and her idea for an exterminating method.*]
	-新聞を読む（R:Japanese）	- Read news papers

English, and (3) an American novel titled *Nights in Rodante*. She went to Italian and Russian restaurants with her friends and colleagues, and took one of her clients (Maltese-French background) to a traditional Japanese teahouse and a temple in Tokyo. Therefore, although it can be argued that a Skype chat and reading French news online are not typically urban practices, reading books on a commuting train, eating in various ethnic restaurants in a city with menus in different languages, and having the opportunity to meet or be exposed to people of various backgrounds may be more typically urban. (In a rural city in Shizuoka, for example, the majority of non-Japanese are Japanese Brazilian and linguistic and cultural diversity is less intense). By the same token, Takeshi's engagement in diversified linguistic practices in Tokyo by mingling with 'foreigners' at different parties may be typically urban. Satoko chose a university in Tokyo and moved from a rural city with a population of 190,000. As a high school student, she immersed herself in the worlds of English and violin when her father remarried. English gave her a sense of belonging and a different life perspective. For Satoko, therefore, moving to Tokyo to study English at a university was for her a lifestyle change and a movement out of a small city. A city is a place where varied people, languages, and objects converge and diverge at a fast speed.

The major part of this chapter was devoted to explicating creative and productive linguistic practices and resources. The application of a multilingualism perspective does not seem to do justice to the data from Takeshi and Satoko if we understand the linguistic practice from a point of view of additive monolingualism. From within its view of discrete languages and identity categories, multilingualism cannot elucidate the comprehensive processes in which linguistic repertoires and features produce space. Whether Satoko reading a French novel on the train, or having a Skype chat with a friend in Australia from her Tokyo office, or Takeshi improvising a word while speaking in a suburban apartment in Tokyo, all belongs to the mobile and emerging linguascape of Tokyo. Thus when Satoko typed "c'est un peu difficile, mais it's very fandesuyo" in her office or when Takeshi improvised the word "instollato," the phrases encompass not only the elements of Japanese, English, French, or Italian, but more importantly space, time, and activities. By adapting space and city as a language modifier, metrolingualism (Pennycook & Otsuji 2015) attempts to frame linguistic practices differently from bilingualism, multilingualism, plurilingualism, and other enumerative strategies premised on the notion of discrete languages. Rather than focusing on people-to-language (language as internalized in the individual and individuals being containers of language and being a multilingual person) or language-to-language (code-switching, code-mixing) relations, the focus is on capturing the productive space and time provided by the contemporary city to produce new language identities. Research on metrolingualism questions assumptions about languages as pre-given, discrete entities used by stable communities. Instead, it claims that language emerges from its use and shows how language users manipulate the multilingual resources that are available. Metrolingualism studies examine the relocalization processes of global activities that are particularly available in urban contexts. As Pennycook (2010: 74) shows, the productive capacity of local language practices "not only localize but also transform what it means to be local." In this way, Satoko and Takeshi, taking part in a metrolingual local practice, transform locality and 'urbanity'; their local practices are enabled by the diversity, mobility, and intensity of global activities at hand.

GLOBALIZATION AND METROLINGUALISM

Language, people, and culture have always been mobile. This mobility, however, has intensified in late modernity and within globalization (Blommaert 2010). Accordingly, a transition from statist understandings of language ideologies in which a particular language is associated with a particular cultural, ethnic, or geographical configuration is required, and this can be done by thinking of language as an emergent practice through an interaction between fixed and fluid modes of identities. This chapter has argued that metrolingualism is open to creative linguistic practices across borders of culture, history, and politics and offers a way to move beyond these terms by focusing on everyday-ness. Unlike government policies such as *koku-saika* (internationalization) and *tabunka kyōsei* (multicultural co-existence), that take a top-down approach by focusing on cultural policies that are premised on the discreteness of cultural diversity, metrolingualism takes a grassroots approach to language practice in relation to the city by unpacking how people live with others and live together linguistically. Pennycook (2010: 128) argues

> [t]he local should not be confused with the small, the traditional, the immutable, since it is also about change, movement and the production of space, the ways in which language practice, such as graffiti writing or talking in the city, create the space in which they happen.

Takeshi and Satoko in this paper are part of the ongoing creation of metrolingual Tokyo. Their linguistic performative acts are enabled by urban (Tokyo) and modern society, but at the same time they also produce Tokyo. From metrolinguistic language ideology, therefore, "Quale va bene" and "c'est un peu difficile, mais it's very fandesuyo" are the local language of Tokyo.

NOTES

1. Single quotation marks are used to indicate that such linguistic categorizations need careful consideration.
2. Translation by the author.
3. Transcription was first done by Takeshi and then double-checked by Rosabella. This allows for accuracy in transcription as well as reflection on the conversation. A follow-up interview was conducted while they were checking the transcripts.
4. Translation by Satoko for all her French data.
5. An online acronym for 'Rolling on Floor Laughing.'
6. This is the actual wording from Satoko's blog. Here, again, it is not so much about the correctness but what she says that is the focus.

REFERENCES

Auer, P. (1995). The pragmatics of code-switching: a sequential approach. In L. Milroy & P. Muysken (Eds.), *One Speaker, Two Languages* (pp. 115–135). Cambridge: Cambridge University Press.

Auer, P. (Ed.). (1999). *Code-switching in conversation: Language, interaction and identity*. London: Routledge.

Auer, P., & Wei, L. (2007). Introduction: Multilingualism as a problem? Monolinguaism as a problem? In P. Auer & L. Wei (Eds.), *Handbook of Multilingualism and Multilingual Communication* (pp. 1–12). Berlin: Mouton de Gruyter.

Bailey, B. (2007). Heteroglossia and boundaries. In M. Heller (Ed.), *Bilingualism: A Social Approach* (pp. 257–274). New York: Palgrave Macmillan.

Blackledge, A., & Creese, A. (2008). Contesting 'language' as 'heritage': Negotiation of identities in late modernity. *Applied Linguistics, 29*(4), 533–554.

Blackledge, A., & Creese, A. (2010). *Multilingualism: A critical perspective*. London: Continuum.

Blommaert, J. (2010). *The sociolinguistics of globalization*. Cambridge: Cambridge University Press.

Butler, J. (1993). *Bodies that matter: On the discursive limit of "sex"*. New York: Routledge.

Butler, J. (1997a). *Excitable speech: A politics of the performative*. London: Routledge.

Butler, J. (1997b). *The psychic life of power*. Standford: Standford University Press.

Butler, J. (1999a). *Gender trouble: Feminism and the subversion of identity* (10th anniversary ed.). New York: Routledge.

Butler, J. (1999b). Performativity's social magic. In R. Shusterman (Ed.), *Bourdieu: A critical reader* (pp. 113–128). Oxford: Blackwell.

Canut, C. (2009). Discourse, community, identity: Processes of linguistic homogenization in Bamako. In F. Mc Laughlin (Ed.), *The Languages of Urban Africa* (pp. 86–102). London: Continuum.

García, O., & Wei, L. (2014). *Translanguaging: Language, bilingualism and education*. London: Palgrave Macmillan.

Harrisi, M., Otsuji, E., & Pennycook, A. (2012). The performative fixing and unfixing of subjectivites. *Applied Linguistics, 33*(5), 524–543.

Heller, M. (2007a). Bilingualism as ideology and practice. In M. Heller (Ed.), *Bilingualism: A Social Approach* (pp. 1–21). New York: Palgrave Macmillan.

Heller, M. (2007b). The future of 'bilingualism'. In M. Heller (Ed.), *Bilingualism: A social approach* (pp. 340–345). New York: Palgrave Macmillan.

Heller, M. (Ed.). (2007c). *Bilingualism: A social approach*. New York: Palgrave Macmillan.

Heller, M., & Duchêne, A. (2011). Pride and profit: Changing discourses of language, capital and nation-state. In A. Duchêne & M. Heller (Eds.), *Language in late capitalism: Pride and profit* (pp. 1–21). London: Routledge.

Jørgensen, J. N. (2008). Polylingal languaging around and among children and adolescents. *International Journal of Multilingualism, 5*(3), 161–176.

Maher, J (2005) Metroethnicity, language, and the principle of Cool. *International Journal of the Sociology of Language, 11*, 83–102.

Makoni, S., & Pennycook, A. (2007). Disinventing and reconstituting languages. In S. Makoni & A. Pennycook (Eds.), *Disinventing and Reconstituting Languages* (pp. 1–41). Clevedon: Multilingual matters.

Massey, D. (1991, June 24–29). A global sense of place. *Marxism Today*, pp. 24–29.

Massey, D. (2005). *For space*. London: Sage.

Milroy, L., & Muysken, P. (Eds.). (1995). *One speaker, two languages: Code-disciplinary perspectives on code-switching.* Cambridge: Cambridge.

Møller, J. S. (2008). Polylingual performance among Turkish-Danes in late-modern Copenhagen. *International Journal of Multilingualism, 5*(3), 217–236.

Otsuji, E. (2010). Where am I from: A metro perspective of sense of origin. In D. Nunan & J. Choi (Eds.), *Language and Culture: Reflective Narratives and the Emergence of Identity* (pp. 186–193). New York: Routledge.

Otsuji, E., & Pennycook, A. (2010). Metrolingualism: Fixity, fluidity and language in flux. *International Journal of Multilingualism, 7*(3), 240–254.

Otsuji, E., & Pennycook, A. (2011). Social inclusion and metrolingual practices. *Journal of Bilingualism and Bilingual Education, 14*(4), 413–426.

Otsuji, E., & Pennycook, A. (2014). Unremarkable hybridities and metroingual practies. In R. Rubdy & L. Alsagoff (Eds.), *The Global-local Interface, Language Choice and Hybridity: Exploring Language and Identity* (pp. 83–99). Bristol: Multilingual Matters.

Pennycook, A. (2010). *Language as a local practice.* New York: Routledge.

Pennycook, A. (2012). *Language and mobility: Unexpected places.* Bristol: Multilingual Matters.

Pennycook, A., & Otsuji, E. (2014a). Metrolingual multitasking and spatial repertoires: 'Pizza mo two minutes coming'. *Journal of Sociolinguistics, 18*(2), 161–184.

Pennycook, A., & Otsuji, E. (2014b). Market lingos and metrolingua francas. *International Multilingual Research Journal, 18*(4), 255–270.

Pennycook, A., & Otsuji, E. (2015). *Metrolingualism: Language in the City.* London: Routledge.

Thrift, N. (2007). *Non-representational theory: Space, politics, affect.* London: Routledge.

Wise, A., & Velayutham, S. (2009). Introduction: Multiculturalism and everyday life. In A. Wise & S. Velayutham (Eds.), *Everyday multiculturalism* (pp. 1–17). Houndmills: Palgrave.

Part III
Pedagogical Transition

7 "To Know What It's Like to be Japanese"

A Case Study of the Experiences of Heritage Learners of Japanese in Australia

Robyn Moloney and Susan Oguro

INTRODUCTION

Traditionally, discussions of Japanese language pedagogy have commonly included the notions of Japanese as a Second Language (JSL) within Japan and of Japanese as a Foreign Language (JFL) in educational contexts beyond the nation of Japan. However, the growing global population of Japanese diaspora has seen the emergence of a new group of language learners known as heritage language learners. School-aged children are included within this group and also have specific needs for formal Japanese language instruction as part of their education. As a result, there is a change in understanding of Japanese language learning in formal education contexts. A case study of the experiences of heritage learners of Japanese in Australia is the focus of this chapter.

Within this chapter, the identity development of adolescent Japanese Australians is explored, focusing in particular on the factors that shape the construction of an identity, which includes being Japanese despite not growing up in Japan. Specifically, case studies are presented exploring aspects of identity and language development in two young adults who have grown up in Sydney, Australia, and whose parents are first-generation Japanese migrants. An analysis of interview data traces their family backgrounds, the impact of the opportunities they had to study Japanese in educational settings, and the relationship between their Japanese language literacy and their sense of identification as Japanese. This chapter considers, through its two case studies, how these learners use Japanese as a heritage language, and what their construction of multilingual identities through their language practices may mean.

While the term 'heritage' is defined differently in various contexts (e.g., Brinton, Kagan, & Baukus 2008; Kondo-Brown 2006; Mercurio & Scarino 2005; Valdés 2001), we find the notion of 'Japanese as a heritage language' useful when describing the use of Japanese by children growing up in Australia in families with connections to Japan. Such children either migrated from Japan to Australia in childhood or, as is more commonly the case, were born in Australia with one or both parents Japanese. The children typically have been educated primarily through English but have also had contact with Japanese through their family and/or community. As users of multiple languages, the heritage language learners typically interact in both their heritage language (in this case, Japanese) and the language of the majority community (in this case, English) within different social contexts. Although comparatively smaller than many other ethnic communities in Australia, the Japanese community has grown significantly in recent times. While it is impossible to ascertain precisely how many children are growing up as speakers of Japanese as a heritage language in Australia, previous research (Oguro & Moloney 2010) looking at enrollments of children in Japanese community language schools has pointed to the growing number of children attending, particularly since the mid-1990s. Thomson (2013), drawing on Cardona et al. (2008), also reports that the number of students attending Japanese community language schools in New South Wales increased by 344.9% between 1995 and 2007, although the overall number is relatively smaller at 605 in 2007 compared to languages such as Arabic, Mandarin, or Greek.

The development of heritage language proficiency not only assists children in fulfilling their linguistic needs, but in the process it also contributes to their developing identities. (Carriera 2004). However, provision of appropriate courses of formal study in the heritage language is often problematic, as heritage language speakers do not tend to match the profile of 'native' speakers of the language, nor typical classroom 'foreign' language learners (Kagan 2005; Kondo-Brown 2006). As Valdés (2005) describes, heritage language speakers are a different type of language learner since, unlike learners of Japanese as a foreign language who learn in formal institutional contexts, they typically acquire their language skills in a variety of contexts, including at home, with extended family, and in the community. The language input they receive may be limited to the domestic context, and their understanding of syntax, vocabulary, genre, and many other aspects of language may, without formal study, develop as incomplete and before the emergence of literacy (Montrul 2010). While analyses of the linguistic profiles of heritage language speakers are useful, more recently the argument for deeper and more nuanced considerations of the complex connection between language, literacy, and identity issues has been made (e.g., Lo-Philip 2010). This chapter builds on this by offering two illustrative case studies that explore a sociocultural analysis of the experiences of heritage learners of Japanese in Australia. We first provide a discussion of the relationship between the contested notion of identity and language development, and its application to the particular context of this study.

IDENTITY AND LANGUAGE DEVELOPMENT

We have struggled with the use of the term 'identity' in our observation of what may be constituent elements of identity in the two case studies, and in our analysis of the relationship between identity and heritage language. The concept of identity has been the site of much contention and of division between academic disciplines, which has shaped differences in definition (Lawler 2008). Hall (1990) and Bhabha (1990) have dismantled the notion that an identity can be static or essential. Instead, they support the notion of identity as unfixed, multiple, fluid, and constantly emerging. Linguistic and cultural identities are derived from and maintained through the fluid nature of social interaction and culture. Block (2006) observes that 'identity' is frequently conceptualized in the media as involving an exclusive choice between distinct identity options, implying that there are a finite number of fixed identities from which people can choose. This is in contrast to the interpretation of identity as socially constructed, that is, something that is constructed through interaction and negotiation with others (Cummins 1996, 2000, 2003; Lave & Wenger 1991; McNamara 1987, 1997; Norton 2000).

This study adopts a broad conception of the sociocultural nature of identity examination, where the boundaries between social and cultural identity are blurred. Identity as a sociocultural construct may be marked as dynamic, complex, and contradictory, constructing and being constructed by language and influenced by larger social processes (Norton 2006). As part of this complexity, different aspects of identity may be of different importance to the person at different times (Omoniyi 2006). However, as Fought (2006) found, language is a key element in the process, as it assists individuals in balancing the various roles and aspects of their identities. Bilingual individuals may position themselves between two languages and two (or more) cultures (Kanno 2003) as they create a new hybrid identity for themselves. Doer and Lee (2013) have scrutinized how the heritage language learner is 'constructed' through processes of contestation and negotiation, which shape particular behaviors regarding learning attitudes and performance.

Endeavoring to represent some of this broader conceptualization, scholars have struggled with the limitations of the term 'identity' and have moved to a focus on the process of identification (Block 2006; Omoniyi 2006). Similarly, Lo-Philip (2010) has chosen to use the term 'identity processes' in an effort to reflect the "multiple dynamic relationships between language and social/individual identity" (Lo-Philip 2010: 282), and He (2006) uses the term 'identity' as related to the form of the verb 'to identify.' In this chapter, we believe this is appropriate to the analysis of the two cases where we see that identity is not a collection of fixed attributes, but rather an active process of continual emerging and becoming, an uneven process that identifies what a person becomes and achieves through ongoing interactions with others (Bucholtz & Hall 2004). As Hall (1992) argues, because heritage language users move across languages and cultures, identity is a production that is never complete but always in process. Group membership and "belonging" (Weeks 1990: 88) are important factors that contribute to better learning of the heritage language and essential in shaping student identities (Kanno 2003).

To understand the two young adult heritage learners' negotiation of identity described here, it is also important to consider the ways in which development in a heritage language has been conceptualized in the literature and has shaped approaches to research. A 'correlational' approach (He 2010) has been useful in identifying variables, or correlations, that can be important in heritage language learning (e.g., Gibbons &Ramirez 2004; Jia 2008). This has supported the development of proficiency-based instruments to assist placement in courses and the development of differentiated curriculum (Kondo-Brown 2010). However, He (2010) is critical of this approach insofar as its evaluation of complex constructs in terms of numerical values leads us to think that these variables produce essential, built-in, and unchanging qualities.

An alternative approach to heritage language research, which is the approach taken by this study, focuses on analyzing the organization of communicative practices through which heritage language learners acquire or maintain sociocultural knowledge, interactional competence, and literacy. The forms of language and the sociocultural contexts of language use become symbiotic with each other.

A sociocultural approach changes how heritage language development is perceived and enables it to be understood in new ways (He 2010). Knowing a heritage language does not only mean one commands syntax, but understands a set of continually changing norms and expectations. It is the way in which a heritage language is *used* that will directly impact how learners perceive the language and its culture. Most importantly, to capture the picture of Japanese heritage language culture operating within Australian mainstream culture, we need to engage with a context that encompasses the construction of multiple, compatible, congruent identities, as well as blended, blurred identities in multilingual and multicultural contexts. The aim of these two case studies was to identify the experiences of two heritage learners of Japanese in the Australian context and determine how those experiences have shaped the emergence of identity processes.

Before discussing how the sense of identity as Japanese has developed for the two young adults in this study, some contextual information on the courses in Japanese language available through the education system for heritage learners is now provided.

COURSES OF JAPANESE AS A HERITAGE LANGUAGE IN SCHOOLS

For Japanese Australian children, there is naturally great variability between families in the degree and frequency of contact with Japanese society and community. This variability means that as learners of Japanese as a heritage language, the children differ enormously in the level of exposure to and opportunity to acquire knowledge of Japanese life, culture, history, and language. Our previous research (Oguro & Moloney 2010) has highlighted Australian teachers' perceptions of the limitations of heritage learners' background knowledge of Japan.

Before we turn to the specific experiences of the two learners of Japanese as a heritage language in this study, additional contextual information is required concerning the provision of Japanese courses for adolescents within the school system in the state of New South Wales. The two cases that follow refer to learners' experiences of exclusion from courses of Japanese for the final two years of secondary education. These final two years of schooling culminate in state-wide centrally administered matriculation examinations, the results of which determine access to tertiary education.

At the time of data collection, in the state of New South Wales where this study took place, courses in Japanese available for matriculation study included a course known as 'Japanese Continuers' (Board of Studies NSW 2009) designed for learners who had studied Japanese in junior secondary school (Years 7–10) and who wished to continue in the final two years of schooling (Years 11 and 12). Eligibility criteria exist for students wishing to take the Continuers course and are based on educational experience, history of residency, and use of Japanese outside the classroom. Specifically, students are only accepted for the course if they "do not use the language for sustained communication outside the classroom with someone with a background in using the language" (Board of Studies NSW, n.d.). An additional course in Japanese is available at the senior secondary level and is known as 'Japanese Background Speakers.' The level of literacy in Japanese expected in this course (Board of Studies NSW 2012: 19) corresponds to the level of literacy Japanese required of students who have completed Year 9 in the school system in Japan (Ministry of Education, Culture, Sports, Science and Technology Japan 2008). The course is typically undertaken by students whose first language is Japanese and who have moved to Australia from Japan while junior high school students.

RESEARCH METHODS

This chapter extends our previous work, which examined curriculum provision for heritage speakers of Japanese in Australia (Oguro & Moloney 2010, 2012). The data reported in this chapter are drawn from a larger project involving 52 recent graduates from secondary school who identified themselves as having a 'Japanese Family Background' and related their experiences of studying Japanese at senior secondary school in Australia through an online questionnaire. A specific definition of a 'Japanese Family Background' was intentionally not provided to allow participants to interpret and claim that identity if desired. The data therefore included participants born in Japan, Australia, or elsewhere and with either one or both parents originally from Japan.

At the end of the questionnaire, respondents were also asked to participate in follow-up individual interviews in English to explore more deeply their learning history and attitudes to formal study of Japanese. The data discussed in this chapter were collected from two female participants age 19 and 20, who agreed to be interviewed and have been given the pseudonyms of Akiko and Maki. Their particular stories were selected as they offered more extensive explanations and details of their life experiences and provided a rich data set.

This chapter draws its findings from interview data in which participants described their Japanese learning experiences. The two cases enable the examination of participant voice and perspective, of different life stages, multiple domains of development, and of the co-constructed interactive nature of learning activities. As a qualitative study, it places emphasis on comprehensive in-depth understanding to construct the meaning of particular events to those involved. Its aim is to understand events through the eyes of the participants.

From the transcribed interview data, we constructed chronicled accounts of the participants' experiences, in which the participants' own words are featured (the interviews were conducted in English). In this chapter they are presented as their 'stories.' We then discuss the processes of construction of identities in consideration of themes emerging in the participants' stories. The participants' voices are heard throughout the accounts and in the discussion of identity construction. The study acknowledges the role and assumptions of the researchers as a possible factor impacting on how the data is 'seen' (Russell & Kelly 2002) and interpreted. The nature of the engagement in dialogue, necessary for interview data, involves the researcher participating in 'co-responsible inquiry.' (Glesne & Peshkin 1992; Wardekker 2000)

EXPERIENCES OF THE TWO PARTICIPANTS:
MAKI AND AKIKO

This section offers a summary of the reconstructed narratives for Maki and Akiko respectively. Following this, a discussion of both participants' experiences considers the processes of construction of identity.

Maki's Story

Maki was born in Japan and both her parents are first generation Japanese migrants to Australia. In terms of her early language use, she reported that when she was one year old, the family moved from Japan to Hong Kong where she learned English in nursery school and in her peer play. Her parents communicated with her in Japanese, but she said she replied to them in English, and this pattern continued throughout her schooling. At the age of seven, Maki moved to Australia with her parents, and she entered an

Australian school, continuing her education in English. It was not until the beginning of secondary school that she commenced study of Japanese in a beginner-level course, the scope of which was limited and the language level elementary. She pursued this formal study through Years 7–10 (the first four years of secondary school).

While growing up, Maki said she used Japanese occasionally on the telephone with relatives and also when she made short trips to visit family in Japan. She described her spoken Japanese at that time as competent for a narrow range of family situations, but with errors and without knowledge of social register. For example, concerning her communication with her grandparents, she describes that she felt:

> My grandparents probably want me to talk closer to them. Because I use a *desu-masu* form to them I think they find that uncomfortable because I'm their grandchild and they want me to be closer.

The '*desu-masu*' form she refers to is more formal register of Japanese, not normally used between family members. Maki described this as her "sociable problem," and it led to her decision at age 13 to start attending weekly individual tutoring in Japanese outside-school hours: "I realized I really had to do something about my Japanese because I wanted to be able to communicate with my grandparents mainly, better."

Maki reported continuing to take private lessons in Japanese for three years, and she planned to include Japanese as one of her subjects for her final two years of secondary schooling, culminating in matriculation university-entrance examinations. As described earlier, two courses in Japanese were available options to her in the senior secondary years: the Japanese Continuers Course and the Japanese Background Speakers Course. Maki was deemed ineligible for the 'Japanese Continuers' course, as she was judged by the school system to have a linguistic advantage. She considered taking the Background Speakers Course but was alarmed by the perceived difficulty level of the course designed for native speakers of Japanese:

> I knew I wouldn't be able to keep up. It was also the idea of knowing that the majority of the people who do Background Speakers in Japanese are usually top speakers of Japanese. They would mainly be people who have lived in Japan until quite recently and so I knew I couldn't keep up with them. I've had close to no formal education of Japanese. I just gave up, to be honest.

Without the motivation and purpose of senior secondary study, she discontinued the independent private tutoring in Japanese. Maki expressed anger and regret that she did not study Japanese for her final years of secondary schooling, particularly as she had invested effort in three years of private study and had been personally motivated to develop her level of proficiency in Japanese. She commented that the loss of the final two years of study of Japanese resulted in a loss of language skills:

> What I had done . . . it all disappeared by the end of the Year 12, so I thought that was a waste . . . I wish I had done it because I had improved in writing, especially the kanji. I had actually lost all that because of the two years.

However, when Maki had finished secondary school and entered university, she chose to pick up her Japanese study once again. Although she could have enrolled in higher-level Japanese courses, she chose to do Japanese courses designed for nonbackground speakers, "because I wanted to learn to write again."

Maki said she plans to be a teacher of Japanese and English in Australian schools. She also hopes to live in Japan for a year or more. When asked about her identification, Maki is ambivalent, describing an emerging multiple identity that embraces Australia, Japan, and broader interests:

> Japanese by blood, by nationality I like to consider myself Japanese at the heart as well. I'm very traditional . . . there are parts of me that I picked up from Australia; I think I have different qualities in different things . . . It's kind of difficult to say where I am. But I think I've decided to be Japanese and to stand up for being Japanese as well. I describe myself as being Japanese, with a bit of international qualities.

Akiko's Story

Both of Akiko's parents were born and grew up in Japan, but Akiko was born and has lived her whole life in Australia. Until the age of five, she reported she spoke only Japanese, and she learned English only from the point of entering school. Her contact with a Japanese-speaking community included accompanying her parents on annual visits to Japan and attending a Japanese Community Language Program school every Saturday morning from Years 1 to 9. These schools commonly use curriculum materials identical to those used in the school system in Japan as supplied by the Japanese government. The schools seek to construct an experience of participation in a Japanese-style primary school, including aiming for learners to achieve a level of Japanese literacy and reproducing cultural markers of the Japanese school year, sports, festivals, and carnivals.

Akiko reported that her nine years at the Japanese community school provided her constant enjoyable opportunities to speak Japanese outside the family and read a wide variety of books for pleasure:

> I gained a lot of Japanese, because there was someone to talk to other than my parents, and learning from the books from Japan, and the books from the library there, like manga, I always borrowed books.

Akiko's literacy development in Japanese was thus comparable to children learning the Japanese curriculum in Japan. She acknowledged that she may now still lack some vocabulary for specialist technical details, but otherwise she is competent in speaking, listening, reading, and writing in Japanese:

> We have NHK [Japan Broadcasting Corporation] news, I've listened often, there are words like economic, political, I have to ask my parents, but normal TV is OK, I can understand everything.

In secondary school, Akiko studied Japanese along with Australian beginners, in Years 7 and 8, but she reported:

> They made me quit and do Commerce, since I wouldn't be able to do the Continuers Course in senior years, I would have had to take Background Speakers, and that would be too difficult.

That is, perceived by her school as too proficient for the Japanese Continuers course (to which her classmates would proceed in their senior secondary years), she was excluded from participating even in the Year 9 and 10 Japanese classes and forced to take another subject in its place. Akiko was "very disappointed" by her exclusion from Japanese study at her school. She was also angered by inequities she saw across schools, as she knew of friends who were heritage speakers of Japanese who had been assessed differently and deemed eligible by their schools to take the Japanese Continuers Course. This discrepancy is due to the fact that the entry assessment relies on a subjective decision by each individual institution. The interpretation of the aforementioned entry requirement that the candidates 'do not use the language for sustained communication outside the classroom with someone with a background in using the language' (Board of Studies NSW, n.d.) could vary across institutions.

When starting Year 11, Akiko reported she had inadequate understanding of the options available to her for her senior study subjects. Although her strong linguistic skills in Japanese may have been sufficient to take the Japanese Background Speakers course, she was informed by her school that it would probably be too difficult for her. Akiko did not know how the school assessed her eligibility and made the decisions that impacted her. She said she felt "sad and regretful" that she did not attempt the Japanese Background Speakers course. She reflected that her desire to do a senior course was to consolidate her very significant early investment in Japanese language and to get the accredited recognition of her personal linguistic asset for her future career and her future adult identity: "I had advantage coming from a Japanese family, I could get a better idea, get job in future, benefit for my future."

Akiko's exclusion from a course of Japanese study in her senior secondary years necessitated other subject choices that consequently set her upon a different tertiary career choice path. Despite her high-level Japanese language skills, at the time of interview she was deciding between a graphic arts course and a degree in forensics and biology, neither of which involved utilizing her Japanese language ability. When asked about her identification, Akiko described:

> I am a mixture of qualities from both sides; I love both places. I'd like to work sometime in Japan, but don't think I could live there, because of the environment. I love it here, more space.

This statement, along with the dilemma over her study options, gives a glimpse into her multiple identities as both Japanese and Australia. While she appears to embrace her identification with Australia and Japan, she seems to see Australia as her permanent base and Japan as a destination for temporary residence.

PROCESSES OF CONSTRUCTION OF IDENTITY

In the discussion that follows, an analysis of the experiences of Maki and Akiko illustrates some of the processes of construction of an 'identity as Japanese.' While naturally different for the two individuals, their identification as Japanese intimately involves elements of Japanese language and literacy, grounded in relationships with family, and in their participation in Japanese communities and cultures both within Australia and within Japan. Their experiences also reveal the multiple ways in which their identification as Japanese and/or as Japanese speakers is evaluated by themselves and by others. Our discussion is thus divided into the analysis of the following three themes evident in the two cases:

1. The importance of Japanese language for personal relationships
2. The development of reading and writing skills for participation in aspects of Japanese culture
3. The processes of evaluating 'Japanese identities' within and beyond the borders of Japan

The development of the first two themes is informed by theoretical perspectives evident in the work of Cummins (1996, 2000, 2003) and Gee (1988) respectively. Cummins (1996, 2000, 2003) asserts that supporting migrant children's mother tongue is important not only for the development of their overall literacy, but also for their identity negotiation process involving personal relationships. Gee's (1988) claim is that language and literacy are "the root of people's identities and ultimately about the ways in which people situate themselves in the world" (p. 40). The third theme has emerged and been developed in the course of this study.

The Importance of Japanese Language for Personal Relationships

The effort invested at different times, by both the students and their families, in the acquisition of a Japanese linguistic ability indicates how important this is to them. Both students actively took a variety of opportunities to participate in Japanese language learning activities, such as attending Japanese community school, after-school tutoring, and taking Japanese Language Proficiency tests (administered by the Japanese government). These activities all take place beyond Japan's borders but provide a level of affirmation of Japanese language ability.

The two learners' efforts to develop their Japanese language skills were also stimulated by an ongoing desire to have the linguistic capital to respectfully and appropriately negotiate their roles and identities within their respective Japanese families. The cases reveal that both learners are still strongly connected to families in Japan and return to Japan on a regular basis, as well as that their desire to speak to family is a driving force in their development. For example, Maki stated:

> My relatives are all in Japan. So, naturally I would speak Japanese to them . . . If we don't visit them, we'd give them a call . . . My father's side will occasionally send us things . . . so we'd give them a ring to say thank you.

Maki also noted how she had to learn about the appropriate register to use with her grandparents in order to build a good relationship, as shown earlier in her comment. The motivation to speak with her family members (including her grandmother) in an appropriate register was the principal reason that Maki undertook three years of tutoring in Japanese after school. Furthermore, she indicated her pleasure in being able to use her Japanese language to provide emotional support to a member of her extended family:

> I have a second cousin who's younger than me, she kind of bonded to me. We speak in pretty simple terms though. But she's very mature in the way she thinks. It's easy to talk about difficult things like adult situations.

Maki's experience highlights the importance of knowledge of Japanese for family relationships; however, Akiko's accounts show that it is important for relationships outside the family as well. She greatly valued her nine years of participation in the Japanese Community School and in particular noted that it gave her the opportunity to participate in a Japanese community beyond the family ("there was someone to talk to in Japanese other than my parents"). Her comments reflect the findings of Oriyama (2010) that heritage language users' school-based friendships shape language use, attitudes, and cultural identity.

The examples cited by Akiko and Maki show how the forms of language and literacy become symbiotic with the sociocultural contexts of use. Maki's Japanese literacy learning is a process by which she is socialized for group membership, enacting a particular social role, in her Japanese community (Lam 2000). Akiko also projected the significance of language for family communication into future generations when she stated "My children? Definitely love to keep it bilingual, so they can speak to my parents. Family links drive language a bit."

Maki revealed that her Japanese language ability has led her to develop empathy with others in the heritage learner situation. In addition to enjoying tutoring students as a part-time job, she explained that empathy with learners like her is the driving force behind her choice of university course and her decision to become a Japanese language teacher:

> I actually have a personal interest in acquisition of second languages [. . .] For Japanese, I dropped my level a little bit because [. . .] I wanted to know what it was like, to do a course, not being a Background Speaker.

Finally, in relation to others, Maki reflected on how her knowledge of both languages has empowered her to move into a bridging intercultural ability:

> My knowledge of English and my knowledge of Japanese both sort of interact with each other and they help me explain particular levels of politeness, within the English language and Japanese language as well. You can sort of compare when you know both languages in context properly so I think those will be useful, in terms of a user personally, and as a student.

Maki's comment indicates a self-awareness of the metalinguistic abilities afforded by her being positioned between two languages (Kanno 2003). Maki also sees the value of this knowledge in facilitating others' understandings. This willingness echoes other studies that have found that where there is positive identification with bilingualism, children show themselves as being able and willing to help others through the use of their bilingual skills (Diaz Soto 2002; Martinez-Roldan 2003). For both Maki and Akiko, family and community relationships represent the contexts in which they use and develop their Japanese and also contribute to their ongoing negotiation of identities. As Cummins (1996, 2000, 2003) argues, this allows bilingual minority students' overall development and empowerment.

The Development of Reading and Writing Skills for Participation in Japanese Culture

The stories of Maki and Akiko reveal that both made strong investments in developing their skills in reading and writing Japanese. Their reading and writing skills in Japanese enable them to access aspects of the rapidly changing Japanese popular culture that they see as essential to their development and sense of self. Maki's and Akiko's engagement with Japanese written texts can be described as the "consequences for the identities of its users" (Menard-Warwick 2005: 254).

We look firstly at the role played by development of their level of proficiency as readers of Japanese. Through her nine years of attendance at her weekly Japanese community school, Akiko developed her reading and writing skills in Japanese. As a result, as a young adult she possesses the level of literacy required to participate in Japanese print and music culture:

> I go to book shops in Japan, spend hours picking out books I might want to read . . . I pick up books on the top seller list . . . music is very important, I listen to a lot of Japanese music, on my iPod all the time, I love listening to music, pick out words.

Similarly, despite Maki's later start in language learning, she also attached great value to her Japanese literacy ability by independently choosing to complete the highest level of the Japanese Language Proficiency Test. This test, in worldwide operation since 1984, measures reading and listening abilities and certifies "the Japanese-language proficiency of those whose native language is not Japanese" (The Japan Foundation 2012). The reading component of the test focuses on knowledge of Japanese kanji characters (ideographs). Maki said of her achievement of Level N1: "I think that was something like over a thousand (kanji) to be able to read." Maki's achievement is indeed significant as the description of the linguistic competence for level N1 includes the ability

> to read writings with logical complexity and/or abstract writings on a variety of topics, such as newspaper editorials and critiques, and comprehend both their structures and contents [and] to read written materials with profound contents on various topics and follow their narratives as well as understand the intent of the writers comprehensively. (The Japan Foundation 2012)

Reading, which entails extensive knowledge of kanji, is a vital way to access contemporary Japanese culture. Maki's description of her reading ability suggests an alignment with personal entertainment: "general stuff I read daily would probably be like light novels, or manga, because they're easy to read." Both Akiko and Maki stressed that their enjoyment of *manga* (comics) highly motivated them to read in Japanese. Japanese pop culture, for example, as represented in manga, *anime* (animation), pop music, and online activity, has a huge following both within and beyond Japan and changes very rapidly. It influences fashion, peer play, consumer choices, and popular idiom; it is continually changing, affecting social norms and expectations. However, as various Japanese pop culture products are reg-ularly commodified globally, they are no longer exclusively symbolic of Japan or Japaneseness (see Burgess and Armour, in this volume). The global commodification allows heritage learners of Japanese easy access to these products both physically and psychologically (Iwabuchi 2002). Akiko's and Maki's stories suggest that their consumption of these media play a signifi-cant role in shaping their emerging and fluid perceptions of Japanese culture and of themselves as members of a desirable media culture.

Lo-Philip (2010) points out the research evidence of the two-way nature of learners' relationship with literacy. It is well established that language and literacy socialization impacts learner identity (e.g., Bell 1997; Lam 2000, McKay & Wong 1996); but it is also interesting that the identi-ties that learners bring, and future identities that learners desire to pos-sess, affect their language and literacy choices and development (e.g., Bell 1995; Kinginger 2004). He (2006) underlines that the content of a text has a direct impact on how the learner perceives the culture and how he/she consequently positions him/herself.

Both students also make ongoing effort to sustain and develop their writ-ing abilities in Japanese. Maki explained:

> I try to keep a diary, first of all. I try to write it in Japanese only because otherwise I don't write in Japanese. . . . otherwise I talk to my friends in Japan in a text or email. When I'm at uni now, I would write reports or necessary assignments in Japanese.

Akiko also reported writing online in Japanese, describing that within her peer group she uses: "Letters and email. Just recently my friends, we started a blog, for fun, writing in Japanese about ourselves. We all have about the same level of kanji." Again, these examples show the element of fun group membership afforded by a level of literacy in Japanese. It is clear that for both Maki and Akiko the desire to read and write is the key to their ability to access the enjoyment and stimulation of the literature and media of their peer group in Japan. Both have indicated the significance of this in their lives. Wang (2004) has commented on the role of having meaningful interaction in the heritage language which in turn generates more capital. This leads to a stronger desire to create a voice for the design of a heritage language identity and ultimately fosters high levels of heritage language lit-eracy acquisition. For Maki and Akiko, their abilities and engagement in reading and writing in Japanese illustrate that language and literacy interact with identities and how they identify themselves (Gee 1988).

The Processes of Evaluating Japanese Identities

Akiko and Maki have been successful to varying degrees in acquiring the language skills to sustain relationships in Japanese and access elements of

Japanese media culture, both of which contribute to their sense of identity as Japanese. However, their sense of identity as Japanese is not necessarily fixed nor is it necessarily similar to identities of peers who have grown up within Japan, but it emerged through their life trajectories. Indeed, because they have grown up beyond Japan's borders, their stories show how their Japanese identities have been questioned throughout their lives by different people and institutions. The following section explores how their Japanese identities have been evaluated.

In terms of their oral communication, Akiko's and Maki's stories related how their spoken Japanese has been evaluated by their families, mostly through telephone interactions. Akiko's attendance at Japanese Community Language School means she would have been evaluated for nine years against the learning goals of the school. Maki deliberately sought out the evaluation of the Japanese government through the accreditation of the Japanese Language Proficiency Test. It can be assumed that these experiences would have constructed largely positive evaluations of their 'Japanese identity' and membership in the language community.

In secondary school, however, the students' Japanese abilities were evaluated by their teachers and by the eligibility criteria prescribed in the school system and placed them outside the desirable profile for their chosen course of Japanese. This was a point of confusion and negative frustration for both Akiko and Maki, as their Japanese background became a liability for them. The external evaluation of them, the exclusion from Japanese study, and the subsequent reduction in choices of tertiary training and adult careers seem to have been a site of divergent transformation for both students. The choice of senior secondary subjects for matriculation is a critical point in adolescent life, where personal alignment and investment with certain subjects strongly impacts their thinking and choices. Students are already constructing a future self in meaningful pathways to a job and further studies. Kalakoski and Nurmi (1998) have noted how adolescents' identity exploration and commitment seem to be affected by these kinds of institutional transitions that they face.

The role of schooling in fostering Japanese heritage language identity has been examined by Oriyama (2010, 2011). She found that heritage language proficiency does not always correspond to the degree of identification with the heritage language group and culture. Many students in Oriyama's study, even though they attended full-time, Japanese-medium schools and had high-level proficiency in Japanese, identified as Australian. Oriyama concluded that formal schooling (whether Japanese or Australian) seemed to have more influence on identity and heritage language proficiency than parentage or home background. In the case of Maki and Akiko, however, the school that each attended provided little support to their desire to develop their Japanese language skills. Outside-school instruction, family, and peers appear to be much more cogent and positive influences on their identities.

Both Maki and Akiko also conduct ongoing self-evaluation of their Japanese identity. Maki's self-evaluation of her Japanese identity against native speaker models identifies areas of language that she feels she can improve, and she perceives that being in Japan will give her access to deeper experience of 'being Japanese':

> I'd really like to go back after I've graduated from university for a year or so and live there. Possibly more depending on how I feel. Sort of, live in Japan, because I've never done that before. To know what it's like to be Japanese. Hopefully, by doing that, I could improve in my Japanese.

This statement suggests Maki may not have identified herself as Japanese in the past but is envisaging a shift in identification. This may confirm the findings of Oriyama (2010) who noted the later change in identification in adolescent heritage speakers. Maki aligns her new identification with improvement in her language ability. Just as language learning is a lifelong activity, so too is identity development never complete but always in process (Hall 1992).

Akiko, despite a chosen career path that does not immediately involve using Japanese language, said she may return later in her career to her love of Japanese graphics and that her Japanese identity is: "still important to me . . . I will continue as an adult, will still be going back often, see my grandparents, make friends over there, keep bonds." Both Maki and Akiko exemplify shifts in their identification at different times in their lives. They remain young Australians participating in the Australian education system and broader community within which their Japanese language abilities and family connections have helped them construct multiple identities.

CONCLUSION

This chapter has examined the stories of two young Japanese Australian women in relation to their Japanese language skills and their developing and changing identities. It has illustrated, through an analysis of their stories, that their Japanese language development has a strong association with their sense of identity as Japanese. The stories highlight that Japanese language ability is developed around two key purposes: for relationships with family and friends and for accessing specific aspects of the culture of Japan. The stories also illustrate that their Japanese identities are subject to processes of evaluation, by others and by themselves, both within and beyond Japan.

Both students exemplify shifts and movements between their Japanese and Australian selves, a sense of ongoing multiple development. They express the desire to continue their relationship with Japan, spend time in Japan as they want to learn more about it, enjoy it more deeply, improve their Japanese language skills, and build greater linguistic and social capital. Although of limited scope and sample, these case studies show varying experience and outcomes in heritage language users within one community. While these two students shared superficially similar family structures, they show significant differences in family language choices and subsequent outcomes in their heritage language development and later education choices.

The narratives suggest that the participants vary in their processes of constructing multiple identities encompassing both Japan and Australia. Maki, with her later and comparatively weaker Japanese language development, now wants to mobilize her Japanese identity, study Japanese at tertiary level, become a Japanese teacher, and thereby acquire both a personal and professional identity associated with her Japanese heritage. Akiko, with her strong language ability, identifies as both Japanese and Australian. While she has currently moved into a career path not involving Japanese, her narrative suggests personal confidence in her multilingual identity, which may in the future re-emerge as a professional asset. These students represent emergent and transitional Japanese identities; both are invested in Japanese language and culture and shaped by their education and life in Australia.

It is appropriate that the relationship between identity and heritage language and literacy development is an emerging focus (Lo-Philip 2010) in research efforts to achieve a more complex understanding of heritage language learners. Heritage language learning is constitutive of identity accomplished in everyday social practices. The research reported here illustrates the value of a sociocultural approach that can encompass the function of social contexts within which language learning and identity construction takes place. The analysis of these two cases has opened up a richer and more detailed perspective than may have been possible with a purely correlational approach. The examination of the social and cultural contexts of the students' developing language abilities and identities has allowed us to track and interpret their uneven trajectories of growth and change.

Despite the uneven trajectories of these students, the study offers a moving illustration of the value of the investment by families in heritage language. The development of Japanese identities beyond the borders of Japan, through family heritage settings and consumption of Japanese popular culture, opens up new and more ambiguous notions of identity. At the same time, heritage learners also need to be recognized and included in appropriate school curriculum provision. The two women did not receive institutional support to extend their language abilities, which seems to be affecting their career options as well as identity negotiation process. The case studies indicate that learners of Japanese as a heritage language need to be positively supported by both institutional and familial practice to embrace their learning experiences and their ongoing identity construction processes. The introduction of a new heritage student category to the courses available at the senior secondary level in New South Wales, where the case studies took place, is a welcome development. It is hoped that a more nuanced grasp of heritage speakers' development within their families and communities will lead to respectful valuing of their multiple abilities and identities, both within Australia and in Japan. The diverse international field of heritage language research calls for this recognition and provision in many different linguistic contexts.

REFERENCES

Bell, J. S. (1995). The relationship between L1 and L2 literacy: Some complicating factors. *TESOL Quarterly, 29,* 687–704.

Bell, J. S. (1997). *Literacy, culture, and identity.* New York: Peter Lang Publishing.

Bhabha, H. K. (1990). The third space. In J. Rutherford (Ed.), *Identity, Community, Culture, Difference* (pp. 207–221). London: Lawrence and Wishart.

Block, D. (2006). Identity in Applied Linguistics. In T. Omoniyi & G. White (Eds.), *The Sociolinguistics of Identity* (pp. 34–49). London: Continuum.

Board of Studies NSW. (2009). *Japanese Continuers Stage 6 Syllabus.* Sydney: Board of Studies NSW.

Board of Studies NSW. (2012). *Japanese Background Speakers Stage 6 Syllabus.* Sydney: Board of Studies NSW.

Board of Studies NSW. (n.d.). *Assessment Certification Examination.* Retrieved on November 21, 2013, from: http://ace.bos.nsw.edu.au/

Brinton, D., Kagan, O. E., & Baukus, S. (Eds.). (2008). *Heritage language education: A new field emerging.* New York: Routledge.

Bucholtz, M., and Hall, K. (2004). Language and identity. In A. Duranti (Ed.), *A Companion to Linguistic Anthropology* (pp. 369–394). Oxford: Blackwell.

Cardona, B., Noble, G., & Di Biasse, B. (2008). *Community languages matter! Challenges and opportunities facing the community language program in New South Wales.* Parramatta, NSW: University of Western Sydney.

Carreira, M. (2004). Seeking explanatory adequacy: A dual approach to understanding the term "heritage language learner." *Heritage Language Journal, 2*(1), 1–25.

Cummins, J. (1996). *Negotiating identities: Education for empowerment in a diverse society.* Ontario: California Association for Bilingual Education.

Cummins J. (2000). *Language power and pedagogy: Bilingual children in the crossfire.* Clevedon: Multilingual Matters.

Cummins, J. (2003). Bilingual education: Basic principles. In J. Dewaele, A. Housen, & L. Wei (Eds), *Bilingualism: Beyond basic principles* (pp. 56–66). Clevedon: Multilingual Matters.

Diaz Soto, L. (2002). Young bilingual children's perceptions of bilingualism and biliteracy: Altruistic possibilities. *Bilingual Research Journal, 26*(3), 599–610.

Doerr, N., & Lee, K. (2013). *Constructing the Heritage Language Learner: Knowledge, power and new subjectivities.* Boston: Mouton de Gruyter.

Fought, C. (2006). *Language and ethnicity.* Cambridge: Cambridge University Press.

Gibbons, P., and Ramirez, E. (2004). *Maintaining a minority language: A case study of Hispanic teenagers.* Clevedon: Multilingual Matters.

Gee, J. P. (1988). Discourse systems and aspirin bottles: On Literacy. *Journal of Education, 170*(1), 27–40.

Glesne, C., and Peshkin, A. (1992). *Becoming qualitative researchers: An introduction.* White Plains: Longman.

Hall, S. (1990). Cultural identity and diaspora. In J. Rutherford (Ed.), *Identity, Community, Culture, Difference* (pp. 222–237). London: Lawrence & Wishart.

Hall, S. (1992). The question of cultural identity. In S. Hall, D. Held, & A. McGrew (Eds.), *Modernity and Its Futures* (pp. 273–325). Cambridge: Polity Press.

He, A. W. (2006). Toward an identity theory of the development of Chinese as a heritage language. *Heritage Language Journal, 4*(1), 1–23.

He, A. W. (2010). The Heart of Heritage: Sociocultural dimensions of heritage language learning. *Annual Review of Applied Linguistics, 30,* 66–82.

Iwabuchi, K. (2002). *Recentering globalization: Popular culture and Japanese transnationalism.* Durham: Duke University Press.

The Japan Foundation. (2012). *The Japanese Language Proficiency Test.* Retrieved on November 26, 2013, from: http://www.jlpt.jp/e/about/levelsummary.html

Jia, G. (2008). Heritage language development, maintenance, and attrition among recent Chinese immigrants in New York City. In A. W. He & Y. Xiao (Eds.), *Chinese as a Heritage Language* (pp. 189–203). Honolulu: National Foreign Language Resource Center/University of Hawaii Press.

Kagan, O. (2005). In support of a proficiency-based definition of heritage language learners: The case of Russian. *International Journal of Bilingual Education and Bilingualism, 8*(2–3), 213–221.

Kalakoski, V., and Nurmi, J. (1998). Identity and educational transitions: Age differences in adolescent exploration and commitment related to education, occupation, and family. *Journal of Research on Adolescence, 8*(1), 29–47.

Kanno, Y. (2003). *Negotiating bilingual and bicultural identities: Japanese returnees betwixt two worlds.* Mahwah: Lawrence Erlbaum Associates.

Kinginger, C. (2004). Bilingualism and emotion in the autobiographical works of Nancy Huston. *Journal of Multilingual and Multicultural Development, 25*(2–3): 159–178.

Kondo-Brown, K. (Ed.). (2006). *Heritage language development: Focus on East Asian immigrants* (Studies in Bilingualism Series 32). Amsterdam: John Benjamins.

Kondo-Brown, K. (2010). Curriculum development for advancing heritage language competence: Recent research, current practices and a future agenda. *Annual Review of Applied Linguistics, 30,* 24–41.

Lam, W. S. E. (2000). L2 literacy and the design of self: A case study of a teenager writing on the internet. *TESOL Quarterly, 34*(3), 457–482.

Lave, J., and Wenger, E. (1991). *Situated learning: Legitimate peripheral participation.* Cambridge: Cambridge University Press.

Lawler, S. (2008). *Identity: Sociological perspectives.* Cambridge: Polity Press.

Lo-Philip, S. W. (2010). Towards a theoretical framework of heritage language, literacy and identity processes. *Linguistics and Education, 21,* 282–297.

McNamara, T. (1987). Language and social identity: Israelis abroad. *Journal of Language and Social Psychology, 6,* 215–228.

McNamara, T. (1997). Theorizing social identity: What do we mean by social identity? Competing Frameworks, competing discourses. *TESOL Quarterly, 31*(3), 561–567.

McKay, S. L., & Wong, S. C. (1996). Multiple discourses, multiple identities: Investment and agency in second-language learning among Chinese adolescent immigrant students. *Harvard Educational Review, 66*(3), 577–608.

Martinez- Roldan, C. (2003). Building worlds and identities: A case study of the role of narratives in bilingual literature discussions. *Research in the Teaching of English, 37*(4), 491–510.

Menard-Warwick, J. (2005). Both a fiction and an existential fact: Theorizing identity in second language acquisition and literacy studies. *Linguistics and Education, 16,* 253–274.

Mercurio, N., and Scarino, A. (2005). Heritage languages at upper secondary level in South Australia: A struggle for legitimacy. *The International Journal of Bilingual Education and Bilingualism, 8*(2–3), 145–159.

Ministry of Education, Culture, Sports, Science and Technology, Japan. (2008). *Guidelines for National Language Teaching at Junior High School.* Retrieved from http://www.mext.go.jp/b_menu/shuppan/sonota/990301/03122602/002.htm

Montrul, S. (2010). Current issues in heritage language acquisition. *Annual Review of Applied Linguistics, 30,* 3–23.

Norton, B. (2000). *Identity and language learning: Gender, ethnicity, and educational change.* Harlow: Longman.

Norton, B. (2006). Identity as a sociocultural construct in second language education. In K. Cadman & K. O'Regan (Eds.), *TESOL in Context* [Special Issue], 22–33.

Oguro, S., & Moloney, R. (2010). An alien from their own language: The case of Japanese in New South Wales. *Babel, 44*(2), 22–31.

Oguro, S., & Moloney, R. (2012). Misplaced heritage language learners of Japanese in secondary schools. *Heritage Language Journal, 9*(2), 70–84.

Omoniyi, T. (2006). Heirarchy of identities. In T. Omoniyi & G. White (Eds.), *The sociolinguistics of identity* (pp. 11–33). London: Continuum.

Oriyama, K. (2010). Heritage language maintenance and Japanese identity formation: What role can schooling and ethnic community contact play? *Heritage Language Journal, 7*(2), 76–110.

Oriyama, K. (2011). The effects of sociocultural context on heritage language literacy: Japanese-English bilingual children in Sydney. *International Journal of Bilingual Education and Bilingualism, 14*(6), 653–681.

Russell, G. M., and Kelly, N. H. (2002). Research as interacting dialogic processes: Implications for reflexivity. *Forum Qualitative Research, 3,* 3.

Thomson Kinoshita, C. (2013). 'Idōsuru kodomo' ga tokubetsu dewa nai basho: Ōsutoraria de nihongo o manabu daigakusei no fukugengo to jiko imēji. [Where 'children on the move' are not special: multilingualism and self-image of university students of Japanese in Australia]. In I. Kawakami (Ed.), *'Idōsuru kodomo' to iu kioku to chikara: kotoba to aidentitī* ['Children on the move' as memory and power: language and identity] (pp. 145–165). Tokyo: Kurosio.

Valdés, G. (2001). Heritage language students: Profiles and possibilities. In J. K. Peyton, D. A. Ranard, & S. McGinnis (Eds.), *Heritage Languages in America: Preserving a National Resource* (pp. 37–80). Washington: Center for Applied Linguistics.

Valdés, G. (2005). Bilingualism, heritage language learners, and SLA research: Opportunities lost or seized? *The Modern Language Journal, 89*(3), 410–426.

Wang, S. C. (2004). *Bi-literacy resource eco-system of intergenerational transmission of heritage language and culture: An ethnographic study of a Chinese community in the United States.* Unpublished Ph. D dissertation, University of Pennsylvania, Philadelphia, PA.

Wardekker, W. L. (2000). Criteria for the quality of inquiry. *Mind, Culture, and Activity, 7*(4), 259–272.

Weeks, J. (1990). The value of difference. In J. Rutherford (Ed.), *Identity, Community, Cultural Difference* (pp. 88–100). London: Lawrence and Wishart.

8 Transcending the Role of Japanese Language Education
A Humanistic Approach in Australian Learning Contexts

Jun Ōhashi and Hiroko Ōhashi

INTRODUCTION

This chapter reflects on emerging humanistic roles of Japanese language education that go beyond the conventional norms of teaching the language and culture to nonnative speakers of Japanese in a context of Japanese language education outside of Japan. As the overarching objectives of the book suggest, this chapter problematizes the traditional views on the roles of second/foreign language education and its goals, and it extends possible educational roles of Japanese language in tertiary education institutions in Australia. Specifically, the chapter draws from two case studies where humanistic values of the language education beyond communicative competence are explored in each situated local context.

The notion of 'communicative competence' provides hypothetical accounts for the nature of language use and what is required for successful communication. Various models of communicative competence have been proposed. The choice of model, therefore, often guides what should be taught and learned in a given second language pedagogy. Canale and Swain (1980) have elaborated on Hymes's (1972) model of communicative competence consisting of two key components: linguistic and sociolinguistic competence. Since Canale and Swain introduced the new concept of strategic competence, it has been adopted by researchers such as Bachman and Palmer (1982), Johnson (1989), Tarone and Yule (1989), and Bachman (1990) in their models. Bachman's (1990) model of communicative competence constitutes linguistic (grammar), discourse (textual), pragmatic, and sociolinguistic components, and he highlights the interdependent nature of those components, stating that "the various components interact with each other and with the context in which language use occurs" (Bachman 1990: 81). The model of communicative competence, which was put forward by Canale and Swain (1980) and elaborated by Bachman (1990), has been most influential and has been adopted and adapted by researchers in the areas of testing and second/foreign language pedagogy. However, the notion of communicative competence as the ultimate goal for second/foreign language teaching and learning falls short of what is needed in a rapidly globalizing world with increased cross-cultural contacts where diverse cultural expectations are encountered. Kramsch (2006) argues that learners' abilities should extend beyond communicative competence as this ability is often interpreted as merely a learners' ability to exchange information efficiently in their second/foreign languages. To be more specific, efficiency in communication and knowing what to say accurately in a manner expected in a given situation is not enough to equip learners with the ability to bridge gaps between people from different sociocultural and historical backgrounds and expectations:

> the exacerbation of global social and economic inequalities and of ethnic identity issues, as well as the rise in importance of religion and ideology around the world have created historical and cultural gaps that a communicative approach to language teaching cannot bridge in itself (Kramsch 2006: 251).

Taking on Kramsch's position, it is the authors' contention that the second/foreign language learning process potentially provides the students with ample opportunity to reflect on self by exploring meaning making through a common target language that demands they think and behave according to a target culture. If such experience can develop students' sensitivities to the perspectives of others and their needs, it should be utilized to achieve wider educational goals.

   This paper discusses two case studies on Japanese language education conducted in Australian tertiary institutions in an attempt to extend educational values of the language. Specifically, in response to Kramsch's problematization of the communicative competence approach in the globalizing world, the two case studies aim to seek alternative attributes that students should develop through second/foreign language learning to close what Kramsch (2006: 251) calls "historical and cultural gaps." The first case study discusses an attempt to connect international and local students through intercultural learning in their common target language, Japanese. The second examines a project that aims to provide students with activity/task-based learning opportunities where employability skills are integrated and to empower Technical and Further Education (TAFE) students to follow mainstream pathways.

JAPANESE LANGUAGE EDUCATION IN AUSTRALIA

According to the statistics conducted by the Japan Foundation in 2009, the number of Japanese language learners has reached 3,651,000 around the world (The Japan Foundation 2009). In Australia, Japanese has been one of the most popular Language Other Than English (LOTE) subjects for the last two decades. According to the Japan Foundation (2011), Australia is the fourth biggest country in terms of the number of learners of Japanese language after Korea, China, and Indonesia. Australia's geographical proximity to Asia and economic dependence on neighboring Asian countries (Yamanaka 2007) contribute to the permeation of Asian languages through Australia; however, the popularity of Japanese language is in part a consequence of Australia's educational export to Asian countries. For instance, international students at a university in Australia where the first case study was conducted make up 28% of the entire student population, and the vast majority (75 %) of these students are from the following six countries: China, Malaysia, India, Singapore, Indonesia, and Hong Kong. Of the 600 students who enrolled in the ab initio Japanese language course at the same university in 2011, 63% were international students. This particular context of Japanese as a LOTE creates a space where international and local students meet on a large scale. Ōhashi (2009) illustrates that Japanese language classrooms provide educational institutions with a space where students are emancipated from assumed hierarchy due to a gap in English proficiency. Such a space can facilitate the students' self-reflexivity and help them explore, imagine, and construct a new reality and identity (Kramsch 2009).

Japanese language education has come to play a significant role in Australia as the Australian government has identified the importance of engaging with Asia. The recent 312-page white paper issued by the former Gillard Labor government entitled *Australia in the Asian Century* (2012) gives us a positive blueprint of Australia's future engagement with Asian countries, and it endorses the promotion of Asian languages. However the focus is primarily given to Australia maximizing economic gain by engaging with fast-developing Asian countries. The Prime Minister's foreword states: "Thriving in the Asian century therefore requires our nation to have a clear plan to seize the economic opportunities that will flow and manage the strategic challenges that will arise" (Australia in the Asian century 2012: ii). Such an ideological stance is not new, but the ongoing association between Asian languages and the nation's economic gain devalue the significance of the humanistic values of the young Australians' language learning experiences.

RESEARCH CONTEXTS

This chapter discusses some initiatives in Japanese language education in two tertiary institutions. What the two institutions have in common is that they both have aims beyond Japanese language acquisition. The significance of the two case studies lies in the provision of specific examples echoing

Kramsch (2006) and Kramsch, Howell, Warner, & Wellmon (2007) advocating second/foreign language curricula that go beyond communicative competence. They also echo Lo Bianco and Slaughter's (2009) claim that language learning contains special qualities, such that the learner's sense of self is challenged and extended.

The first case is situated in the context of an Australian university and it explores an educational role that Japanese language can play outside of Japan. The Australian Universities Quality Agency (AUQA 2010) has identified the lack of interaction between the international and the local students as problematic.[1] The first case addresses this issue. Specifically, it explores how 'intercultural learning' can be integrated into the core of the Japanese language curriculum to redress a widening divide between local and international students and to maximize the potential educational value of 'intercultural learning.' Here 'intercultural learning' is defined as a process where students mutually learn about something unfamiliar (other cultures) to question something familiar (one's culture and self). The importance of the self-reflexivity is also described by Kramsch (2009: 18) as "[we] only learn who we are through the mirror of others, and in turn, we only understand others by understanding ourselves as Other."

The second case study is situated in the Technical and Further Education (TAFE) sector in Australia. According to the statistics compiled by the Australian Bureau of Statistics in May 2012, 2.8 million students were enrolled in study for a qualification, and 27% of them were at the higher education institution, while 18% were at TAFE institutions.[2] Therefore, TAFE institutions, which focus on vocational training, are also significant in tertiary education. The ratio of international students to local students is smaller in TAFE institutions than in higher education. However, TAFE serves the specific purpose of transforming students into a 'work-ready' workforce and giving noncurrent, school-leaver/mature-age applicants alternative entry pathways to higher education. Here the main focus is given to providing the education and training that is required to meet the vocational needs of students. Therefore, this second example shows that the vocational education training (VET) quality framework has to be embedded into the Japanese language curriculum. TAFE also provides those who could not get a place in the higher education sector with a pathway and a second chance to go back to mainstream tertiary education the following year. The curriculum, therefore, is also required to provide students with a solid academic foundation. Equally importantly, since some students in TAFE are underprivileged in various ways (Powles & Anderson 1996) and regard themselves as 'underperformers,' there is a need to help them increase their self-confidence, particularly those who use a TAFE program as a transitional process to access mainstream opportunities in education or career. The case study examines activity/task-based approaches to combine Japanese language and employability skills to increase confidence in students' transition into mainstream pathways.

THEORETICAL UNDERPINNINGS OF THE CASE STUDIES: BILDUNG VERSUS AUSBILDUNG

According to Kramsch et al. (2007), Germany's traditional educational value of Bildung (the ongoing processes of self-formation and inner growth by interacting with the outside world) came under attack when societies demanded a development of practical and efficient skill-based competence (Ausbildung). They argue that the interrelationship between these two values is relevant to an understanding of the current higher education scene. Kramsch et al. (2007) also illustrate the situation of teaching of German in American universities and argue that the tension between the two competing values is reflected in a divide between "culture and language, knowledge and skills in FL [foreign language] education in the United States" (p.171).

Researchers such as Richard and Rogers (1982), Lo Bianco, Liddicoat, and Crozet (1999), and Lo Bianco and Slaughter (2009) have identified some significant qualities of language and its learning process. Language is "a vehicle for the realization of interpersonal relations and for the performance of social transactions between individuals" (Richard & Rogers 1982:156), and the significant nature of language is its ability to "[shape] human interactions and relations" (Lo Bianco et al. 1999: 10). The learning process of second/foreign languages is therefore significant as "[t]here are special qualities that language learning contains, (. . .) they potentially challenge and extend the sense of self of the student" (Lo Bianco & Slaughter 2009: 64). Lo Bianco and Slaughter argue that languages are associated with the ultimate purposes of education because of the nature of languages, which "are intimately linked to the essentially humanistic, cultural and intellectual reasons for making education compulsory" (Lo Bianco & Slaughter 2009: 64). Making a linguistic choice in a foreign language requires an understanding of the sociocultural norms of the target language, and the learners are required to reflect on their first-language norms and their presentation of self in their target language in intercultural communication. They are constantly required to think from a perspective of cultures other than their own. Therefore, learning a foreign language provides the learners with opportunities to reflect on self between the first-language and the target-language norms and to develop their sensitivity to others' needs and a sense of empathy. Such attributes of foreign language learning can have a positive impact on the learners' self-formation and inner growth, and the notion of Bildung is therefore relevant in second/foreign language education and needs to be emphasized. This potential benefit of language learning is, in fact, emphasized in the *Draft Shape of the Australian Curriculum: Languages*, which was published in January 2011 by the Australia Curriculum, Assessment and Reporting Authority (ACARA).[3] Lo Bianco and Slaughter's (2009) rationale for the special quality of language learning is also quoted there. In the following two case studies, Japanese as a LOTE is taught not only for language acquisition, but also for the learners' formation of self and inner growth.

CASE STUDY 1: AB INITIO JAPANESE COURSE IN AN AUSTRALIAN UNIVERSITY

As briefly discussed earlier, one of the issues the university faces is a lack of interaction between local and international students. We also need to recognize the diversity within each group. As Marginson and Sawir (2011) describe, referring to a survey report (AEI 2007), local students' indifferent attitudes toward international students, and the lack of English language skills of some of the international students may also contribute to the insufficient interactions between the two groups. Marginson and Sawir (2011) also refer to a survey conducted by UK Council for International Education (2004), which suggests that English language competence is important for international students in networking with local students.

> Of native-English-speaking international students, two-thirds had UK friends, compared to 36 percent of the students from English as a second language backgrounds, and 29 percent of those from English as a foreign language backgrounds. (Marginson & Sawir 2011: 113)

This suggests that those international students who do not use English as a communicative tool in their home countries may face higher hurdles in making local friends. However, none of the research on integration of international students looked into possible roles of LOTE subjects in improving interactions between local and international students. Japanese language, as one of the most popular LOTEs, particularly among international students, provides a substantial space where both local and international students, as well as various ethnic groups from within or outside Australia, can interact free from native/nonnative English speaker power inequality and stereotypes. Japanese language classrooms where students from diverse cultural backgrounds meet provide them with great educational opportunity.

Simple Sentences May Reinforce Stereotyping

Implementation of a curriculum that systematically integrates awareness raising of cross-cultural self-reflexivity is necessary even in the ab initio Japanese course. For example, ab initio language courses introduce simple sentence structures with basic vocabulary items, which, in fact, promote simplistic stereotypes about social categorization (i.e., I am Australian. She is Japanese. He is Chinese.). Therefore, we are reminded that ab initio language courses have a long-lasting impact, either negative or positive, on students' intercultural learning. If successful, the learners will have solid ground to challenge stereotypes about any social categorization by accessing information about the complexity and heterogeneity of a given group. If unsuccessful, they will have reinforced stereotypical images about otherness.

The basic syntactic structure "A *wa* B *desu*" ('A is B') is introduced in all Japanese ab initio courses. In the textbook, which is used as one of the course materials in the first case study, there are some pattern practice sections, and one of them lists nationalities, such as Japanese, American, French, Chinese, etc. Examples are "*Kare wa america jin desu. Kanojo wa nihonjin desu*" ('He is American. She is Japanese') and so on. The negative structure, "A *wa* B *dewa arimasen*" ('A is not B'), is introduced in a later section. The introduction of the simple affirmative sentence, "A *wa* B *desu*," is commonly found in a hypothetical scenario where international students from various cultural backgrounds meet and introduce themselves on a Japanese university campus.

"*Watashi wa* Mearii *desu*. America *jin desu*." (I am Mary. I am American).
"*Watashi wa* Wan *desu*. Chūgoku *jin desu*." (I am Wang. I am Chinese).

Such common self-introductions often found in Japanese language textbooks in fact assume a fixed notion of nation-state: one country, one culture, one language. A pattern practice exercise of this kind only reinforces simplistic stereotyping, which prevents the learners from knowing and expressing more about the transnational reality globalization has created.

Australia is an ideal location where the conventional understanding of nation-states can be challenged.[4] For example, there are diverse Chinese background Australians, some identifying themselves as Chinese and some Australian. There are Anglo-Australian students who identify themselves as Australians but many of them have diverse ancestral roots. Looking at individual students, one can easily understand the complexity involved in one's identities, and the heterogeneity among students both local and international. For example, there is an international student from Hong Kong, whose mother is Taiwanese and father is Mainland Chinese, who claims himself as Hong Konger. A local student whose mother is of Egyptian-Italian descent and father a second generation Greek identifies herself as Australian.

In the ab initio subject, to foreground the complexity of individual's identity and make the students feel comfortable in talking about their cultural backgrounds, the following example of Mary's (pseudonym) story was used (in English).[5]

Mary's mother is Korean and her father is Iranian. Mary was born in Melbourne, but she and her parents moved to Botswana when she was three. Mary came back to Melbourne to study. She is an Australian citizen, but she is more attached to Botswana.

First, such transnational identity as reality should be foregrounded in introducing intercultural learning beyond the notion of nation-states. Students are then asked to put this into spoken Japanese as much as they can. At this stage they only know 'A is B' structure, and only a quarter of the hiragana have been introduced. The following Japanese spoken text may represent their level of Japanese at this stage.

> *Mary no okāsan wa kankoku jin desuga, otōsan wa iran jin desu. Mary wa Ōsutoraria jin desu. Botsuwana mo Mary no kuni desu.*
> (Mary's mother is Korean, and her father is Iranian. Mary is Australian, but Botswana is also her country.)

After a couple of weeks, students revisit the self-introduction with negative sentence structure, "A *wa* B *ja arimasen* (A is not B)", for example:

> *Watashi wa Chūgoku shusshin desu ga Chūgokujin ja arimasen*
> (I am from China, but I am not Chinese.)

> *Haha wa Taiwan-jin desu. Chichi wa Chūgoku-jin desu. Watashi wa Taiwan-jin ja arimasen Sorekara Chūgokujin ja arimasen.*
> (My mother is Taiwanese, and my father is Chinese. I am not Taiwanese. And I am not Chinese.)

> *Ōsutoraria-jin desu.*
> (I am Australian.)

With the negative sentence structure, the students can reflect on transnational identities through the medium of Japanese language. However, students' limited Japanese language repertoire forces them to resort to rather simplistic semiotic indexations using 'A is B' and 'A is not B' structures, but opportunities can be created to share stories of transnational identities in class using English.

The significance of intercultural learning has been clearly articulated in the recent *Teaching and Learning Languages: A Guide* (Scarino & Liddicoat 2009), which is designed to lead language teachers of Australian secondary schools in new directions. In particular, it is highlighted that understanding other 'cultures' is not gaining knowledge about other cultures but the whole process of engaging with other cultures and discovering something new/different/unfamiliar and then reflecting on one's own culture because of it.

> Understanding culture as practices with which people engage becomes centrally important. This means that in the language classroom it is not just a question of learners developing knowledge about another culture but of learners coming to understand themselves in relation to some other culture. (p.19)

What is significant about the guide for language teachers is the fact that intercultural learning is recognized as a process in which individual learners transform themselves into people who are more self-reflexive and sensitive to others' needs. By embedding intercultural learning into the language curriculum, we add very important values to it and provide opportunities for students' self-cultivation and self-improvement.

Embedding Intercultural Learning into Curriculum

In this section, we examine intercultural learning through a semester long project in the ab initio subject. The issues to be addressed are 1) how can intercultural learning be integrated into the language curriculum, 2) how can it be embedded into an already crammed ab initio Japanese language subject, and 3) how can the transnational ideology underlying the project be received by students?

In 2012, a cultural discovery project (see Appendix) consisting of a set of tasks was added to the assessable components of an ab initio Japanese subject in an Australian university. 450 students enrolled in this subject and had four contact hours per week for a semester of 12 weeks. The contact hours consist of a one-hour lecture and two seminars of 90 minutes each (one focusing on conversational skills and the other on reading and writing skills). For the seminars, the cohort was broken down into twenty small groups of about twenty-two students. Three assembled tasks that were related to intercultural learning were incorporated. First, students were asked to pair up with someone who had a different cultural background to work on a set of tasks, one in the middle of the term and the other at the end of the term. In many cases, local students paired up with international students, including pairs of an Australian-born Chinese and international students from mainland China or other Asian countries. There were some 'local-local' and 'international-international' pairs; but in those cases, students were encouraged to pair up with someone from a different cultural background.

Task 1 required students to prepare a conversational script of about 20 conversational turns, including self-introduction and its associated ritualistic expressions. They were also expected to include as many target grammar and vocabulary items as possible in the script. Typically, students found their partners within a few weeks and started working together for Task 1 in Week 6. Students told the teaching staff that they met outside of classrooms many times, such as in the library, unused classrooms, and cafés to prepare and practice their conversational scripts. As they were not allowed to see their written scripts during their presentations, they had to get together and rehearse their 20-turn dialogues many times. This task changed the classroom dynamics and seating arrangements of the students in class as the task required them to go beyond their comfort zone and interact with an unfamiliar partner within and outside of the classroom.

Task 2 was a guided essay in Japanese and English. A grade of 10% was given for students' oral presentations (Task 3). Section one of the task overlaps with the Task 1 self-introduction; however, students were required to update their self-introduction by incorporating new grammar and vocabulary. Section 2 required students to write about how they spend their weekends. They were expected to demonstrate their accurate use of various verbs and locative particles *de* and *ni*. Students did not know how their classmates spent weekends, and the project gave them an incentive to learn about the 'everyday' practices of their peers and their lifestyles. Section 2 also required students to write about their cultural festivals and how they celebrated them. Festivals such as Chinese New Year, Moon Festival, Kasada festival in Indonesia, Hari Gawai in Malaysia, Easter, and Christmas were featured. This section potentially required a lot of vocabulary beyond the expected level of students' knowledge of grammar and vocabulary at the time, and we gave them some extra support during class hours. Section 3 required the students to interview their intercultural partners to learn and discover what was new to them and realize diverse ways of doing things and reflect on their own culture. Section 3 also asked the students to describe their learning experiences with their intercultural partners through the semester in English. It gave students an opportunity to freely reflect on their intercultural learning.

Task 3 is an oral presentation of Task 2. It was intended to be a summary of the project, but turned out to be an extended version of their written work as students did not have to observe a word limit for the oral presentation but were given only four to five minutes for their presentations.

The cultural discovery project created ample opportunities for the students to interact with other students who possess invaluable resources for their intercultural learning. It also offered genuine reasons to connect those who would not have sought each other out and generated cross-cultural interactions through Japanese as a medium.

Student Feedback

To address the third issue in the implementation of intercultural learning, namely, how the transnational ideology underscoring the project has been received by students, it is also important to look into the students' feedback.

Voluntary and anonymous online subject experience surveys are conducted toward the end of a semester in every subject offered in the university. After the particular semester when the intercultural learning had been implemented, 264 students (59%) responded positively to quantitative questionnaire items: "Overall, this subject has been intellectually stimulating" and "Overall, this subject has been well-taught." The survey used the Likert-scale and the points given to the following responses were: 1-strongly disagree, 2-disagree, 3-neither, 4-agree, 5-strongly agree. Mean scores for these questions were 4.3 and 4.2 respectively. Of those who responded to the quantitative questionnaires, 150 students (57%) responded qualitatively to "What were the best aspects of this subject?" and 140 (53%) responded to "What aspects of this subjects do you believe should be improved?" The students' responses for these questions will be investigated in the text that follows.

"What were the best aspects of this subject?"

Only ten students (6.6%) referred to the cultural projects in this question. While cultural projects may not have been perceived as the best aspect of the subject, some valued collaborative nature and intercultural dimension of the cultural projects:

> "Working with partners is very helpful because we are able to give each other help or advice about the work we have to do."

> "I can make friends with people from different background."

> "Working with partners. It allowed me to view things from a different perspective and different ways to approach the material being studied."

A student showed approval to the aim of the cultural projects:

> "The aim of the subject to bring cultural unity and awareness is commendable."

Despite the low number of responses on the project, these positive comments support/reassure us of the importance of the notion of Bildung (the ongoing processes of self-formation and inner growth by interacting with the outer world). They suggest that these students valued their learning experience beyond achieving Ausbildung (practical and efficient skill-based competence).

However, more students referred to the cultural projects in response to the following question:

"What aspects of this subject do you believe should be improved?"

Eighteen students (12%) referred to the cultural projects. There were two key themes in their feedback: 1) more Japanese culture and 2) tasks were too difficult.

1) More Japanese culture

> "I do not like to describe my culture, I prefer to learn more about Japanese culture."

> "Sometimes, we are taught about other cultures instead of the Japanese culture."

"Maybe can change the culture project into something other project about discovering Japan."

"Growing up in multicultural Australia, cultural diversity within my own life had already been explored during school. I would rather learn about the Japanese culture instead."

These comments represent the students' expectations about the Japanese language subject. They would rather learn about 'Japanese culture' than the cultures of their peers. Those students tend to believe other cultures are something they learn about as knowledge. In relation to the notion of Bildung, it was intended that the students reflect on self, their social norms, and values during the cultural discovery project through the negotiation processes of intercultural communication in Japanese. While learning about other cultures (such as partners' common activities during weekends, cultural festivals that are specified in the task), as knowledge was not the ultimate goal, the comments noted earlier indicate that the principle of intercultural learning was not embraced by all students.

The following student expressed his/her view of language learning as a development of Japanese language skills (Ausbildung). The student values Japanese language skills more than the processes of intercultural learning.

"Cultural aspects are too highly emphasized to the detriment of the basic Japanese skills learning."

The scant reference to the cultural projects indicates that they were insignificant for the students' needs. Students were more concerned about their state of Japanese language and cultural acquisition, but they did not intend to learn about classmates' cultures through the medium of Japanese language. There seems to be a tension between these students and the educator over ideologies of language learning. It is quite understandable that when they chose to study Japanese language, learning about cultures of classmates was beyond their thinking. As students wish to learn more about Japanese culture, it would be desirable to use Japanese cultural phenomena explicitly as a starting point. Students' cultures may be shared in relation to a targeted Japanese cultural phenomenon.

2) Tasks were too difficult

"I guess the cultural project is too difficult to do, because our vocabulary is limited and thus it's hard to form sentences."

"Finish a report and an oral on culture event is tooooo hard for Japanese 1."

"It required new words in Japanese that I think is out of Japanese 1 level."

Five students responded qualitatively, expressing that the written cultural project was difficult because of the perceived gap between what they are capable of handling and what is required. It was not intended that students use grammatical structures beyond the beginners' level, but they were required to search for some lexical items necessary to describe the cultural events they had chosen. It appears that adequate scaffolding is essential for them to feel confident in fulfilling the task. This is one of the challenges in implementing intercultural learning at an ab initio level, especially where there are constraints in terms of resources and contact hours. It can also be said that the cultural project is not perceived as prominent in relation to the core language acquisitional curriculum. It will be necessary to clearly link the cultural project with the target grammar points and lexical items and scaffold students' intercultural learning with clear instructions and some examples.

Intercultural learning has been embedded into the curriculum of ab initio Japanese language subject with the inclusion of the cultural discovery project consisting of tasks amounting to 35% of the total assessments. The students' feedback on the subject was positive overall, however, only a small number of students referred to the cultural project positively or negatively. It can be said that Ausbildung is a common ideology held by students in the Australian learning context in the present study, and Bildung achieved by learning about classmates' unfamiliar cultures may be beyond their expectations.

CASE STUDY 2: EMPOWERING TAFE STUDENTS THROUGH AN INTENSIVE JAPANESE LANGUAGE PROGRAM

The second case study will further explore the aforementioned notion of humanistic values of the second/foreign language learning in the context of a Japanese intensive program in a TAFE sector at an Australian university. It will discuss another powerful role of second language teaching in that context, seeking what language education can possibly do in order to guide students to "update themselves" (自己変容 *jikohen'yō*) (Hosokawa et al. 2004: 19–21) through a new language. As mentioned earlier, students in TAFE sometimes regard themselves as being underprivileged in various ways (Powles & Anderson 1996), and this belief often has a strong impact on students' confidence and self-esteem. Some students are not financially comfortable and consider the TAFE program as the only pathway to a better future.[6]

Taking these factors into consideration, the intensive TAFE Japanese language course sees a role not only in developing students' communicative competence in the language, but also in helping students as members of society assume a more positive outlook as they further their education and increase their employability by learning Japanese.

Embedding Employability Skills into Curriculum

The process of language learning can be seen as a transition period from present to future and from classroom to broader real life. If these links between present and future and classroom and real life are not made, learning a language as an academic subject alone cannot fulfil the goals of TAFE in this context. However, if the course is able to facilitate its learning pathways in order for the students to attain attributes that are required as a member of society, they will be more confident and ready for their future.

Figure 8.1 illustrates how the combination of employability skills (adapted from the Employability Skills Framework, Commonwealth of Australia 2006) and personal attributes developed in the workplace lead to the required skills as a member of society. These are employability skills, but they can be interpreted widely as community skills that are able to represent one's social capability in a wider community-based environment. The direction for the program's pathways are derived from this idea, and this belief serves as a basic principle for TAFE.

Although the TAFE language qualification assessment is based on language competence with employability skills, the skills demonstrated earlier are crucial in forming not only a work-ready person but also a responsible member of the community/society.

The VET (Vocational Education Training) framework is thus distinctly different from any equivalent found in the higher education sector. The

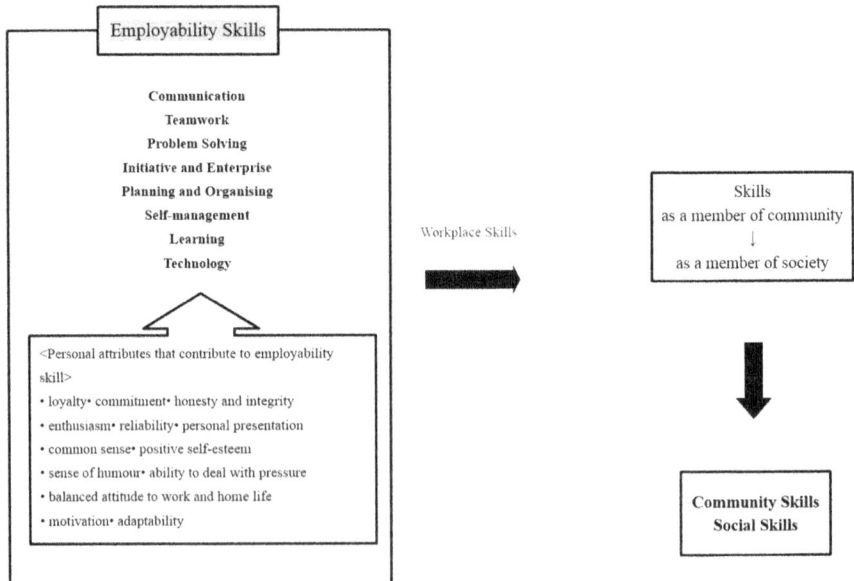

Figure 8.1   Employability skills (adapted from Commonwealth of Australia 2006) and Basic Principles of TAFE Intensive Japanese Language Program

conventional knowledge-based delivery of language material is not fit for achieving the objectives of the course. There has been a strong need to embed workplace essential skills into the generic communication skills in the program. Therefore, the students are provided, in addition to their day-to-day language acquisition training using a prescribed textbook, with opportunities where they can develop some targeted workplace skills as they engage in task-based social activities in the classroom and beyond. Some of these activities include:

- in-country study tours and internship programs
- off-campus language immersion camps with native speakers
- language exchange sessions with native speaker students
- hosting study tours from Japan
- leading/mentoring secondary school students on their visit to the institution

We will look at one of the examples, off-campus language immersion camps, and discuss how it is implemented and what outcomes are reached.

Off-Campus Language Immersion Camps

Annual off-campus language immersion camps are held for the TAFE students who started learning Japanese as zero-beginners and have completed the first half of the program amounting to 14 weeks of 18-contact hours a week. They are joined by Japanese students coming from a Japanese sister university. They spend two nights and three days in a historic seaside village located 120 km southwest of Melbourne. There they engage in social and cultural activities as a way of putting their language into practice. All activities at the camp are student-led and student-centered, and thus the whole camp environment is suitable for the students to develop the aforementioned community skills in practice, using only the target language. While teachers make the initial arrangements, such as setting up dates, booking accommodation, or liaising with teachers from the sister university, all other arrangements are expected to be organized by the students. For each activity that students organize, they are reminded that they should divide each one into three stages, 1) preparation, 2) action, and 3) reflection, to maximize their learning outcome in relation to the employability skills.

Preparation
Prior to the camp, the two groups of students meet to have a couple of preparation sessions where they discuss and decide how they will run the camp. Teachers also participate in these sessions to observe student decisions and give suggestions if necessary. These discussion sessions are initially guided by the teacher in English, using handouts (see Figure 8.2) to clarify the goals and objectives of the camp in terms of both linguistic and personal skills. The handouts also guide students to realize the important role of the language

Broader Goals:

- To take and/or share responsibility in all aspects of the camp, from planning to completion of the camp with your fellow students from the course, students from sister universities and teachers.
- To develop life and social skills through active involvement with the organizational process and sharing of responsibility
- To make this valuable experience both worthwhile and fun

Targeted skills:

Linguistic skills with Communication strategies and appropriate use of the language;

- Provide and seek information, explanations, instructions and advice
- Participate in a casual conversation
- Negotiate a problematic exchange
- Complete necessary documents

Personal skills:

While trying to find your definition of 'good'

- Be a good communicator
- Be a good member of the team
- Be a good problem solver
- Be a good leader

Camp Responsibilities:

Expected Challenges

Understand what is going on	Understand what is spoken/heard
Manage time	Manage 自分 (self)

Find your role/job to improve situations you are in

Manage activities in limited time

Be prepared for the unexpected

Participate actively- Have a go; get out of your comfort zone

Figure 8.2   Preparation: Excerpt from Camp Handout

and other factors, while reminding them of the fact that language is not learned for its own sake.

This stage is followed by a student-led discussion in Japanese to decide on items, such as responsibilities, rosters throughout the camp, activities to be done, the leader of each activity, and the preparation required for each activity. Students also discuss a scheduled timetable, food and cooking responsibilities, and transportation.

Action

During the camp, students follow the program they have designed and take responsibility for their own activities and duties. Figure 8.3 is an example of scheduled timetable of a camp, which was written by the students. This is an English translation of the original written in Japanese.

The students take and share responsibility in all camp activities with their peers and teachers especially when things do not go as expected. The students face numerous challenges they need to overcome to accomplish their own tasks. Their challenges are not limited to their language skills but extend to their community skills. However, students are not always aware of the fact that these skills (beyond language skills) are also important to succeed in their social lives. Therefore, they are asked to take time to reflect on themselves and their camp experiences and to write their reflections in the third stage.

Reflection

To encourage self-reflection while ensuring linguistic developments in Japanese, a writing task is given to students. They are required to write about the camp: where they went, who they met, what they did, what they had to do in preparation, and so on. They have to include the following:

- 一番楽しかったこと　　　一番たいへんだったこと
- (What was the most enjoyable event? What was the most troublesome event?)

- 後悔していること
- (What do you regret)

- 来年キャンプに行く学生にアドバイス
- (Any advice to future students who will participate in the camp?)

In completing this task, students are required to use Japanese vocabulary and expressions they have learned, such as volitional＋と思う (*to omou* 'think that . . .'), ／〜たり〜たりする (*tari tari suru* 'do A, B, and so on'), ／〜ばよかった (*ba yokatta* 'should have done X'), /たら (*tara* 'if/when'), / 〜てあげる・くれる・もらう (*te agaeru; kureru; morau* [auxiliary verbs of giving and receiving]), etc.

2012 Language and Culture Immersion Camp Schedule   * Names in Japanese script indicates names of Japanese students

29 August (Wed)	Activities	Leader Organiser
8:00		
9:00		
10:00		
11:00		
12:00		
13:00		
14:00	集合・部屋わり Assemble / ミーティング Meeting	先生 Teachers
15:00	運動会 Athletic games	先生 Teachers
16:00	お茶 Afternoon tea / アクティビティ Activity	Jess・Pamela
17:00	自由時間 Free time	料理準備はん ① Preparation Group1
17:45	Assemble in kitchen	Preparation Group1
18:00	夕食料理開始 マスターシェフ Start Cooking/Master chef	全員 All
19:00	夕食・かたづけ Dinner/Clean-up	全員 All
8:30	ぼんおどり Traditional Japanese dancing	しょうた・もえ

30 August (Thurs)	Activities	Leader Organiser
8:00	ラジオたいそう / 朝食 Breakfast / かたづけ Clean-up	
9:00	ミステリーゲーム Mystery Game	先生 Teachers
10:00	アクティビティ Activity / お茶 Morning tea	Angela・Tim
11:00	アクティビティ Activity / 自由時間 Free time	John Mat Max
12:00	昼食準備 Lunch Preparation	料理準備はん ② Preparation Group3 / Assemble in kitchen
13:00	昼食・かたづけ・昼休み Lunch/Clean-up/Break	全員 All
14:00	アクティビティ Activity	Mary・Eric・けん / よし・Kim・Alex / あき・Heidi・Sarah
15:00		
16:00	お茶・自由時間 Afternoon tea/Free time	
17:00	アクティビティ Activity	料理準備はん ③ Preparation Group4
17:45	Assemble in kitchen	Preparation Group4
18:00	夕食料理開始 マスターシェフ Start Cooking/Master chef	全員 All
19:00	夕食・かたづけ Dinner/Clean-up	全員 All
8:30	自由時間 Free time	

31 August (Fri)	Activities	Leader Organiser
8:00	ラジオたいそう / 朝食 Breakfast / 料理準備はん ③ Preparation Group5 / かたづけ Clean-up	ゆうか・ゆきお・Anna / 料理準備はん ② Preparation Group2 / Assemble in kitchen / まち・じゅん
9:00	Amazing Race	先生 Teachers
10:00	かたづけ Clean-up	
11:00	反省会 Reflection (Questionnaire)	
12:00	チェックアウト Check-out	全員 All

Figure 8.3 Camp Program

In addition, a survey is conducted in order to elicit each student's reflections on the camp activities. It is conducted in English so that students are able to express themselves more freely in their first language. The questionnaire says:

List the following items;

1) Three best aspects of the camp.
2) Three challenges you experienced in the camp and what did you do to overcome the challenge?
3) Things learned from attending the camp in terms of personal development?

In 2011, out of all 18 of the Australian TAFE students, 16 of them found that using Japanese spontaneously in context was the most challenging. Many of them, however, obtained a sense of achievement after completing various difficult tasks and finding their own solutions. The following is a list of some of the students' comments in response to the third question in the reflection discussed earlier.

> "I'm also grateful I was given an opportunity to discover within myself qualities I was not aware I had or was capable of."
> "I've learnt many valuable skills in communication, leadership and teamwork."
> "Immersing one's self (sic) in leader-based activities, especially in a cross-cultural context, enabled me to gain confidence as well as insight into the qualities a leader should possess."

This seems to have led to an improved sense of achievement and confidence in speaking Japanese and beyond:

> "I learnt that both Japanese and Australian groups were struggling together at the camp. Therefore I did not have to be self-conscious about my mistakes. I became more confident after the camp."
> "I became confident in trying to say things in both English and Japanese."
> "I have the motivation and now the confidence to study even harder."

The students appeared to have developed not only their knowledge of the Japanese language but also their social and community skills through active involvement in organizing activities and taking on responsibilities. The Japanese language immersion camp provided the students with ample opportunity to facilitate their self-reflexivity, extend their sense of self, and boost their confidence by fulfilling a series of challenging tasks. This is exactly what Bildung aims for, and it is one of the special qualities that language learning can offer (Lo Bianco & Slaughter 2009).

Role of Language Learning for Self-Esteem

Many researchers claim that there is a very strong connection between what happens inside the learner (psychological and cognitive state) and how much she/he learns in a language classroom (Brown 1994, de Andrés 1999; Gardner & Clement 1990). Brown (1994) also linked learners' self-esteem to one of the important qualities needed to be a good language learner. It was also observed that the sense of achievement leading to self-esteem motivated and encouraged students to learn more of the language after the camp. Conversely, it can be the special qualities of language learning that play an important role in the learners' inner growth, mental development, and boosting of self-esteem. The underprivileged learners are able to 'update themselves' (自己変容 *jikohen'yō*) through a target language toward their objectives. While studying, students grow as people, and they can be expected to develop much-needed community skills and form strong bonds and friendships with their classmates. As the feedback from the off-campus language immersion camp illustrates, the confidence and development of self-esteem is not restricted to their language competence. This appears to have occurred through social activities where the target language is more than a mere tool of communication (our emphasis):

> "I used to feel immensely disappointed with myself, if I got the smallest thing wrong, *but now I don't.*"
> "I have gained more *confidence* within myself and the language that I am learning and I have come out of my shell a bit more, daring to do more things that I wouldn't normally do. Since I am a very shy person, the camp has helped a lot."

The following comment suggests the student's identify transformation is occurring alongside the development of confidence in language and leadership skills:

> "During the immersion camp I faced many challenges including overcoming language barriers and resolving/avoiding conflict. I've learnt many valuable skills in communication, leadership and teamwork. The time I spent with the students was an amazing experience and I've definitely *changed as a person (for the better).*"

Among the comments of the 16 students who voluntarily handed in their feedback after the completion of the course, the term 'confidence' appeared eight times and was the most frequently used expression to describe their achievements. In addition to this number, there were students who did not use the word 'confidence' specifically but highlighted their improved confidence as their significant achievement together with their language acquisition.

However it should also be noted that four of 18 Australian TAFE students were expressing their feelings of uncertainty and anxiety as responses to 2), i.e. three challenges experienced in the camp and what they did to overcome the challenge.

"I often had very little idea of what was going on and what was planned for the day."

"I did not know how I could start conversation or how to find interesting enough topics to talk about with the Japanese students during the free time."

Despite the more informal atmosphere compared to that of the classroom activities, this fear of uncertainty is largely related to the fear of making mistakes and students' lack of confidence or self-esteem. It is not easy nor simple to determine whether the lack of confidence is related to the lack of language or social/community skills. Nevertheless, foreign language anxiety may have a negative effect on students' self-esteem, confidence (cf. Horwitz, Horwitz, & Cope 1986), and performance at the camp in general. There seems to be a need for addressing the negative aspect of language anxiety, in addition to the importance of the role of an educator, in implementing language programs utilizing its educational role guided by the principle of Bildung.

The discussion has so far focused on possible educational roles and values of the language education; however, it does not explain the impact of gaining self-esteem on students' linguistic developments. The camp is no doubt a confidence-booster for many students, however, it is not known to what extent the self-esteem and linguistic competence are correlated.

One of the students indicated that, through the camp activities, she gained sensitivity to others' needs and a sense of empathy. This is also one of the significant qualities of learning beyond communicative competence and evidence of inner growth:

"It [the camp] made me really aware of quiet/shy/younger peers who weren't comfortable speaking (either language) being left out of activities, and I know I will try to make things inclusive for everyone in a similar situation in the future."

There is much more anecdotal evidence of their learning beyond language acquisition. However, students' overwhelmingly positive comments about their gaining confidence may be the reflection of their dissatisfaction toward their previous educational contexts. It also has to be said that those students have been extremely lucky to have 18 contact hours a week in learning Japanese in a small class environment. Organizing activities and tasks beyond conventional classroom context requires extra preparation and coordination. However the underlining principles of the above activities could be applied in any type of language education setting.

CONCLUSION

Two cases have been drawn from different tertiary institutions where Japanese language is taught not only for language acquisition, but also for the learners' formation of self and inner growth. In the first case, intercultural learning is called upon in order to connect/bridge students of various backgrounds by incorporating collaborative cultural projects into assessments. In the second example, an activity/task-based approach is implemented to integrate employability skills into the core language curriculum. It provided TAFE students with opportunities to gain self-esteem, which comes with their study/work-ready status. Communicative competence is no longer the single most important goal for the language learners in the 21st century, and the educational value of Bildung, which underlines the students' self-formation and inner growth, becomes equally important.

However, some challenges in the humanistic approach to Japanese language education were identified in examining student feedback in both cases. For some students, the idea of intercultural learning and the principle of Bildung may clash with their inclination toward Ausbildung. Language anxiety may affect development of confidence and self-esteem.

Additionally, as discussed in the previous section, the method of assessment needs reconsideration. The issue is, specifically, how can we assess the outcome of Bildung linguistically together with their language acquisition? In the first case study, the cultural discovery project, the learners' linguistic repertoire is very limited and it would be difficult to link linguistic expressions with the learners' developments in relation to Bildung. However, intercultural communication is encouraged by including tasks and activities where local and international students work together. As they move on to the higher levels, linguistic items and content will reflect their intercultural learning and their inner growth in their target language. It is important to continue to have specific assessments that reflect the values of Bildung throughout the degree course. In the second example, the reflective writing task illustrates that the instruction specifically requires students to reflect on self in relation to activities that are directly related to employability skills. However, for both cases, it will be necessary to clearly link the projects with the target grammar points and lexical items to scaffold students' learning processes by providing them with clear instructions.

New roles of Japanese language education in two tertiary institutions have been explored in this chapter, with the premise that Japanese language education should go beyond aiming solely at communicative competence. The roles of language education discussed earlier are the reflections of the local contexts in question, and the chapter illustrated how language education can be a tool to enhance the universal educational value of Bildung in various local contexts. While this endeavor is in line with the proposed paradigm shift away from the language teaching ideology premised on language acquisition as cognitive mastery of 'language system' (Canagarajah 2007), this chapter also identified a tension between learners and teachers over ideologies of language learning. It is hoped that second/foreign language education will empower students in constructing and imagining a new reality and identity to live through the 21st century in nurturing humanistic values in various local contexts.

Appendix

Cultural discovery projects (35% of the total assessment)
  Task 1(10%): Oral dialog presentation WEEK 6
  Create a conversational script that includes 1) self-introduction + any topics with which you can demonstrate your ability to use new grammar items, vocabulary, and cultural understanding. Conversational turns should be around 20.
  Task 2 (10%): Cultural discovery project: Oral presentation WEEK 11
  Task 3 (15%): Cultural discovery project: Guided essay in Japanese and English WEEK 12
  http://www.newworldencyclopedia.org/entry/Nation-state
  Read the definition of a 'nation-state'[7] and understand the historical and political meanings of the notion. The 'nation-state' is a relatively new idea, and it has been instrumentally used to promote a single national identity for various reasons. Such a notion as the force of forming a single national identity is challenged in the globalizing world.

Section one (100 characters)

Reflect on your own identities in biographic terms (based on the series of events making up your life):
  What is your name and where do you come from? If you moved from one country to another, please describe. What nationality do you identify yourself as? (Nationality is often defined by your citizenship, however, sometimes by ethnicity, place of residence, or individual's sense of belonging.)

Section two (150 characters)

Describe how you typically spend your weekends. What are the things that many people of your society do during the weekends. Do you celebrate any festivals? What are they? Describe how people celebrate those festivals.

Section three (180 characters)

Throughout the semester you have been learning Japanese with your classmates coming from various parts of the world. First, write about your intercultural partner in the manner that you described yourself in sections one and two in Japanese. Describe, in English, what you have learned from your partner or other classmates with various cultural backgrounds. How would it affect your worldview and understanding of your own culture.

NOTES

1. Fincher and Shaw (2011) illustrate that international and local students create separate spaces for socializing in Melbourne.
2. http://www.abs.gov.au/ausstats/abs@.nsf/Products/6227.0~May+2012~Main+Features~Participation?OpenDocument
3. The draft was made available for comments between the January 31 and April 7, 2011. Also the draft *Foundation to Year 10 Australian Curriculum: Languages* was released for public consultation during May 2013.
4. Australia's population born overseas exceed one-quarter of the total population in 2008. http://www.abs.gov.au/ausstats/abs@.nsf/0/92C0101965E7DC14CA25773700169C63?
5. Mary is a research participant from one of the authors' research on international students in progress.
6. http://www.brimbankweekly.com.au/news/local/news/general/tafe-funding-cuts-second-chances-denied/2571040.aspx
   The article shows that TAFE is a one of very few pathways for disadvantaged students to pursue a better future. The article features a story of a woman who came out of poverty after gaining confidence and skills at a TAFE course. She says, "I had no confidence or skills until I did TAFE and I ended up going on to do a bachelor of arts at the University of Western Sydney."
7. New World Encyclopedia http://www.newworldencyclopedia.org/entry/Nation-state

REFERENCES

Australian Education International, AEI. (2007). *2006 International student survey: Report of the consolidated results from the four education sectors in Australia*. Canberra: Department of Education, Employment and Workplace Relations. Retrieved on April 1, 2011, from https://www.aei.gov.au/research/Publications/Documents/ISS_2006_CONS.pdf

Australian Universities Quality Agency, AUQA. (2010). *Report of an Audit of the University of Melbourne*. Retrieved on November 10, 2010, from http://teqsa.gov.au/sites/default/files/auditreport_uom_2010.pdf

Bachman, L. F. (1990). *Fundamental considerations in language testing*. Oxford: Oxford University Press.

Bachman, L. F., & Palmer, A. (1982). The construct validation of some components of communicative proficiency. *TESOL Quarterly, 16*(4), 449–465.

Brown, H. D. (1994). *Principles of language learning and teaching* (3rd ed.). Englewood Cliffs, NJ: Prentice-Hall.

Canagarajah, A. S. (2007). Lingua franca English, Multilingual communities, and language acquisition. *Modern Language Journal, 91*(5), 921–937.

Canale, M., & Swain, M. (1980). Theoretical bases of communicative approaches to second language teaching and testing. *Applied Linguistics, 1,* 1–47.

Commonwealth of Australia. (2006). *Employability Skills: From Framework to Practice.* Retrieved on March 10, 2010, from http://www.nssc.natese.gov.au/__data/assets/pdf_file/0010/69454/Employability_Skills_From_Framework_to_Practices.pdf

de Andrés, V. (1999). Self-esteem in the classroom or the metamorphosis of the butterflies. In J. Arnold (Ed.), *Affect in Language Learning* (pp. 87–102). Cambridge: Cambridge University Press.

Fincher, R., & Shaw, K. (2011). Enacting separate social worlds: 'International' and 'local' students in public space in central Melbourne. *Geoforum, 42,* 539–549.

Gardner, R. C., & Clement, R. (1990). Social psychological perspectives on second language acquisition. In H. Giles & W. P. Robinson (Eds.), *Handbook of Language and Social Psychology* (pp. 495–511). Chichester: John Wiley & Sons.

Horwitz, E. K., Horwitz, M. B., & Cope, J. (1986). Foreign language classroom anxiety. *The Modern Language Journal, 70*(2), 125–132.

Hosokawa, H., Take, K., Tsumura, N., Hoshino, S., Hashimoto, H., & Ushikubo, R. (2004). *Kangaeru tameno Nihongo: Jissen hen.* Tokyo: Akashi shoten.

Hymes, D. (1972). On communicative competence. In J. B. Pride & J. Homes (Eds.), *Sociolinguistics* (pp. 269–293). Harmondsworth: Penguin.

Japan Foundation. (2011). *Survey report on Japanese-language education abroad 2009.* Japan Foundation. Retrieved on November 28, 2011, from http://www.jpf.go.jp/j/japanese/survey/result/dl/survey_2009/gaiyo2009.pdf

Johnson, K. (1989). *The second language curriculum.* Cambridge: Cambridge University Press.

Kramsch, C. (2006). From communicative competence to symbolic competence. *The Modern Language Journal, 90,* 249–252.

Kramsch, C. (2009). *The multilingual subject: What foreign language learners say about their experience and why it matters.* Oxford: Oxford University Press.

Kramsch, C., Howell, T., Warner, C., & Wellmon, C. (2007). Framing foreign language education in the United States: The case of German. *Critical Inquiry in Language Studies, 4*(2), 151–178.

Lo Bianco, J., Liddicoat, A., & Crozet, C. (1999). *Striving for the third place: Intercultural competence through language education.* Melbourne: Language Australia.

Lo Bianco, J., & Slaughter, Y. (2009). Second languages and Australian schooling. *Australian Education Review.* Melbourne: ACER.

Marginson, S., & Sawir, E. (2011). *Ideas for intercultural education.* Basingstoke: Hampshire.

Ōhashi, J. (2009). Natural conversation reconstruction tasks: The language classroom as a meeting place. *Journal of Multidisciplinary International Studies. PORTAL, 6,* 1–15.

Powles, M., & Anderson, D. (1996, November 25–29). *In the balance: Participation and access in TAFE.* Paper presented to Educational Research: Building New Partnerships. Conference jointly organised by Education Research Association, Singapore and Australian Association for Research in Education Singapore Polytechnic, Singapore. Retrieved on January 5, 2012, from http://www.aare.edu.au/96pap/anded96053.txt

Richard, J., & Rogers, T. (1982). *Approaches and methods in language teaching.* New York: Cambridge University Press.

Scarino, A., & Liddicoat, A. J. (2009). *Teaching and learning languages. A Guide.* Melbourne: Curriculum Corporations. Retrieved on May 10, 2012, from www. deewr.gov.au/Schooling/Programs/Documents/Guide.pdf

Tarone, E., & Yule, G. (1989). *Focus on the language learner.* Oxford: Oxford University Press.

Yamanaka, M. (2007). Asia, Australia kankei no kakudai to shinka, *Australia Kenkyuukiyou, 33,* 65–80.

UK Council for International Education. (2004). *International students in UK universities and colleges: Broadening our horizons: Report of the UKCOSA survey.* London, UK: UKCOSA.

9 Assimilation Versus Multiculturalism

Struggles Over the Meaning of 'Tabunka Kyōsei' in Education for Language Minority Children in Japan

Sumiko Taniguchi and Cheiron McMahill

INTRODUCTION

In this chapter we question the extent to which the Japanese educational system can be said to tolerate or promote multiculturalism in relation to its language educational policies and programs for language minority (hereafter LM) children in the era of increasing globalization. Through a critical ideological approach, we problematize the ideological underpinnings of existing policies and programs and then examine how these ideologies manifest themselves in social practices at the local level, taking as one example the struggles by a grassroots initiative to promote a strong form of multiculturalism as 'multilingualism for all' in public schools.

The term '*kokusaika*' or 'internationalization' has been used extensively since the 1980s in Japanese policy documents to describe mainly transnational exchange. Internationalization in education has aimed to promote international understanding and to develop foreign language proficiency needed for international communication (Ministry of Education, Culture, Sports, Science and Technology [hereafter MEXT] 2013). However, '*kokusaika*' often implies Westernization with a focus on learning English (Kubota & McKay 2009; see also Kubota, this volume), which is out of keeping with the reality that most newcomers to Japan are not English-speakers but migrant workers and their families from South America (Brazil and Peru, in particular) (Immigration Control Office 2005). These migrants began to enter Japan due to the revised Immigration Control Law in 1990, which allowed foreigners of Japanese descent and their spouses and dependents to legally live and work in Japan.

Most LMs in Japan are spread out over a wide area for their work and enroll their children in local schools; thus they have accelerated ethnic and linguistic diversity in local communities. This demographic change has been regarded as '*uchinaru kokusaika*' (internationalization within Japan) and has been cited as a sign of mainstream Japanese society becoming more multilingual and multicultural. The need to integrate these newcomers as residents ('*seikatsusha*') into the host community has also led to policy and program initiatives both at national and local government levels (Ministry of Internal Affairs 2006).

Since the 1990s, these initiatives have increasingly adopted the new term '*tabunka kyōsei*' to describe their goals and activities, alongside and gradually as a replacement for '*kokusaika*.' The term '*kyōsei*' originated from the term 'symbiosis' in ecology. Symbiosis signifies a close relationship between two organisms of different kinds that benefits both organisms. Thus '*tabunka kyōsei*' can be translated to English as 'multicultural coexistence' or 'multicultural living in harmony.' As such, it implies some form of multiculturalism; and if used in education, some form of multicultural education (i.e., education aimed at inculcating positive views on diversity within Japan) among not only minorities but also among the Japanese majority.

However, we hold that '*tabunka kyōsei*' has mainly been used to implement policies and programs that do not support multiculturalism or multilingualism but in fact are coercive and assimilative for LMs (Ueda & Yamashita 2006). As evidence of this is the fact that publicly funded programs for LM children address only their acquisition of Japanese language and assimilation to Japanese culture. They lack any measures regarding the maintenance and improvement of LMs' mother tongues and recognition of their cultural heritages and identities (Kanno 2008; McMahill 2010a). Finally, they do not mention, and thus exempt, the Japanese majority from any requirement to change themselves by learning about their LM classmates' languages, cultures, and situations in Japan.

We argue here that the official goal of '*tabunka kyōsei*' is a positive word clothing the old agenda of assimilating minorities rather than diversifying Japanese society. We further find two main types of beliefs based on biased assumptions or knowledge to bolster the assimilationist goals of '*tabunka kyōsei*.' The first belief is that newcomers are following a linear trajectory of migration and acculturation from their homeland to the host community of Japan. The second belief is that the bilingualism/biculturalism of LM children is irrelevant to their educational success in Japan and could even be a deficit or disability (MacSwan 2000). Aforementioned arguments on the ideological underpinnings of existing educational policies and programs are presented in the first section.

In the second section we present a case study that connects the dominant language ideologies on the macrolevel of educational policies with their manifestation in the microlevel of social practices. We take a nonprofit organization's (NPO) implementation of a multilingual educational project as an example to examine how dominant ideologies are contested, accommodated, and negotiated at several different levels. At the same time, we scrutinize the presence of resistance as well as the promotion of multilingual education by LMs.

DOMINANT IDEOLOGIES IN LANGUAGE EDUCATIONAL POLICIES AND PROGRAMS FOR LM CHILDREN

Theoretical Framework

We adopt a critical language ideological approach to educational policies and programs for LM children in Japan. By 'critical' we mean that language educational planning, policies, and programs are not neutral, but work to legitimize particular language ideologies and are mediated by relations of power (McCarty 2004; Wiley 2000). As such, educational policies and programs constitute "deliberate efforts to influence the behavior of others with respect to the acquisition, structure, or functional allocation of their language codes" (Cooper 1989: 45).

However, we take the position that it is not only the dominant groups or institutions that have language ideologies. We define language ideologies as systems of belief shared by a group or social class about the identity and position of the groups, as well as to how the statuses, functions, or uses of languages promote or threaten its interests (van Dijk 1998). As such, while language ideologies are used to establish and maintain hegemonic interests, they can also be used to 'counter' hegemony and work for social justice and equality; for the sake of clarity, we refer to such efforts in this chapter as "counter-ideologies" (van Dijk 1998: 130).

Certain individual or group social actors are also powerfully positioned by their institutional membership as gatekeepers and brokers (van Dijk 1995). Such dominant elites can demand complicity with and hence reproduce dominant language ideologies by controlling the access of weaker groups, such as minorities and foreigners, to material and symbolic resources (Foucault 1979). Nevertheless, we take the view that this power is not absolute or unilateral. This is because language ideologies as well as power relations are not static or complete but are constantly being challenged, appropriated, and recontextualized in a dialectical process of negotiation (Ricento 2000).

The construction, reproduction, and contestation of language ideologies can be revealed not only in written policies and official documents, but also in social practices including discourse, such as the actions, talk, and text of social actors (Bourdieu 1991; Gal 1998; van Dijk 2000). As such, discourse itself can be analyzed critically to obtain evidence of the language ideologies being constructed. In this chapter, we draw in particular on critical analysis of discourse structures i.e., the specific forms of language use in spoken or written texts including lexical choice, omission, foregrounding, backgrounding, and speech acts, i.e., the differential access of certain social actors to speech acts such as permits, allowances, determinations, and warnings (Gee 2012; van Dijk 1998, 2008).

Policies of Assimilation

The increase in foreign resident newcomers in Japan has generated concern for the education of '*gaikokujin jidō/seito*' or 'foreign children' in public schools (Cabinet Office 2010, 2011). The response of MEXT, which is largely in charge of the educational programs of school children at the national level, can be seen in ideological terms as assimilative and supporting the dominance of Japanese nationals by defining 'foreign' children's educational needs foremost as assistance in acquiring Japanese as a second language (hereafter L2) and Japanese culture. It is necessary to point out here that how to refer to such children is itself an ideological choice. Although the lexical label 'foreign' used by MEXT implies 'non-Japanese citizens,' MEXT conflates citizenship status with language ability. We problematize the government's usage by using single quotation marks around 'foreign' in contrast with our usage of the lexical label throughout this chapter of 'language minorities' (LMs) or 'newcomers,' meaning a person who uses a language other than Japanese as a first, home, or heritage language. In fact, some LM children are fluent in Japanese and/or do possess Japanese nationality.

One major reason MEXT has been able to persist in an assimilative policy is that non-Japanese citizens are exempted from compulsory education (Kanno 2008; Nihongo Kyōiku Seisaku MastāPuran Kenkyūkai 2010). On the one hand, their admission to public schools is not blocked; 'foreign' children are free to enter public school if their parents wish to enroll them. As the "Guide for Foreign Students to Start School" prepared by MEXT (2011) states, "Japanese public elementary and secondary schools accept foreign children free of charge, the same as Japanese students, if they wish to enter, and the opportunity of receiving the same education as Japanese students is guaranteed to foreign children."

However, as the words "wish to enter" indicate, while Japanese-national children have a constitutional right and obligation to attend school for nine years, foreign national children do not. Though free to enter the public school system, "they are also free to leave or not to come in the first place" (Kanno 2008: 16). As Kanno (2008: 16) points out, "the fundamental aim of Japanese public education is to foster Japanese citizens; as such, providing education to non-Japanese children is seen as 'doing a favor' (Sakuma 2006)." As a consequence, schools are not obligated to take into account the previous learning experiences, languages, cultures, and future trajectories of 'foreign' national children.

It is a circular argument taking the dominance of Japanese language and cultural identity as the unchangeable status quo for public education, normalizing a medium-of-instruction policy that then "determines which social and linguistic groups have access to political and economic opportunities, and which groups are disenfranchised" (Tsui & Tollefson 2004: 2). As Japanese is exclusively used as the medium of instruction in government-approved schools, without Japanese language proficiency, 'foreign' children are not able to participate in the classroom. MEXT also emphasizes "*tekiō shidō*" or instructing 'foreign' students in how to adapt to Japanese school culture and rules and get along with Japanese students but not providing any concurrent instruction for the majority Japanese (Ōta 2000). Indeed, both Japanese language acquisition and cultural adaptation constitute two of the three most important measures that MEXT proposed for making public schools more accessible to 'foreign' students.[1] (MEXT 2010) To implement these recommendations, Japanese as a Second Language (JSL) curricula (MEXT 2003, 2007) and teaching materials have been developed (e.g., Tokyo University of Foreign Studies 2006), and schools with large numbers of foreign nationals can apply for extra teachers of JSL, although there is currently no special requirement or qualification to become a JSL teacher in the public schools.

As Gottlieb (2012) points out, the omission of certain goals in official educational policy and program funding also reveals ideological motivations: in the case of Japan, this can be seen in the absence of any initiative to maintain and develop LMs' first languages, cultures, and identities. Some may argue that in areas with large numbers of LM children, bilingual support teachers who speak the children's first language (hereafter L1) are working as part-timers in many JSL classrooms. However, the use of the L1 is sanctioned only in the service of acquiring the Japanese language or giving psychological support (Ogawa 2002). Literacy or academic development in the L1 is not officially approved; and if it happens, it is carried out surreptitiously (McMahill & Muramoto 2011).

The risk of this JSL-centered policy, attested to by LM parents, is the attrition of children's first language (L1) and culture. The phrase "children who require Japanese language instruction" suggests that children have other languages besides Japanese (Ishii 1999: 148). However, their other languages are often considered problems rather than assets. Although the importance of maintaining and developing LM children's first languages, cultures, and identities has been advocated by many scholars (e.g., Cummins 1996; Kanno 2008; McMahill 2010a), and first language maintenance classes have been in operation in some local areas (e.g., Ishii 1999), compared to JSL programs, less attention and little or no public financial support have been allocated to L1 maintenance programs.

Popular Beliefs Bolstering Japanese-Only Policies

As we have discussed, the real aim of maintaining the advantage of the Japanese majority is often masked by 'commonsense' arguments that newcomers becoming monolingual in Japanese and assimilating to Japanese cultural norms is 'for their own good.' Two of the most common beliefs to justify this can be identified. 'Beliefs' here refers to the constituent parts of ideologies, subsuming knowledge and opinion (van Dijk 1998). These are: 1) that newcomers, including economic migrants, are increasingly 'settling down' in Japan, and therefore urgently need to acquire Japanese; and 2) that JSL instruction does not need to or should not take the first or heritage languages or the bi-/multilingualism of students into account for various reasons, including feasibility, fairness, and efficacy. In relation to the last point, we will touch on the popular belief that using or developing the first language or heritage language risks producing a population of semilingual or double-limited children whose cognitive and literacy skills are undeveloped or '*chūto-hampa*' (not fully developed) in any language (McMahill 2010b).

Firstly, the belief that migrants are 'settling down' is based on the assumption that newcomers are following a unidirectional trajectory of migration and acculturation from their homeland to Japan. The unidirectional perspective presupposes the urgency of abandoning one's first language and culture in order to learn the second and acculturate to the target language group, "whether this abandonment is termed 'acculturation' or 'integration.'" (Pavlenko 2002: 279) The following report from MEXT on policies for enriching the education of 'foreign' children clearly shows the priority given to Japanese language instruction and adaptation justified by the assumption of permanent immigration to Japan:

> As foreigners in our country continue to stay longer and settle down here, it is essential that foreign children attend school and acquire the Japanese knowledge and skills they need to achieve a happy life in our country as members of society; this is also exceedingly significant for the stability and development of our own nation's society (MEXT 2008a).

Key self-serving assumptions here are that LM children *should* or *can* stay on, assimilate, and become full members of Japanese society and that if they do not, it may have a destabilizing effect on Japanese society, and Japanese language acquisition plays a pivotal role in this successful assimilation.

However, it is noteworthy that there have been numerous government surveys indicating the unstable employment conditions of foreign nationals who are bound to have an impact on their family's stability and thus their children's education. Most foreign residents in Japan are limited to positions as dispatched workers and temporary contract employees (Cabinet Office 2010), meaning that although it is illegal to discriminate on the basis of nationality in employment, these workers are the first to be let go in times of economic downturn and the last to be hired when the economy improves (Yasuda 2010). In a 2006 Ministry of Land, Infrastructure, Transportation and Tourism (MLITT) survey of 738 foreign national residents of the North Kanto region, only 3.1% said they owned their own homes in Japan; just 26.4% of respondents said they were directly employed at their workplaces; and only 28.6% made a single entry to Japan, while most had been back and forth between their countries of birth and Japan multiple times (MLITT 2006). The children of these workers by necessity have "indeterminate future trajectories" (Kanno 2008: 42) that preclude permanent immigration to Japan.

The second belief supporting the irrelevance of L1 maintenance and development for LM children is the supposed negative effect of L1 on L2 acquisition. Foreign students' maintenance of their L1 is popularly understood to delay their acquisition of Japanese (Gunma Ken Tabunka Kyōsei Suishin Kondankai 2010). Further, policy is guided by the principle of egalitarianism (*byōdōshugi*) (Moorehead 2012), meaning all students should be treated equally. Since students are from a variety of language backgrounds, it is unfair to support only those who speak major foreign languages, such as Portuguese and Spanish. If it is not possible to support every language, doing so for only some languages will lead to inequality and discrimination, "creating a language minority within language minority" (Itō 2011: 15).

Going even further, the term 'double-limited' is currently used interchangeably with 'semilingual' in the Japanese media and academia to blame the very bilingual and bicultural ability of such children for their affliction, rather than the lack of appropriate support for their bilingualism (McMahill 2010b). As more 'foreign' children drop out of school, such children are coming to be labeled as educational 'problems' as opposed to resources. It is the LM children who are assumed to need 'fixing,' not the school system.

This deficit theory of LMs (MacSwan 2000) can be seen creeping into educational policy. In accordance with the revision of the Basic Act on Education (*Kyōiku kihon hō*) in 2006, for example, a Basic Plan for the Promotion of Education (*Kyōiku shinkō kihon keikaku*) was proposed in July, 2008, including special education to address the special needs of 'foreign' students and Japanese students returning from sojourns abroad. A provisional translation of the passage from the MEXT website states:

Promoting Special Education to Address Special Needs

Paragraph 2, Article 4 of the revised Basic Act on Education newly provides for assistance for the education of *persons with disabilities*. From the viewpoint of assisting their autonomous efforts for independence and social participation, the government is promoting Special Needs Education that intends to improve their abilities and let them overcome difficulties in living and learning based on the understanding of individual educational needs and providing appropriate guidance and assistance. In addition, education for *foreign students and other students with special needs* will be promoted (italics added) (MEXT 2008b).

The Basic Plan allows more flexibility in public education so more appropriate support can be given to meet students' needs. In so doing, it makes special needs education and the education of 'foreign' students into two exceptions to the principle of egalitarianism in Japanese public education (Moorehead 2012), which is important in order to establish special programs.

At the same time, however, it is problematic that services for 'foreign' students are being justified in education policy by educational laws regarding children with disabilities. This might strengthen the misconception that LM children have a kind of 'language disability' in that they may not have acquired the Japanese language to the level of their Japanese monolingual peers.

To sum up this section: we have argued that the dominant language ideologies on the macrolevel of educational policies and programs for LMs are assimilative and are bolstered by two types of popular beliefs related to newcomers and multiculturalism, which do not necessarily reflect the complex statuses and aspirations of the LMs themselves. Such policies result in the devaluation of the multiple languages and cultures of minority children and their identities.

COUNTER-IDEOLOGIES AT THE LOCAL LEVEL

In this section we focus on the ways in which the dominant language ideologies on the macrolevel manifest themselves in social practices at the local level. Specifically, we describe one example of a nonprofit organization's (NPO) struggle to promote a counter-ideology valuing the languages and cultures of minority children as resources for developing multilingualism and multiculturalism for everyone in Japan.

The language program examined here is an after-school minority language project for elementary school students called the Dream Club, which was conducted by the Multilingual Education Research Institute nonprofit organization or NPO, better known as the International Community School or ICS. It was a grassroots organization founded by immigrant parents, teachers, and their Japanese friends in 2000 to create and implement community-based, multilingual educational programs and services in Gunma Prefecture. ICS was one of the first NPOs to be legally registered and run by mainly foreign residents in Japan.

Its founding counter-ideology asserted the need for and value to all of greater multilingualism and multiculturalism in Japan in the face of increasing globalization. To these ends, ICS accepted students of any language background and ethnicity, including Japanese, although the majority of students were Brazilian or Peruvian foreign or dual nationals. Its projects included a full-time school for K–12 in Portuguese, Spanish, Japanese, and English, after-school and Saturday classes in English, Spanish, Portuguese, Japanese, and Urdu; and a multilingual counseling and advocacy service.[2] Along with many volunteers, the paid staff of ICS averaged about thirteen people each year and consisted mainly of Brazilian, Peruvian, and Japanese nationals, but with significant participation by immigrants from the Philippines, Pakistan, Iran, the U.S., and Vietnam. All events and meetings were conducted in a mixture of Portuguese, Spanish, Japanese, and English.

ICS planned to start the Dream Club in order to foster awareness of and interest in the heritage or first languages of minority children as worthy subjects of study for all children, meaning for Japanese children as well, within the public elementary schools. At the time of the Dream Club, ICS was located in G City (pseudonym), the area with the greatest number of foreign residents in Gunma.[3] ICS had conducted an after-school, multilingual homework club on its own premises since 2000, but the number of participants was always limited by the difficulty of providing free transportation after school from the public schools to ICS and then to the children's homes each day.[4] For this reason, and also to spare children the tiring bus ride, ICS had been trying for some years to get permission to hold classes in the public schools themselves.

This step entailed ICS staff deciding to take their educational project outside the building ICS rented and controlled as an NPO into institutional space controlled by the Japanese government. At this point, ICS formulated two goals for the Dream Club related to challenging the dominant language ideologies in the government schools: to sanction the use of the children's mother tongues within the usual 'Japanese-only' space of the schools and to attempt to raise consciousness and change attitudes by exposing a wider range of principals, teachers, and students, both minority and Japanese, to the counter-ideology of 'multiculturalism and multilingualism for all.'

ICS, however, lacked the institutional power that MEXT and government schools possess, what Tsui and Tollefson (2004: 17) call "conditions for implementation," i.e., "legitimation of policies, adequate provision of resources, and strong institutional support." Therefore, ICS staff undertook many discursive strategies to project their approach as something aligned with the ideology of the grant provider to secure the support, both material and political, necessary to implement the program. In the following sections, we will examine accommodation, negotiation, and conflict between dominant ideologies and counter-ideologies manifested at three different levels: 1) the level of conception and funding, 2) the local institutional level, and 3) the classroom discourse level.

Accommodation to Japanese Institutions at the Level of Conception and Funding

Language ideologies reflect and construct relations of power and inequality between groups with different interests, and when encoded in law, determine the rights and institutional identities of social actors (van Dijk 1998). The result is that powerful social actors or groups are invested by their institutional membership with the ability to control and manipulate those in a weaker position, i.e., to compel them to act in the interests of the powerful and against their own best interests (van Dijk 2006). Before even beginning the Dream Club, ICS was in a powerless position in terms of institutional identity and material resources vis-à-vis Japanese government institutions, because MEXT maintained criteria for school recognition that denied it along with other non-Japanese language medium institutions from legal school status and funding.[5] As an NPO carrying out educational activities rather than a school, ICS relied on membership fees, tuition payments, and short-term public and private grants and subsidies to operate its projects and pay its administrators and teachers, who depended on ICS for their livelihood. However, the public schools made not charging students any fees a strict condition of allowing ICS to use public school classrooms for the Dream Club, and ICS had no choice but to act against its own interests and accept the school board's policy and look for grants for funding.

However, in 2011, ICS could not locate any funding sources for NPOs in Japan in support of the mother tongue or heritage language education of minorities. With reference to speech act theory, which examines the differential access of certain social actors to speech acts (van Dijk 1998), public and private grant agencies were positioned as institutional actors with the power to prohibit multilingual/multicultural education by omitting it as a legitimate goal of the social welfare and educational activities they would fund. The closest match were grants available through the Agency for Cultural Affairs (*Bunkachō*), part of MEXT, for integrating foreigners as '*seikatsusha*' or residents via Japanese language education (Agency for Cultural Affairs 2013), based on the ideological assumption we discussed in the first section that foreigners are settling down in Japan and therefore urgently require instruction in practical Japanese. Within the various options available for the 2011 grant year, ICS selected the grant category of "*Nihongo kyōshitsu secchi un'ei*," or, establishing and operating JSL classrooms for foreign residents, as it was the only one that would fund actual language instruction. At this point, then, in order to get funding, ICS had no choice but to officially align its own goal of multilingual education with the economically powerful funding agency's goal of JSL education to assist foreigners in settling down in Japan, becoming empowered as members of society, and full participants in social life (Agency for Cultural Affairs 2011).

At the level of writing the grant application, grant writers at ICS also used various discursive strategies such as 'backgrounding,' 'lexical choice' and 'speech act' (van Dijk 1998; 2008) to overtly accommodate and covertly counter the funding agency's ideologies. For example, these grants were aimed in principle at adult foreign residents, but could include children as long as the parents were involved in some way. Further, the grants were aimed at foreign nationals, but Japanese nationals were not explicitly forbidden.

Firstly, ICS used the strategies of lexical choice, 'vagueness' as well as 'backgrounding' in its grant application by slipping in the inclusion of Japanese participants as "サポーター" (supporters) and clarifying that this meant Japanese classmates and their parents in parentheses as follows:

受講対象者：群馬県Ｇ市の公立小学校に通う外国人生徒1年生〜3年生とその保護者及びサポーター（興味ある日本人の同級生と保護者の任意参加も自　由）。

English Translation: Intended participants: 1st to 3rd grade foreign students attending G City, Gunma Prefecture public elementary schools and their parents and supporters (Interested Japanese classmates and their parents may also participate freely as their own volition.).

Secondly, the application foregrounded the operation of a Japanese language classroom as its main goal, and backgrounded its actual main objective of teaching the L1s and cultures of minority children by downgrading it to a strategy for more effectively achieving this goal as follows:

保護者も参加可能で、子どもの母国語・母国の文化を知ることを通して多文化な視点の支援も行う日本語教室の設置と運営。

English Translation: To establish and operate a Japanese language classroom in which parents could also participate, and which supports children from a multicultural perspective through being aware of their mother tongues and mother countries' cultures (ICS grant report[6] 2011: 1)

Thirdly, ICS stated its grant objectives in a very general way as "自尊心を高め" (raising self-esteem) and "自立的な適応力を向上させる" (improving students' autonomous power of adaptation) in conjunction with the official goal of raising Japanese communication ability and empowerment, while deliberately not specifying that it believed the most effective way to do this was by supporting the L1 and home cultures of students:

目的：外国人の子どもの日本語コミュニケーション能力と自尊心を高め、学校生活における自立的な適応力を向上させること。また、将来の進路についての 選択肢に関わる日本語能力を得ること。

English Translation:

Objectives: To raise the Japanese communication ability and self-esteem of foreign children and improve their autonomous ability to adapt to school life. Also, to allow them to obtain the Japanese language ability needed for future education and employment (ICS grant report 2011: 1) (see footnote 6).

Thus ICS endorsed the agency's goal of improving Japanese ability without promising to actually teach Japanese, while remaining silent about its intention to in fact teach the L1s of students as a way to indirectly improve their academic learning in Japanese outside of the Dream Club.

Lastly, ICS did not include its fundamental ideology in the grant application, i.e., that multilingual education in which Japanese along with LM children learned and appreciated the minority languages and cultures of their classmates was the key to preventing racial bullying and discrimination in Japan and an aim of all ICS activities. It did state bullying as a main reason for foreign children not attending school or leaving Japan, but backgrounded the prevention of bullying by listing it as the last of five needs of foreign children in the Dream Club grant application. In so doing, it stressed rather the ability of ICS staff to communicate with parents and to act as mediators with the school if necessary to revolve claims of bullying as follows:

> いじめの予防の必要性：母国への帰国という事態や不登校となる主
> 要な原因のひとつとして、いじめがある。当教室への親の参加機会
> を積極的に提供し、母国語を解する教授者のもと、親自身の体験学
> 習や親子との面談を行うことのできる教室が学内にあれば、問題が
> 大きくなる前に解決できる。いじめはデリケートで話しにくいこと
> であるので、学校関係者以外の中立的な第三者であることにより予
> 防をむしろ行いやすい。

> English Translation: The necessity of preventing bullying: One of the main causes for the fact that [foreign children] return to their countries and/or are truant from school in Japan is bullying. This problem could be solved before it gets too big if there were a classroom in the school in which [foreign] parents are actively given opportunities to participate in experiential activities and can consult with teachers who speak their languages. Bullying can be an emotional and hard to discuss topic, so a neutral third party who is not involved with the school might be even more effective in preventing it.

In the end, ICS's application was approved; not only the first year, but later for a second year.

Negotiation at the Local Institutional Level: District Politicians, School Districts, and Principals

After securing funding, ICS needed to undertake negotiations at the local institutional level, such as with school districts and school principals in order to implement the Dream Club project at the site of local public schools which are controlled by the Japanese government. This process revealed the negotiation of ideologies, as well as the power relations that marginalize and disempower LM groups.

Firstly, ICS cooperated with the ideological aim of a Japanese power broker, a local politician, in order to obtain permission from the Superintendent of Education of G City to approach the principals of its municipal elementary schools. This city councilor represented the district in which ICS was located and was concerned with the situation of out-of-school foreign students, who had dropped out of junior high school but were too young to legally work and who were often in danger of being recruited by criminal gangs for the purpose of shoplifting and burglary. This councilor wished to provide educational and social welfare activities to help prevent the school truancy of foreign students and had approached ICS earlier to offer his support.

The councilor set up the meeting with the superintendent, something ICS did not have the clout to do on its own, and he also attended the meeting with ICS representatives. Going along with the councilor's belief that foreign youth lacked sufficient support for staying in school, ICS appealed for permission to conduct an after-school club that would increase foreign students' self-esteem and school attendance, also thus helping to prevent truancy (and by implication, delinquency) in the future. The superintendent gave his approval and personally called each school to ask for their cooperation, although he added that it would be up to each individual principal as to whether to allow the club at their schools. This was a significant achievement, as it was the first time in Gunma Prefecture that an NPO led by mainly foreign parents and teachers had gotten the endorsement of the superintendent to use public school facilities for their activities. However, it also meant that members of the ICS staff allowed themselves to appear compliant with a dominant discourse of deficit in which LM students themselves are blamed, this time as potential delinquents, for their educational and social problems.

Secondly, ICS staff then approached four elementary schools (herein referred to as Schools A, B, C, and D) with the largest concentrations of foreign students. While these school principals had already been phoned by the school superintendent, and under that pressure from above agreed to a meeting and nominally agreed to host the Dream Club, problems of access and scheduling and intended participants were immediately raised. The official school calendar and activity schedule was "fixed" and "could not" be modified for nonschool functions. Further, public school teachers had to be already on duty during the Dream Club in order to take responsibility for student safety on the school grounds. The principal and vice-principal of each school did not want to ask teachers to stay later and supervise the facilities for activities they considered non-school-related. Principals agreed to ICS's request to allow Japanese students to attend the Dream Club, while insisting that the Club was "meant for only 'foreign' students." Here the principals and vice-principals also imposed the 'deficiency' theory as a condition of the Club going forward, maintaining that only LM need 'special' education to allow them to better adapt, rather than all children needing multicultural and multilingual education.

In addition, each school revealed their apprehensions about collaborating with 'foreigners' by stipulating that a Japanese coordinator at ICS, and by implication not a foreign staff member, be appointed as the official go-between between ICS and the school in order to "avoid misunderstandings."

In the end, the four public schools would only agree to allow younger children (grades 1–3 or six to nine years old) to join in the Dream Club on those afternoons when older children (grades 4–6) already had a once-a-week, after-school club activity. This meant that the Dream Club could only recruit from half of the students in the school and had to dilute its content to fit within one hour from 3:00 to 4:00 p.m., once a week or less, depending on the school calendar. Furthermore, the grant for the Dream Club from the Agency for Cultural Affairs only covered two out of the three school terms, further shortening the amount of instruction. As a result, the Dream Club met for a total of 138 hours in the public schools as follows:

Figure 9.1 shows that the hours varied widely depending on the school, related to differences in the frequency of club activities for older children at each public school and also perhaps the willingness of each school principal to insert the Dream Club into the schedule.

The number of students who participated at each school also varied greatly depending on whether the school administrators actively distributed and collected Dream Club flyers and sign-up sheets, as well as on the frequency with which the Club met. It is clear that School A, which had the most supportive principal and where the Club met almost every week, also had the greatest participation (Figure 9.2).

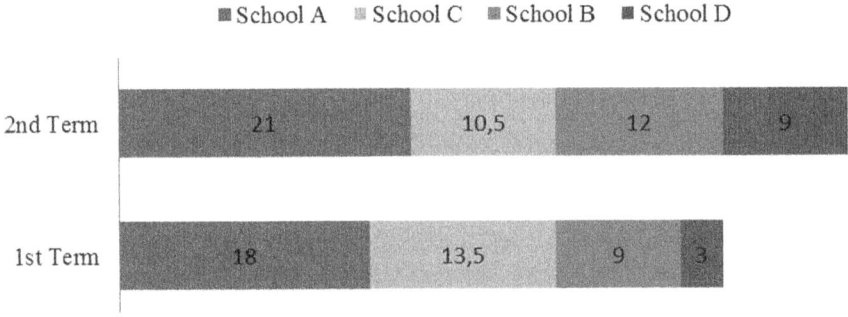

Figure 9.1 Hours Dream Club Held at Each School

School	A	B	D	C
Number of participants	30	7	6	2

Figure 9.2 Number of Participants at Each School

In this way, the principals exercised their institutional power to control the contextual conditions of the Dream Club, i.e., to severely limit the hours, scope and number of participants, and recruitment of participants in the Dream Club at their schools, while still officially cooperating with it in accordance with the request of the superintendent of schools. If ICS as the supplicant had not accepted these limitations, the principals could have used that as an excuse to not cooperate at all, so ICS agreed.

However, ICS had some mitigating power through its position in the LM community to approach sympathetic Brazilian and Peruvian teaching assistants at three of the elementary schools in their own languages outside of school hours. ICS even used the covert strategy of paying a small honorarium to Brazilian and Peruvian teaching assistants at the elementary schools to pass out flyers to LM students and their parents and talk to them about the Dream Club. In the end, a total of 69 foreign students participated in the Club over the year (27 Peruvians, 25 Brazilians, 3 dual Peruvian-Brazilian nationals, 8 Vietnamese, two Americans, two Pakistanis, one Thai, and one Filipino), along with a total of 16 Japanese.

Ideological Conflict at the Level of Public Image

As was mentioned before, ICS adapted its mission and goals for the Dream Club to the ideology of the Agency for Cultural Affairs that the greatest need of foreign nationals is greater acquisition of Japanese language and culture because it believed this was necessary to obtain funding. However, at one point, ICS went outside the government power structure and used the mass media to publicly assert its counter-ideology that not only JSL for foreigners, but an appreciation for multiculturalism and multilingualism, was necessary for the whole society. This was possible because ICS was contacted by a young Japanese reporter who was sympathetic to discrimination against ethnic minorities in Japanese public schools. This reporter was following up on a case of suicide a year before in which a middle school student with a Filipina mother had committed suicide after being taunted with racial slurs in her school for years. The reporter wished to interview someone at ICS to see if foreign residents believed the local educational authorities had taken any concrete steps to prevent such racial bullying.

Because School A seemed to be the most successful example of the Dream Club, with School A's permission, ICS invited a reporter to observe it and take photos for a Japanese newspaper. McMahill used the interview to construct School A as a model example of proactively tackling the issue of school bullying by allowing the Dream Club—in that Japanese children participating in the Club could experience being a linguistic minority and develop empathy for minority classmates—which could then serve to prevent school bullying toward foreign children.

The reporter published this, and the vice-principal of School A immediately called the Japanese coordinator at ICS when the article appeared in order to lodge a complaint. He said that he and the principal at School A were upset by the comments, as they gave the public the impression that Japanese children had something to learn from the Dream Club, whereas it was supposed to be aimed only at foreigners, again echoing the 'deficit' argument regarding LM. The vice-principal also expressed his displeasure with the article, which he thought implied that bullying might exist at School A, which was not the case; here he refused to legitimize ICS's counter-ideology of LM as victims of Japanese bullying. ICS was asked to take care not to make similar comments in the future as a condition of continuing the Dream Club. The power of the vice-principal as an institutional actor can be seen in his ability to issue this ultimatum to ICS. However, in this case, because the article was already published and there was no call to retract it or publicly apologize, ICS did succeed in using the existence of the Dream Club to put its counter-ideology out in public by using the mass media.

Accommodation at the Classroom Discourse Level: Making Minority Language Instruction Comfortable for the Language Majority

We already mentioned in the first section that the ideology of egalitarianism in education has been used as an excuse in Japan not to support L1 education. ICS in its grant application, as well, did not mention any specific community language for this reason.

In practice, however, to challenge the dominance of Japanese and English and also to reflect and value the cultural and linguistic diversity actually present at each of the schools, ICS made the decision to teach using mainly Portuguese, Spanish, and Vietnamese, hoping to attract participants from these language groups along with their friends. ICS teachers took turns preparing lessons so that the initial presentation of each class's themes would alternate between each of these three main languages and cultures, after which children would split into their own L1 groups for communication and literacy practice. Japanese children could join any of the L1 groups they liked. English was only used on two occasions: when a Filipino and an Australian teacher each prepared and led the lesson.[7]

In addition, although Japanese explanations and translations were provided to facilitate the participation of Japanese students who wanted to join the class, care was taken to always present the lessons first in the target language and to only use Japanese as a supplement. The intent was to position the minority language as the 'default' and natural language of instruction, putting Japanese monolingual speakers in the weaker position of having to listen to a language they did not know and be forced to rely on nonverbal cues to get the gist, while waiting for a Japanese translation. At the same time, they saw their bilingual classmates following and participating in both languages and could gain a new appreciation of the advantages of knowing another language.

However, accommodating the participation of Japanese students, teachers, and administrators diminished the use of the L1 for LM children. LM children whose Japanese friends came to class would frequently stop to interpret for them or were interrupted by them with questions or comments in Japanese. Given that the Dream Club met for only one hour a week at each school, any time or attention not spent on a minority child's own home language(s) was a loss of an opportunity.

Dilution of LM instruction can also be inferred in the program evaluations made by the students and their parents. The results show that, although the overall evaluation of the program was positive, they perceived a greater benefit in terms of interest in their countries of origin and cultures and motivation toward school rather than specifically toward the mother tongue as shown in Figures 9.3 and 9.4 that follow.

Thus the case of the Dream Club seems to support Gottlieb's (2012) assertion that "The concept of community languages has not yet entered into the language policy process" in Japan (p. 155). The obstacles the project faced resulted in the time and focus spent on L1 fluency and literacy being watered down so that the main benefits to minority participants appear to have ended up being more social and psychological than educational.

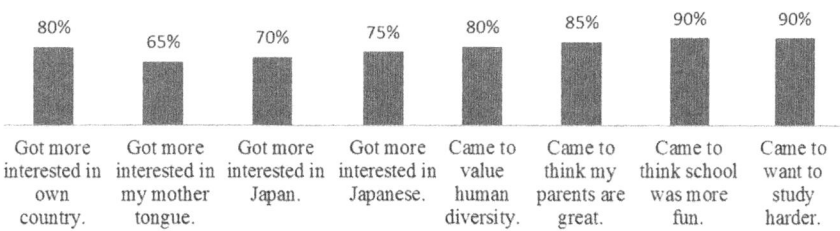

Figure 9.3   Student Evaluations of How the Dream Club Affected Them N=20

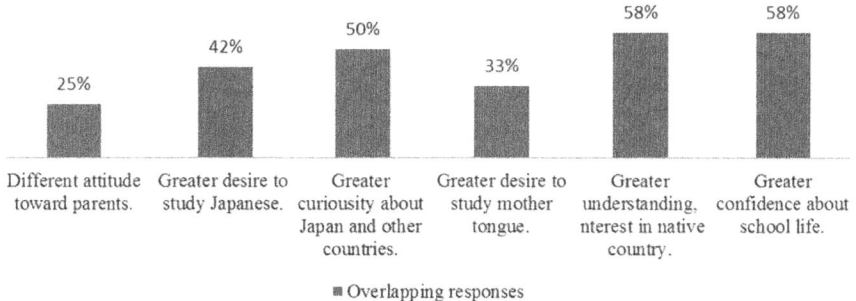

Figure 9.4   Parents' Evaluation of What Their Children Gained N=12

CONCLUDING REMARKS

In this chapter, we have discussed the dominant institutional language ideologies in publicly funded language educational policies and programs for LM children in Japan and examined how these ideologies manifest themselves in social practices at the local level by looking at the case of a multilingual and multicultural project called the Dream Club conducted by an NPO at the site of local Japanese public schools. We conclude that language ideologies supporting JSL instruction, while paying lip service to multiculturalism, are aimed at assimilation under the assumption that foreign nationals should settle down and stay in Japan. Minority languages and cultures are only tolerated as a means to that end and only for LM children, not for the Japanese majority. Further, special educational assistance to such children is justified within the rubric of deficiencies or 'disabilities.' ICS, as a grassroots organization, in challenging these language ideologies was forced into the position of supplicant and became to some extent controlled by and complicit with the beliefs and interests of institutions of government grant agencies, city educational officials, elementary school administrators, staff, and even students.

Nevertheless, the Dream Club project did go forward, did mainly focus on an appreciation of minority languages and cultures and include Japanese students, and did include oral communication as well as literacy practice in the L1s of LM students. As such, it provides a case of ideologies being contested and negotiated, however covertly, not only by LM groups, but within Japanese institutions themselves. This is because although ICS took the initiative, it could not have implemented it without the existence of some alternative sources of power for minorities, including sympathetic members of government, concerned politicians and educational officials, dissenters in the mass media, and solidarity among some members of the LM communities. Evidence such as increasing opportunities for citizens' groups to obtain funding, more accessibility to the local public schools, and growing interest in non-English languages and cultures of immigrants by some Japanese children and their parents all indicate the potential for creating educational programs to recognize and support minority children's home languages, cultures, and identities. It is hoped that the shift toward valuing diversity as a resource gradually leads to an opening up of the Japanese educational systems to transformation and equal participation by newcomers.

NOTES

1. The third is improving the environment for receiving/orienting 'foreign' pupils/students and providing a support system for their further education and employment.
2. McMahill was a founder and chair of the board of ICS and this description of ICS is based on her 2006 PhD research (McMahill, 2006), while information on the implementation of the Dream Club is drawn from her

participant-observation notes, ICS internal documents, public documents and meeting notes. Taniguchi served as a member of the board of the NPO from 2010–2012 and also served on the steering committee for the Dream Club.
3. According to Gunma Prefectural statistics, 10,443 of the 207,264 residents of G City as of December 31, 2011, were foreign nationals accounting for 24.7% of foreign nationals in Gunma Prefecture. The largest national group was Brazilians, followed by Chinese, Filipino, Peruvian, and Korean (http://www.pref.gunma.jp/04/c3600057.html, retrieved on 7 May, 2013).
4. Because most foreign parents either worked long hours and could not transport their children to and from ICS or did not own cars, ICS had to operate two school buses for which parents paid on a sliding fee basis.
5. There are many obstacles to international or ethnic schools receiving recognition in Japan, but the first is that full-time academic schools are required to follow MEXT's curricula in order to be recognized.
6. This report can be accessed at the following website: http://www.bunka.go.jp/kokugo_nihongo/kyoiku/seikatsusya/h22/pdf/h22_kyoushitsu_gunma_03.pdf
7. The Dream Club curriculum included learning and transforming traditional stories from various countries along with the students, to engage the students in discussion and literacy activities, and to better reflect their experiences and concerns as minorities in Japan.

REFERENCES

Agency for Cultural Affairs. (2011). *Seikatsusya to shite no gaikokujin ni taisuru nihongo kyōiku no hyōjuntekina karikyuramuan katsuyō no tame no gaidobukku* [Guidebook for utilizing standard JSL curriculum plan for foreigners as residents]. Retrieved on May 7, 2013, from http://www.bunka.go.jp/kokugo_nihongo/kyouiku/nihongo_curriculum/pdf/curriculum_guidebook_ver05.pdf

Agency for Cultural Affairs. (2013). *Seikatsusya to shite no gaikokujin no tame no nihongo kyōiku jigyō* [JSL education project for foreigners as residents]. Retrieved on May 2, 2013, from http://www.bunka.go.jp/kokugo_nihongo/kyoiku/seikatsusya/index.html

Bourdieu, P. (1991). *Language and symbolic power* (J. Thompson, Ed.; G. Raymond & M. Adamson, Trans.). Oxford: Polity Press.

Cabinet Office. (2010). *Nikkei teijū gaikokujin shisaku ni kansuru kihon hōshin* [Basic policy on measures for foreign residents of Japanese descent]. Retrieved on May 10, 2012, from http://www8.cao.go.jp/teiju-portal/eng/policy/pdf/eng-full_text.pdf

Cabinet Office. (2011). *Nikkei teijū gaikokujin shisaku ni kansuru kōdō keikaku* [Action plan on measures for foreign residents of Japanese descent]. Retrieved on May 10, 2012, from http://www8.cao.go.jp/teiju-portal/eng/policy/pdf/eng-full_text_action.pdf

Cooper, R. L. (1989). *Language planning and social change.* Cambridge: Cambridge University Press.

Cummins, J. (1996). *Negotiating identities: Education for empowerment in a diverse society.* Ontario: California Association for Bilingual Education.

Foucault, M. (1979). *Discipline and punish: The birth of the prison.* New York: Knopf Doubleday Publishing Group.

Gal, S. (1998). Multiplicity and contention among language ideologies: A commentary. In B. Schieffelin, K. A. Woolard, & P. V. Kroskrity (Eds.), *Language Ideologies: Practice and Theory* (pp. 317–331). New York: Oxford University Press.

Gee, J. P. (2012). *Social linguistics and literacies: Ideologies in discourses* (4th ed.). London, New York: Routledge.

Gottlieb, N. (2012). *Language policy in Japan: The challenge of change*. Cambridge: Cambridge University Press.

Gunma Ken Tabunka Kyōsei Suishin Kondankai. (2010, March 17). *Gunma ken tabunka kyōsei suishin kondankai gijiroku* [The minutes of the proceedings on the promotion of multicultural co-existence in Gunma]. Unpublished.

Immigration Control Office. (2005). *Tōroku gaikokujin tōkei* [Foreign registration statistics]. Retrieved on May 22, 2013, from http://www.immi-moj.go.jp/toukei/index.html

Ishii, M. (1999). Tayōna gengo haikei o motsu kodomo no bogo kyōiku no genjō [Situation of first language education for children from various language backgrounds]. *Chūgoku kikokusha teichaku sokushin sentā kiyō, 7,* 148–189.

Itō, T. (2011). Gunma ni okeru chiiki nihongo kyōiku no arikata: Kadai no kashika ni mukete. [State of Japanese language education in Gunma: Toward identifying tasks]. *Gunma kenritsu joshi daigaku kokubungaku kenkyū, 31,* 13–29.

Kanno, Y. (2008). *Language and education in Japan: Unequal access to bilingualism*. London: Palgrave/Macmillan.

Kubota, R., & McKay, S. (2009). Globalization and language learning in rural Japan: The role of English in the local linguistic ecology. *TESOL Quarterly, 43*(4), 593–619.

MacSwan, J. (2000). The threshold hypothesis, semilingualism, and other contributions to a deficit view of linguistic minorities. *Hispanic Journal of Behavioral Sciences, 22*(1), 3–45.

McCarty, T. L. (2004). Dangerous difference: A critical-historical analysis of language education policies in the United States. In J. W. Tollefson & A. B. M. Tsui (Eds.), *Medium of Instruction Policies: Which Agenda? Whose Agenda?* (pp. 71–93). Mahwah, NJ: Lawrence Erlbaum.

McMahill, C. (2006). *Valuing minority children and their languages in Japan: A case study of a Portuguese, English, and Japanese community language school*. PhD thesis, Lancaster University. Available through UMI.

McMahill, C. (2010a). Results of a local survey of students who returned to Brazil from Japan: Looking back on educational experiences during the stay in Japan. *Daitō Bunka University Keiei Ronshū (Management Journal), 19,* 133–149.

McMahill, C. (2010b, December 7). "Jikan no mondai dake" to makkō hanron. Mikkumeehiru Daito Bunka Daigaku kyōju ni kiku- anata no tonari no gaikokujindaburu rimiteddo (3). ["Just a matter of time": Professor McMahill of Daito Bunka University argues head-on against the term "double-limited (3)."] Interview in *Naigai Kyōiku* 6042, 2–3.

McMahill, C. & Muramoto, E. (2011). *Impacto Educacional sobre as Crianças Retornadas do Japão: Considerações a partir das Famílias Nikkeis Retornadas* [Educational impact on returnee children: Considerations from returned Nikkei families]. Paper given on September 27, 2011 at the International Symposium on Estudos Japoneses na América Latina—Diálogos, Perspectivas e Projetos Conjuntos, Association of Brazilian Japanese Studies, Sao Paulo.

Ministry of Education, Culture, Sports, Science and Technology. (2003). *Gakkō kyōiku ni okeru JSL karikyuramu no kaihatsu ni tsuite saishū hōkoku: Shōgakkō hen* [The final report on the development of the JSL curriculum in public schools: Elementary school level]. Retrieved on May 10, 2012, from http://www.mext.go.jp/a_menu/shotou/clarinet/ 003/001/ 008.htm

Ministry of Education, Culture, Sports, Science and Technology. (2007). *Gakkō kyōiku ni okeru JSL karikyuramu Chūgakkō hen* [Development of the JSL curriculum in public schools: Junior high school level]. Retrieved on May 10, 2012, from http://www.mext.go.jp/a_menu/shotou/clarinet/003/001/011.htm

Ministry of Education, Culture, Sports, Science and Technology. (2008a). *Gaikokujin jidō seito kyōiku no jūjitsu hōsaku ni tsuite hōkoku* [Report on policies for enriching

the education of foreign children]. Retrieved on May 15, 2012, from http://www.
mext.go.jp/b_menu/shingi/chousa/shotou/042/houkoku/08070301.htm
Ministry of Education, Culture, Sports, Science and Technology. (2008b). *Kyōiku
shinkō kihon keikaku* [Basic plan for the promotion of education]. Retrieved on
May 15, 2012, from http://www.mext.go.jp/english/lawandplan/1303463.htm
Ministry of Education, Culture, Sports, Science and Technology. (2010). *Teijū gaikokujin no kodomo no kyōiku nado ni kansuru seisaku kondankai no iken o
fumaeta monbukagakushō no seisaku no pointo* [Major points of policies of
MEXT in accordance with the opinions of the council for education of the children of foreign residents]. Retrieved on May 15, 2012, from http://www.mext.
go.jp/b_menu/shingi/chousa/kokusai/008/ toushin/1294066.htm
Ministry of Education, Culture, Sports, Science and Technology. (2011). *Gaikokujin no tame no shūgaku gaido* (Guide for foreign students to start school).
Retrieved on May 30, 2012, from http://www.mext.go.jp/a_menu/shotou/clari
net/003/001/009.pdf
Ministry of Education, Culture, Sports, Science and Technology. (2013). *International education.* Retrieved on November 10, 2013 from http://www.mext.go.jp/
english/elsec/1303533.htm
Ministry of Internal Affairs and Communications. (2006). *Chiiki ni okeru tabunka
kyōsei suishin puran ni tsuite* [On the plan for promoting multicultural
co-existence in local communities]. Retrieved on May 12, 2012, from http://
www.soumu.go.jp/kokusai/pdf/sonota_b6.pdf
Ministry of Land, Infrastructure, Transportation and Tourism. (2006). *Kokudo shisaku sōhatsu chōsa Kitakantōken no sangyō iji ni muketa kigyō jichitai renkei
ni yoru tabunka kyōsei chiiki zukuri chōsa hōkokusho* [Report on developing
multicultural co-existence areas by cooperate and local government to sustain
industries in North Kanto region]. Retrieved on June 12, 2013, from http://www.
mlit.go.jp/kokudokeikaku/souhatu/h18seika/ 04kitakantou/04kitakantou.html
Moorehead, R. (2012). Remedial language education and citizenship: Examining
the JSL classroom as an ethnic project. In N. Gottlieb (Ed.), *Language and Citizenship in Japan* (pp. 98–116). New York: Routledge.
Nihongo Kyoiku Seisaku Mastāpuran Kenkyūkai (Ed.). (2010). *Nihongo kyōiku
de tsukuru shakai* [Society created through JSL Education]. Tokyo: Koko
Shuppan.
Ogawa, S. (2002). Nyūkamā no kodomo ni taisuru nihongo kyōiku, bokokugo
kyōiku, bobunka hoji kyōiku [Japanese language education, first language and
culture maintenance education for children of new comers]. *Gunma ken Ōta,
Ōizumi no shō chūgakkō kokusaika no jittai to motomerareru kyōin shishitsu no
sōgōteki kenkyū (Comprehensive studies of conditions of internationalization at
elementary and junior high schools of Ota and Oizumi in Gunma Prefecture and
quality of teachers),* 1–22.
Ōta, H. (2000). *Nyūkamā no kodomo to nihon no gakkō* [Newcomer children in
Japanese public schools]. Tokyo: Kokusai Shoin.
Pavlenko, A. (2002). Poststructuralist approaches to the study of social factors in
second language learning and use. In V. Cook (Ed.), *Portraits of the L2 user*
(pp. 275–302). Clevedon: Multilingual Matters.
Ricento, T. (Ed.) (2000). *Ideology, politics, and language policies: Focus on English.*
Amsterdam: John Benjamins.
Sakuma, K. (2006). *Gaikokujin no kodomo no fushūgaku* [Non-school-enrollment
of foreign national children]. Tokyo: Keisō Shobō.
Tokyo University of Foreign Studies Center for Multilingual Multicultural Educa-
tion and Research. (2006). Gaikoku ni tsunagaru kodomo no tame no kyōzai
[Educational materials for children with non-Japanese ethnicity]. Retrieved on
May 30, 2012, from http://www.tufs.ac.jp/blog/ts/g/cemmer/social_02.html

Tsui, A. B. M., & Tollefson, J. W. (2004). The centrality of medium-of-instruction policy in sociopolitical processes. In J. W. Tollefson & A. B. M. Tsui (Eds.), *Medium of Instruction Policies. Which Agenda? Whose Agenda?* (pp. 1–18). Mahwah, NJ: Lawrence Erlbaum.

Ueda, K., & Yamashita, H. (Eds.). (2006). *Kyōsei no naijitsu* [Reality of mutual co-existence]. Tokyo: Sangensha.

van Dijk, T. A. (1995). Aims of critical discourse analysis. *Japanese Discourse, 1*(1), 17–27.

van Dijk, T. A. (1998). *Ideology: A multidisciplinary approach.* London: Sage Publications.

van Dijk, T. A. (2000). *Ideology and discourse. A multidisciplinary introduction.* Catalunya: Universitat Oberta de Catalunya (UOC). Retrieved on November 18, 2013, from http://www.discourses.org/UnpublishedArticles/Ideology%20and%20discourse.pdf

van Dijk, T. A. (2006). Discourse and manipulation. *Discourse and Society, 17*(2): 359–383.

van Dijk, T. A. (2008). *Discourse and power.* New York, NY: Palgrave Macmillan.

Wiley, T. G. (2000). Continuity and change in the function of language ideologies in the United States. In T. Ricento (Ed.), *Ideology, Politics, and Language Policies: Focus on English* (pp. 67–85). Amsterdam: John Benjamins.

Yasuda, K. (2010). *Sabetsu to hinkon no gaikokujin rōdōsha* [Foreign workers of discrimination and poverty]. Tokyo: Kōbunsha.

Epilogue

10 Japan-in-Transition
Reflections and Futures

*Ikuko Nakane, Emi Otsuji, and
William S. Armour*

The chapters in this book have explored languages and identities in an increasingly mobile world. By scrutinizing the discourses, practices, and ideologies of internationalization (*kokusaika*) in Japan since the 1980s and of globalization, this collection has aimed to uncover key aspects of Japan-in-transition represented by the continuum from internationalization to globalization. It has focused on how the modernist discourse of internationalization has been resisted, defied, reinforced, or reproduced within the Contemporary Period of globalization in Japan. The central themes concerning languages and identities in relation to Japan-in-transition were approached through critical discussions of global trends, policies, and public discourses, as well as through the analysis of associated local practices. The three categories, namely cultural, ideological, and pedagogical transitions, provided a comprehensive account of the transitional phenomena. The underlying stance of the book was to move away from the binary understandings of the global-local and top-down, bottom-up practices and show how these seemingly dichotomized practices are in fact dynamically forming and informing each other.

For example, the section on cultural transition explored how national identity has absorbed the shift from 'hard power' to 'soft power' and how this, in turn, has affected Japan's positioning globally and on the policy level (Burgess), as well as more locally in the Japanese language educational domain, particularly in the identities of Japanese language teachers and learners (Armour). The local multilingual practices were critically examined in chapters on the ideological transition with reference to language ideologies, both at the policy and grassroots levels. This was done by firstly looking at the gap between the ideology of English as an international language and actual multilingual practices found in international business communication (Kubota), secondly by denaturalizing the ideology of Japanese language as it relates to language proficiency and genres in the legal context (Nakane), and thirdly by problematizing language ideologies of 'multilingualism' in Tokyo that are still premised on a monolingual mind-set (Otsuji). The final three chapters investigated the transition in language pedagogy from various perspectives. The first area investigated was the impact that personal and institutional levels of language-learning contexts have had on identity negotiation of heritage learners of Japanese in Australia (Moloney & Oguro). The second area introduced a proposal for a humanistic approach to language education in multicultural contexts in tertiary education sectors in Australia (Ōhashi & Ōhashi), and finally a critique of language-education policy in Japan (Taniguchi & McMahill).

The case studies conducted both in and outside Japan demonstrated an ambivalence between 'global' and 'local,' and have highlighted the importance of exploring the processes of Japan-in-transition beyond 'Japan-and-the-rest-of-the-world' dichotomy. There was also an observation presented throughout the book of a need to problematize the monolithic relationships between language, national identity, and citizenship in the era of a mobile world. Under these circumstances, what it means to be Japanese, to speak Japanese, or to teach/learn Japanese has been refashioned. The flexible link between language, national identities, and citizenship means that the notions of Japan and Japanese language can no longer be confined by monolingual and monocultural mind-sets. Nevertheless, while awareness of multiculturalism and multilingualism within Japan has risen and policies to support and integrate the increasing number of migrants have been implemented, the realities of transcultural identities and language practices now found commonly in Japan do not seem to have fully shifted from the 'us' and 'them' ideologies of internationalization. The chapters presented in this book, indeed, have demonstrated the instability of identification, by fixing and unfixing the 'self' and the 'other' on the local as well as on the global level.

Therefore, the core message of this volume is not that the 'Japanese language' or 'Japanese identity' exclusively belong to 'Japan the nation,' 'Japanese citizens' or 'the Japanese race,' but that we should seek and understand the flexible ways in which they unsettle, undo, resist, reinforce, reproduce, or refashion each other. Much as the world resides in Japan, one can find Japan everywhere in the world, constantly transforming and transcending itself. We hope that the chapters in this book have provided vivid examples of such processes through the exploration of languages and identities in a mobile world.

It was not possible to include in this volume discussions of language and identity issues other than in Japan, China, and Australia. Further research is needed in other parts of the world, for example, countries such as Malaysia, Indonesia, or Thailand, where there are increasing numbers of Japanese nationals (Ministry of Foreign Affairs 2013), for a more comprehensive understanding of how transcultural flows have impacted on languages and identities in association with Japan.

With the 2020 Tokyo Olympic Games in sight, English-language education will be compulsory to younger-year levels, which is one of Japan's globalization strategies. As mentioned in the opening chapter, this reform ignores the diversity of languages used in the international community by uncritically assuming that English is the lingua franca of the world, thereby reinforcing a narrow, monolingual view of globalization. Furthermore, the 'Cool Japan' policy continues the nation's attempt to promote the 'Japan brand.' It remains to be seen whether the gap between the growing trans-cultural trends of globalization and the ideology of one language, ethnicity, and citizenship will subside in the near future. We hope to have increased a critical awareness of how, in Japan-in-transition, local and global as well as policy and everyday practices are connected.

REFERENCE

Ministry of Foreign Affairs. (2013). *Annual report of statistics on Japanese nationals overseas.* Retrieved on August 23, 2014, from http://www.mofa.go.jp/mofaj/files/000017472.pdf

Contributors

William S. Armour is an Honorary Senior Lecturer in the School of Humanities and Languages, UNSW, Australia. He has taught both Japanese language and Japanese area studies courses for over two decades as well as courses in intercultural communication. His previous research has focused on identity and foreign-language learning, and representations of masculinity in Japanese 'manga.' His present research includes the exploration of Japanese language education, in particular the use of Japanese mass culture products such as 'manga' and 'anime' in the classroom, a project investigating the links between Japanese mass culture products and how they might motivate individuals to study Japanese language and area studies, and a study into how Japanese typefaces are used in 'manga.'

Chris Burgess is a Professor at Tsuda College, Tokyo, where he teaches Japanese and Australian studies. His research focuses on migration, globalization, and multiculturalism in contemporary Japan. His most recent publications include a chapter on Japanese language education and migrants in Nanette Gottlieb's *Language and Citizenship in Japan* (Routledge 2012) and a forthcoming paper on Japan's push to secure and foster global human resources in globalization, societies, and education.

Ryūko Kubota is a Professor in the Department of Language and Literacy Education in the Faculty of Education at the University of British Columbia, Canada. Her research draws on critical applied linguistics, critical multiculturalism, critical race theory, and critical pedagogy. She is a coeditor of *Race, Culture, and Identities in Second Language: Exploring Critically Engaged Practice* (Routledge 2009) and *Demystifying Career Paths After Graduate School: A Guide for Second Language Professionals in Higher Education* (Information Age Publishing 2012). Her publications also appear in many edited books and academic journals, e.g., *Applied Linguistics, Critical Inquiry in Language Studies, Linguistics and Education,* and *TESOL Quarterly.*

Cheiron McMahill is a professor of English as a Foreign Language at Daito Bunka University, Japan. She obtained her PhD in Applied Linguistics at Lancaster University and founded and ran a nonprofit multilingual community school for the children of foreign workers for thirteen years in Gunma, Japan. She is currently working to establish an awareness of, and support services for, linguistic and ethnic minority students at Japanese universities.

Robyn Moloney is a Senior Lecturer in the School of Education, Macquarie University. She teaches preservice language teachers in the areas of literacy and language pedagogy and supervises postgraduate research projects in language education. Her research interests include language learning pedagogy, teacher narratives, heritage language learners, and intercultural education. Recent publications include *Language Teacher Narratives of Practice*, coedited with Associate Professor Lesley Harbon for Cambridge Scholars Publishing (2013) and a range of journal publications examining the teaching of Chinese as a Foreign Language.

Ikuko Nakane is a Senior Lecturer at the Asia Institute, the University of Melbourne. She holds a PhD in Linguistics from the University of Sydney. Her research focuses on lay-professional interaction in legal contexts, silence in intercultural communication, and diachronic changes in Japanese with a focus on gender, class, and regional identities. Her publications include *Silence in Intercultural Communication: Perceptions and Performance* (John Benjamins 2007); *Interpreter-mediated Police Interviews* (Palgrave Macmillan 2014), and articles in journals such as *Applied Linguistics*, *Journal of Pragmatics*, *Japanese Studies* and *Asian Studies Review*.

Susan Oguro is a Senior Lecturer in International Studies and Education in the Faculty of Arts and Social Sciences at the University of Technology, Sydney. Her research interests and publications are in diverse areas of the field of education, including heritage languages, curriculum and pedagogy, preservice teacher education, intercultural education, and human rights education.

Hiroko Ōhashi is the Coordinator of Japanese Studies at the RMIT University. She has been spearheading ideas of adding value to Japanese language teaching by incorporating the Engagement and Leadership program involving the Career Development and Employment unit. She envisions its wider educational values help students access new communities, cultivate cultural reflexibility, and grow to imagine positive selfhood through social interaction and interpersonal relations. Her research interests include second-language acquisition, curriculum design, and discourse analysis. Her coauthored journal articles and book chapters have been published by Oceania Education Studies, Osaka Municipal University Press, and the University of Michigan Press.

Jun Ōhashi teaches Japanese language at the University of Melbourne. He has been coordinating the beginners' Japanese language subject for the last three years. He believes in humanistic values in language education, and his interest in teaching the language goes beyond the learners' language acquisition. His other research interests include gendered and generational variation of speech act realization, cross-cultural investigation of public signs and exhortations, and group identity formation in sports media discourse. He is the author of *Thanking and Politeness in Japanese* (Palgrave Macmillan 2013) and research articles published by *Journal of Pragmatics, Multilingua, Japanese Studies* and others.

Emi Otsuji is a Senior Lecturer at University of Technology, Sydney. Her research interests include language and globalization (metrolingualism and multilingualism), the performativity theory of language and identities, and critical pedagogy in language teaching. Her work (with Alastair Pennycook) on metrolingualism assumes that the use of mixed languages is a norm, which ultimately links language practices to the urban environment. Emi has published a number of book chapters and articles for journals including *Applied Linguistics, International Journal of Multilingualism and Multiculturalism, International Journal of Bilingual Education*, and リテラシーズ (Literacies).

Sumiko Taniguchi has been teaching Japanese as a second language and is currently teaching academic Japanese to international students at Chuo University, Tokyo, Japan. She obtained her PhD in adult education at the University of Technology, Sydney. Her research interests include child/adult multilingual and multiliteracy development and narrative approach to learner development. She also teaches teacher-education courses for Japanese as a second language.

Index

Test (JLPT); *see also* background
  speaker
Japanese Language Proficiency Test
  (JLPT) 131–3, 135
Japanese Speaking Background (JSB)
  see background speaker

kanji 46, 69, 128, 133–4
kizuna 30; *see also* Japanese; national
  identity
Koizumi Junichiro, 22–3
kokusaikai *see* internationalization

L1 *see* first language
language xiii, 1–9; acquisition 143–6,
  154–5, 160–2, 171–2; dichotomized categories of 8; language
  skills 4, 6; learner 43, 67, 122–3,
  160–1; learning 38–9, 40–6,
  50–2, 59–65, 71, 121–124,
  131–8, 142–5, 152–4, 159–62
language proficiency *see* proficiency
language minority (LM) children
  xiv, 167–74, 178–84; *see also*
  minority children
language maintenance 9, 168; first language maintenance program 9,
  168, 171–3
lay judge *(saiban-in)* 78,
  96–7
learner empowerment 39
learning English: for intercultural communication 67; for leisure 62;
  for self-fulfillment 64; for status
  64–6; for work/career 62, 68;
lingua franca *see* English
linguistic practice: everyday 101; fluidity in 108, 110, 115; *see also*
  liquid life
liquid life 39–40
liquid modernity 39–40
literacy 85–6, 95–6, 121–2, 171–2,
  182; and identity development
  128–34, 137; *see also* identity
Lowy Institute 43–4

manga *see* popular (pop) culture
mass media 37–40, 46–7, 181–4;
  coverage of Japan 16–18
media and new technologies 1–2, 37–40,
  44, 49–51
metrolingualism 8, 101–2, 109–12,
  115–16; and globalization
  116

MEXT (Ministry of Education, Culture,
  Sports, Science and Technology)
  72, 167, 170–6
migrants 20, 30; assimilation of 168,
  170–4; economic 172; Japanese
  121–9; labor 79; non-English
  speaking 60, 167–8; non-
  Japanese 167–8; *see also*
  immigrants
minority children 167–8, 174, 176–7,
  184; *see also* language minority
  (LM) children
mobility 72, 79, 101–3, 113–16;
  cultural 115–116; demographic
  2–5
multicultural coexistence *(tabunka
  kyōsei)* 4–5, 116, 167–8, 173
multicultural education 168, 175–6
multiculturalism 174–5 181, 192; in
  Australia 42; and the Japanese
  education system 167–8; and
  policy 184
multilingual 101–2, 113–15, 191;
  see also courtroom; *see also*
  education
multilingual courtroom *see* courtroom

Nariaki, Nakayama 15, 30
national interest doctrine *(kokueki-ron)*
  24
nationalism 6, 18, 25, 30; *see also*
  brand nationalism
nationality 2, 128, 147; as basis for
  discrimination 172; Japanese xiv,
  170
nation-state 5, 25, 109, 147
neoliberal: belief 61, 70–1; society 61
newcomers 63–5, 78–80, 167–8,
  170–4, 184
non-Japanese Speaking Background
  (NJSB) *see* background speaker

pedagogy xiv–xv, 43–4, 50–2, 121,
  135, 141, 191
policy 3–7, 49, 72; education 60, 72,
  173–4; English-only 61; immigration 167–9; economic 19–21,
  23–24
popular (pop) culture xiii, 1, 6–8;
  anime and manga xiv, 47–50,
  133; commodification of 28–9,
  134; and identity 128, 133; as
  motivator in education 37, 46–9,
  51–2, 128, 133